EXCELLENCE vs. EQUALITY

Can Society Achieve Both Goals?

Allan C. Ornstein

Routledge
Taylor & Francis Group

NEW YORK AND LONDON

First published 2016
by Routledge
711 Third Avenue, New York, NY 10017

and by Routledge
2 Park Square, Milton Park, Abingdon, Oxon OX14 4RN

Routledge is an imprint of the Taylor & Francis Group, an informa business

© 2016 Taylor & Francis

Library of Congress Cataloging in Publication Data
Ornstein, Allan C.
Excellence vs. equality : can society achieve both goals? / Allan C. Ornstein.
pages cm
Includes bibliographical references and index.
ISBN 978-1-138-94089-5 (hardback) -- ISBN 978-1-138-94090-1 (pbk.) -- ISBN 978-1-315-67398-1 (ebook) 1. Equality. 2. Common good. 3. Income distribution. 4. Social stratification. 5. Social mobility. 6. Educational mobility. I. Title. II. Title: Excellence versus equality.
HM821.O76 2016
305--dc23
2015013849

ISBN: 978-1-138-94089-5 (hbk)
ISBN: 978-1-138-94090-1 (pbk)
ISBN: 978-1-315-67398-1 (ebk)

Typeset in Bembo
by Saxon Graphics Ltd, Derby

Printed and bound in the United States of America by Publishers Graphics, LLC on sustainably sourced paper.

Dedication

To Adrian and Sophia

The future belongs to you
Make the most of it
Get your priorities straight
Act on them
Ask the right questions
Go beyond what's in front of you
Look far into the distance
Play the long game

CONTENTS

INTRODUCTION

Excellence vs. Equality: Consider This

So much has been written in the last ten years about growing inequality and lack of opportunity that one might think that writing another article or book related to this subject would be pretty much a matter of pushing the reader into cruise control, or even worse some kind of stupor. To be sure, there are too many books on the subject to know any of them well, and the quality of our ideas gives way to the quantity of tidbits on the Internet. But the growing gulf between the wealthy and the working people, the rich and rest of us, is only one part of the narrative. A decade of politicians and economists have used their supposedly rational perspective to argue we are becoming two nations: "Wall Street" vs. "Main Street", "1 percent" vs. "99 percent", "Tax Payers" vs. "Takers" (and "moochers"), and "Job Makers" vs. "Workers."

In a high-passion debate we often hear from all kinds of professionals, pundits, and self-styled experts, arguing (1) whether safety nets and social programs are necessary, (2) whether "job creators" should be taxed (and how much), (3) what steps are needed to stabilize the financial system, (4) whether banks and corporations need to be regulated (and to what extent), (5) why we cannot end poverty in America (and in other parts of the world), (6) whether opportunity and mobility still exist for ordinary people in America or elsewhere, (7) how to improve schools, employment, and income and other economic conditions over the long-term, and (8) who should attend college, how do we make colleges more affordable, and how can private colleges provide more *need-based* assistance, while balancing the competitive advantages of awarding *merit-based* assistance, without exhausting their resources.

Now there are different ways to piece together the puzzle. Those who reflect a conservative slant tend to frame their arguments around personal responsibility—such as family structure and family values, school dropouts, drugs and delinquent behavior, lack of individual initiative and lack of perspiration. There is the cry for small government and criticism of government intervention involving welfare, food stamps, health programs and unemployment programs—all that impede mobility and create a culture of poverty (from one generation to the next) in the U.S. Give money to the government in the form of taxes, and it goes into a sinkhole. Obamacare is a debacle, an example of a great sinkhole. If the government would get out of the way of "job creators," the economy would grow and people would prosper. Populist rhetoric about inequality is a "fantasy," used as a method to stir up and organize labor and the liberal base. Income inequality is merely a statistical byproduct of competition—and reflects the success of capitalism. Inequality fosters economic growth by serving as an incentive for those who exhibit excellence in their field of endeavor. Those with talent, intelligence and/or aptitude rise to the top and are entitled to make huge sums of money, whereby lesser individuals fall to the wayside and land at the bottom of the pyramid. Finally, the government is watching you and knows where you are: If you have a "smart" phone, GPS in your car, or use plastic money or a toll-bridge tag (E–Z Pass).

Those on the liberal side tend to frame their arguments around the notion that in a democracy a social contract is supposed to exist between the people and their government; therefore, government programs and government regulation of finance and industry are necessary. The method for remediation and increased mobility is to raise minimum wages, eliminate bad schools, spend more money on education (especially Head Start and pre-kindergarten programs), and legislate equal pay for women. Similarly, there is need to bolster union membership, train unskilled workers and retrain laid-off workers. Raising the alarm about the concentration of wealth, there is growing need to tax the rich and super-rich to help pay for Social Security, education and other social programs—and to avoid a potential oligarchy. Finally, inequality of income tends to reflect inequality of opportunity; it has little to do with personal responsibility, lack of hard work or ability. Conversely, inequality contributes to less opportunity, and in turn less intergenerational mobility. It is not just the concentration of wealth that alarms liberals, but it is also the decline in meritocracy and mobility that concerns them.

With so many people in the U.S. gravitating to opposite sides of the issues on inequality and opportunity, small wonder that polarized passions result in a certain sense of inevitability. Witness the rise of partisan politics in the U.S. Congress and fabrications through attack ads, Occupy Wall Street and the Tea Party, the Heritage Foundation and the ACLU, and the popularity of extreme commentators on cable television like Bill O'Reilly and Sean Hannity on the Right and Chris Matthews and Rachel Maddow on the Left—all firing up their audience and fomenting a public outcry.

Even when the debate on inequality (and lack of opportunity) is broken down from a messy whole into slightly more coherent phrases, there is little incentive to question one's assumptions or to create the ground to compromise. From the

Golden Gate Bridge to the George Washington Bridge, from the Mississippi Delta to the twin cities of Minnesota, the political, social and moral fiber of society is being stretched like a rubber band—and the outcome seems fruitless and disheartening. We are moving toward two worlds, two cultures, two classes—dominant and subordinate—a shrinking middle class and the rise of an oligarchy class in the U.S. (and around the world).

It's not just the drop in standard of living among the working and middle classes that shocks people, it's the geometric rise in the upper ranges of income and wealth for people who have no rational need of more and more. In short, growing inequality around the world, and here in the U.S., is leading to a huge underbelly or underclass and subsequent decline of human rights, democracy and economic productivity. The growing division in society, between the rich and the rest of us, is fueled by what I call the "volatile side" of modern life—technology, media and globalization—which permits a tiny percentage of people to glom most of the wealth produced by the economy. Moreover, we cannot expect growth and prosperity to trickle down from the top, unless of course you are an ideologist or believe in the tooth fairy.

But others are quick to point out that the free enterprise system is the best of all options. It has created more opportunity for the poor and working people than any other system in the world. Even if a society produced perfect equality, and thus eliminated all the advantages of privileged heredity and wealth, it will still inevitably favor certain skills and talents over others. Unless we are advocating equality of results, regardless of ability, aptitude and/or achievement, there will always be differential rewards. Unless we seek to reduce the rewards of competition and talent, as well as the costs of laziness and failure, there will always be a range of differences in terms of money, power and status.

There is no perfect sorting-out process to determine individual performance or merit—and how to distribute rewards. In a society that emphasizes extreme performance, most participants fall to the wayside and wind up feeling inadequate and insecure. In organizations, people of average ability often cooperate to curtail highly talented individuals. In still other societies, where there is more commitment to equality, individual achievement is not fully recognized and rewarded—certainly not at the same level as in more competitive societies. People of average ability are paid the same amount as high-performing people are. Workers are rewarded on the basis of years of experience (seniority) and accumulation of education credits or degrees. Highly talented individuals find themselves at odds with this kind of organization and rarely feel totally fulfilled.

The new economy produces very talented people who are annually paid tens of millions of dollars, as well as very valuable companies with few employees who get paid large sums of money. Meanwhile the majority of Americans do not share in this new wealth. The average full-time worker at Walmart earned $27,000 in 2013, a humiliating wage which forced many of its employees to seek public assistance. However, when Facebook went public in 2013, hundreds of workers became instant millionaires. Then Facebook bought out WhatsApp for $19 billion the following year, and it paid a price equal to $345 million per employee (55 people). The fact is, technological advances are trimming middle-class jobs—while venture capitalists chase tech- and information-based companies with limited jobs. The Department of Labor summed up the situation in 2013: The national earnings of the middle 60 percent of workers had fallen from 53 percent to 45 percent of the economic pie since 1970.

The real losers are the people who vote against their own economic interests because of some racial or cultural rational. Lincoln was wrong, I am sad to say. You really can fool all of the people—at least enough people—with 30-second TV ads and in the time it takes for an election to tip one way or another. If we mix a little history with geography, all nations throughout the centuries are a motley assortment of individuals, and the individual is a mini-nation of individuals—with the vast majority trying to keep their heads above water and struggling to live with some dignity. But having the right to vote is a relatively new concept, not more than a few hundred years old—corresponding with the rise of Anglo law and democracy. Perhaps the reason why ordinary people (or most voters) are misled by their own opinions, is because having no potential or political voice is the historical norm. As late as the American Revolution, only 10 percent of the populace was qualified to vote; that is, you had to be a property holder. In 1776 for example, the richest 10 percent owned more than 90 percent of the property in New York, Philadelphia, Baltimore and Charleston.

Perhaps the biggest problem related to voting, today, is that the majority of people living outside the big cities of America (where there tends to be more tolerance and diversity) see the U.S. landscape declining in terms of people from Anglo-Saxon stock, from whose Founding Fathers conceived the political and social ideals of the nation. Too many people from suburban and rural America see the current change in color and character of the U.S. population as one vast "polygot" mass, a huge pool of indistinguishable black, brown, and yellow people. Instead of welcoming the new immigrants, and recognizing their strength of character and different thinking and innovative thought process, they fear and mistrust these people. Moreover, they see them as a threat to our democracy and way of life. It boils down to a subtle racism, a byproduct of provincial or traditional thinking, played out in voting patterns over cultural, moral and religious issues which hinder the social and economic status of ordinary Americans or what is sometimes referred to as the "silent majority."

And so the above complexity of issues and nuances come together in a simple question: Can a society achieve both excellence and equality? The overall theme and related questions below are perennial in nature and test the isles of time; they cut across centuries of history, as well as nations and empires around the world. How we deal with the questions of excellence and equality determines the nature of our society, the kind of people we are or think we are. By my own temperament—given some seven-plus decades of living—Americans have shown little inclination to discuss the issue of excellence vs. equality because it touches on differences among and within racial and ethnic groups, cultures and classes, men and women, as well as political and social philosophies. The one thing we Americans are not allowed today to say in public is that there are group differences mentally or physically that may be correlated with different outcomes in life.

How do we deal with the tensions and differences between excellence and equality in modern society? How do we view the connection between aptitude and achievement, between equal outcomes and equality of opportunity? If we believe that no person is better than the next, and that we all have basic human rights but different needs and interests, then how should we encourage and reward different athletic, artistic and cognitive achievement? To what extent should we allow these different achievement levels to affect income inequality? How much more should we reward special talent in a given field vs. average performance? How much more shall we reward excellence in medicine, teaching, computer science, baseball, or janitorial work? Unquestionably we can afford to pay a medical researcher $250,000 extra than his peers for his extraordinary abilities, but what can we pay or should we pay an excellent ping-pong player or janitor? How can society reconcile the differences between the strong and weak, the swift and slow runner, the smart and average or below average person?

Are we able to fully grasp the effects and realities of a system that promotes unbridled excellence and unlimited wealth or a system that handicaps achievement and favors one group at the expense of the other to achieve statistical parity? Should we put limits on or handicap those who are strong, swift or smart? Should we redistribute wealth achieved through ability so that slow runners or below average performers can fully participate in society? Should the system provide a host of government benefits and services based on financial need, disability, age or lack of ability?

If as a society we reserve our respect and affection toward especially talented people, entrepreneurs and "job creators," investors and risk takers, and thus provide them with the most rewards, how do we treat and regard ordinary working people who comprise the vast majority of the populace? What kind of respect do the 1 percenters—the entrepreneurs, investors and specially talented ballplayers and entertainers—have, or pretend to have, toward working people who have faithfully worked for other people and have taken responsibility for their lives and family? No society can provide a decent living for every kind of worker, or every kind of talent, but all those who have earned their own success need to celebrate or at least respect the "average" student or "average" worker. Resources must be made available for a broad-based education for low-achieving students and a decent job for provision of the working family in order for a modern society to perpetuate itself and improve.

So, we come to a dilemma: How much *excellence* do we want to stress? How much should we reward excellence? How *equal* do we want to be? On what basis?

Given a diverse society (and world), how do we define both terms? Who defines these terms? Should people, the government or the marketplace be the determining factor? What benchmarks do we use? What are the outcomes when society pushes in one direction (at the expense of the other goal)? Is there a way for reconciling the interdependence and differences between excellence and equality? Obviously, these are not easy questions to answer, given varied opinions from conservative to liberal, from the hard right to socialist and given the possibility that personal feelings might influence our own discussion on the subject.

History, culture and geography, and almost any personal experience or bias, can shape our definition, measures and degree of emphasis on excellence or equality. As benchmarks of excellence and equality change over time, so do our understanding and meaning of the two terms change. To be sure, everyone can use a little more self-understanding. Scholars, pundits and journalists support their meaning and understanding of excellence and equality by selective use of data to build their own arguments and claims on the subject. They tend to exclude data that contradicts their social and political lens and focus on benchmarks and statistical data that support their own beliefs and biases of excellence and equality. The question of how our views influence our judgments on these twin concepts is a central methodological issue among scientists, social scientists and serious authors. It becomes a problem with all new research and publications in democratic societies, especially if they affect the conditions of performance and/ or social mobility of people.

The reader is faced with a similar dilemma. If asked to define or measure excellence or equality, there would likely be a host of different responses with varied reasons. Because we are human beings, we have different life experiences, beliefs, and biases. Every reader, every interpreter labors under this handicap or inevitable need for validity and clarity. Here I am trying to give the reader a glimpse of self-understanding, a moment of doubt and need for reflection. All of us have different opinions about excellence and equality, and see these concepts from different vantage points. Try to keep an open mind and not fall victim to your own self-confirmability or interpretation. Keep an open mind and try to become more self-aware as you explore ways for looking at various forms of excellence and equality.

You might even ask yourself what are you most proud of? As you reflect on your own achievements, where do you feel you have set some standard of excellence? Are you able to say "Wow I really did that"? What performance do you hold in high regard or regret the most? How has that performance impacted on your life? What would you do over if you had the chance? As we go through the stages of life, we might ask: How should parents, schools or the workplace support growth and development of the individual? His or her creativity? Vision? Intuition? Innovation? Most people have a sense of family, school or organizational ownership, but to achieve excellence in their life endeavors they need to own a creative, visionary intuitive, or innovative agenda. They need to be inspired, motivated, and driven to succeed even when people say "no" or are disparaging. In some extreme cases, you must do what you think you cannot do.

But change makes for more change and the historical and social context is always changing; thus the notion and benchmarks of excellence and equality will also change. Just when we think we have agreed on a definition or benchmark for excellence or equality, there is a change of the guard and a new group gains power in society. Different rules and regulations for merit and rewards are implemented. New policies and laws are passed to deal with discrimination or try to remedy the disadvantages some of us start with or claim. Hence, the context, criteria and variations of excellence and equality change over time.

Whatever cards we are dealt, we must learn to deal with them and make the best of the situation. Early setbacks may even have beneficial results. The fields of business and entrepreneurship indicate that failures offer a learning experience and a chance to reflect and improve. Steven Rogers of Harvard University claims that the average entrepreneur fails four times before succeeding. The idea is to pick yourself up, dust off the failures, and start up again. As the Roman philosopher once stated: "Difficulties strengthen the mind, as labor does the body." Most important, in order to achieve, one cannot get buried by self-pity or victimization. The idea is to believe in yourself, despite the "ney"s and "no"s of other people.

The goal is to understand and develop your strengths within the rules established by society, knowing full well that not everyone will begin equally at the starting line and that certain aptitudes or skills will not always be rewarded in the same way. A successful nurse or teacher will not obtain the same monetary awards as a lawyer or physician, much less a professional baseball player or soccer star in the vast majority of societies. Similarly, what was once considered important and rewarded accordingly (i.e., a rider for the Pony Express or a blacksmith) changes as society evolves and changes.

Those who believe that heredity is the dominant factor in determining intelligence, talent or achievement will most likely exhibit a philosophy that coincides with personal responsibility and conservative elements in society. Those who seem convinced that environment is the crucial factor in determining differences in intelligence, talent or achievement tend to believe that differences between individuals are due to social and economic inequalities. It's not easy to settle this controversy because the stakes are high and frank, public discussion is hard to come by given the politically correct society we live in, compounded by the influence of instant media and the litigation-based world we inhabit.

It's essential to recognize that life has its ups and downs, and just about all of us will have to face failures, a lot of misses, and a lot of bumps in the road. The important thing is to be able to get up at bat, take your swing, and get up and try again if you strike out. Being optimistic helps, but being able to learn from our failures so we have a better chance to succeed the next time helps even more.

It's a safe bet that not all readers live in a country where there is a social contract between the government and the people, and that social and economic mobility are part of the fabric of society. It can also be argued there is no such thing as achievement of equality of opportunity, that in every society there will be a privileged group with greater access to opportunity. In the face of such inequality, let us assume for now some range of opportunity at the starting gate wherever you reside—and not just limited to the industrialized world or to a small percentage of the global populace.

To be sure, we are all given a different set of cards to play the game of life. Very few of us will grow up in a four- or five-bedroom house, with three and a half bathrooms in Manhasset, New York or Winnetka, Illinois—or have an Ivy League education. You have to take your background, accept it, and own it, and turn whatever is negative into a positive. This being the case, it means we need to embrace whatever opportunity there is, making the most of it when it comes knocking at our door—not wasting time or making excuses. It means having a sense of responsibility, motivation and drive. On the other hand, you cannot make the most of opportunities if you lack these personal values, if you don't know what you're doing, or if you're afraid to make decisions or act when it's your turn to get up at bat. It also means not getting paralyzed or stymied by bad decisions in the past; it boils down to picking yourself up when there is a dark cloud and saying "I can do it," something like the Eveready battery that keeps going or the little engine that said, "I think I can, I think I can."

For a college student, it means studying and getting to know your field of study, then gaining practical experience first with internships and real-life projects, and then finding a mentor at college and a colleague or supervisor on the job who welcomes you and works with you to develop relevant skills and competencies. In short, you need to move from theory to practice, from being a "me" to a "we," if you work in an organization. You need to feel comfortable with risk, trying new things, and be willing to talk about mistakes and learning from them.

Here it might be advantageous to recognize that college is not for everyone. If we assume that college is the main meal-ticket for success, then it is not surprising that so many parents today are pushing their children in that direction. What society needs is more viable options for success, more diverse and decent jobs for high school graduates, and greater recognition of individual differences and human potential. The primary focus should be on excellence, but there needs to be diversity and recognition of various forms of excellence. Most important, the notion of excellence should begin with children for they are the next generation of inventors, innovators, dreamers, athletes and artists.

Life is unfair and no one with an ounce of smarts should think it is fair. Similarly, the playing field is tilted, and it has always been tilted in favor of the rich and powerful. There is no such thing as equal opportunity, only the hope to be given some chance to succeed and that the log cabin, rags-to-riches folklore is still part of the American fiber. You run the best race you can within the limits imposed on you. The result is usually out of your hands, because external and uncontrollable factors impact on the process and outcome. Indeed, some of us are born with a mom and dad (who is a doctor) and have expectations since childhood of becoming a doctor. Others never knew their father and are forced to support themselves at a young age and have expectations of becoming a plumber or electrician. Some of us are born with brains and courage and others like the Scarecrow in *The Wizard of Oz* lack brains and still others like the Lion lack courage. Some of us are born in wealthy neighborhoods with high property values and well-financed schools and others are born in poor or working-class neighborhoods with financially strapped schools (where the student spending ratio is 4:1). Some of us are born with trust funds and college legacies to Harvard and/or Yale, like the Rockefellers, Kennedys and Bushes. Others are born in modest homes, earmarked into community colleges or state colleges and wind up in debt after college. To be sure, talent is universal, but opportunity and mobility are not.

As we contemplate the idea of "excellence" or "equality" as youngsters or adults, we read into our own aspirations, hopes and dreams our own notion of standards, hard work and achievement. But the more we think that the deck is stacked—even worse, that some are born on third base and others will never get up to bat—then the more we sense there is lack of opportunity and the likelihood of mediocrity. In stratified societies, privilege and wealth determine access to a good education and job. In democratic societies, families at the lower economic levels are handicapped, but those children with ability often find opportunities to succeed, although not everyone with ability will succeed. To be sure, a democratic society needs to provide opportunities for children of ordinary people in order to maximize its human resources and to foster its growth and prosperity. The problem is, we are becoming a society of inherited wealth, not self-made people, just when we thought we had put behind the idea of heredity privilege and old patterns of aristocracies and family, caste and class.

People perceive and define excellence and equality in different ways, largely based on historical context, the norms and goals of society, and their own life experiences and philosophy (or opinions). In a society where there is great inequality and differences in wealth and power, education cannot overcome such wide variations of birth and home background. The best we can hope for is a chance to get up at bat, and that society will find methods to limit the effects of hereditary stratification and allow, even encourage, individual differences in ability and talent to emerge in all phases and pursuits of life. This is no easy method; it requires the passage of policies and laws to help remedy the disadvantages with which many children and youth of ordinary people start at birth. In practice, it suggests a more even playing field and chance to compete and succeed within the norms and goals of that particular society. Every society must work out these policies, based on what it views as fair and just and best for the common good, in order to make full use of its human resources and support human rights among its citizens.

1

THE SEARCH FOR TALENT

We Americans are a "nation on the make." Our democracy has unleashed the energies of all its people, and with this new energy comes the dissolution of a stratified society. According to Walter McDougall in *Freedom Just Around the Corner*, we are "con artists" and "cowboys" and "dreamers" and "inventors," not just because we are a different breed of species or better or worse than other nations, but because Americans have enjoyed immense opportunity to pursue their ambitions and dreams. On the positive side, these distinctions have helped Americans to have faith in themselves—to win the West, to innovate, to expand and make it big—not being fixed by Old World Church or state hierarchies and social or class distinctions that hold people in place and constrain their innovative spirit and energies.

As part of a new culture and society, the humblest and poorest have been able to lift up their heads and face the future with confidence; we have increasingly relied on education as an integral part of this process of becoming. On the negative side, this forceful, driving and imaginative American characteristic has led to political excesses and abuses—nearly wiping out whole civilizations and extracting land from other people and places in order to further and/or protect our "interests." It has also produced some ghastly business ethics—based on greed and creative corruption—highlighted by the Gilded Age, the Wall Street collapse in the 1930s, the dot-com bust in 2000 and the Great Recession of 2007–2012.

Although some observers might criticize the American character, and comment about our flaws and failures, McDougall (and others) maintains that the formation of the "United States is the major geopolitical event of the past 400 years." Imagine some ship flying the Dutch, English or French flag in the year 1600 and then being transported to the present. The difference would astound them. From a primitive and vacant land, we have become "the mightiest, richest, most dynamic civilization in history," exceeding the achievements of not only the European world but also the entire world. We are the most revolutionary country, a society that is constantly changing and reforming and revitalizing itself. To paraphrase Joseph Perkins, a famous orator of Harvard in 1797, we are "the Athens [and Rome] of our age," and until recently "the admiration of the world."

As we try to define our national legacy, we have the Enlightenment on one side with its faith in progress, opportunity and education, as well as democracy with its cherished values of freedom, liberty, equality and faith in the individual. On the other side, we have materialism, consumerism and excess—and education that has been "softened" into entertainment, hustle that has turned into hucksterism, and opportunity that is currently being diverted into financial oligarchism. We have liberals and conservatives, each with their own interpretation of what is right and wrong with society. Somehow it seems to go back to the *isms* of the past and present—between the philosophy and differences of Alexander Hamilton and Thomas Jefferson, Social Darwinism and Social Democracy, and Roman patrician and Greek egalitarian thought. Perhaps it goes back to how we distinguish ourselves from the Old World. Maybe it goes back to how we perceive truth and how we perceive the world around us or how competing ideas in the U.S.—such as elitism vs. egalitarianism, conspicuous consumption vs. common good, perennialism vs. progressivism—impact on schools and society.

Geography and "Smart" Thinking

On a global, much more theoretical level, growth and prosperity among cultures and civilizations can be explained by environment, or by the limits of geographical isolation. Given a make-believe world in which every individual has identical genetic potential, there would still be large differences in education, skills and related occupations and productivity among people because of environmental and demographic differences that over centuries shape human behavior and attitudes.

For Thomas Sowell, the conservative economist, nothing conflicts so much with desire for equality as geography; it is the physical setting—reflected by large bodies of water, deserts, mountains, jungles, forests, etc.—in which civilizations, nations, races and ethnic groups have evolved and produced different cultures. Put simply by Sowell in *Conquests and Cultures*, the people of the Himalayas have not had equal opportunity to acquire seafaring skills, and the Eskimos did not have equal opportunity to learn how to farm or grow oranges. Too often the influence of geography is assessed in terms of natural resources that directly influence national wealth. But geography also influences cultural differences and cognitive thinking, by either expanding or limiting the universe of ideas and inventions available to different people.

In this connection, Richard Nisbett argues in *The Geography of Thought* that geographical isolation can lead to either positive or negative outcomes, and can explain differences in behavior and attitudes over accumulated generations.

Beyond Nisbett, the accidents of geography (and history), where you were born and when you were born, immensely influence innovation, opportunity and human capital. Put in simple terms, had Warren Buffett or Bill Gates been born 500 years ago, they may have likely died on the battlefield, given their physical stature and the European inclination toward war. Had Alex Rodriguez been born 100 years ago, the likelihood is he would have been a factory worker or laborer.

When geography isolates people, say by mountains, a desert or a small island, the people have limited contact with the outside world and, subsequently, their technological and innovative advancement is limited. While the rest of the world trades skills, ideas and values from a larger cultural pool, isolated people are limited by their own resources and what knowledge they have developed by themselves. Very few advances come from isolated cultures, and those that do are usually modified and improved by people who have learned to assimilate and adopt new ideas from other cultures. Until 9/11, we had the advantage of geographical isolation and protection. The isolation did not hinder our progress because of the large influx of immigrants from around the world who not only brought their meager possessions to our shores but also their ideas, values and aspirations.

For two thousand years, before the invention of railroads, trucks and airplanes, water was the key for traveling and exploring. Up to the 1850s, it was faster and cheaper to travel by water from San Francisco to China than overland to Chicago. The Europeans, since the Viking era, understood that geographical isolation could be overcome by the sea or ocean, and, given their capitalistic and conquering zeal and attitudes of superiority, they went out and traded with, and also colonized, other people and other cultures. Subsequently, they made industrial and technological advances by adopting and modifying the idea of other civilizations.

England, France, Portugal, Spain and the Netherlands were tiny countries, compared to China and India, but the Europeans traveled the navigable waterways of their continent as well as the Atlantic and Indian Oceans. They came in contact with many countries and civilizations, including South America, Africa, Egypt, Turkey, India, China, Japan, etc.—and thus gained from their knowledge. But the older and isolated civilizations did not draw knowledge or ideas from the Europeans or from each other and eventually those great civilizations (which were once more advanced, but isolated) were overtaken and conquered by the smaller countries that had expanded their knowledge base.

Once Japan broke from its isolation, and its traditional culture mixed with new ideas, it became one of today's economic powers, and a comparable process is now shaping China and India. Similarly the rise of the United States—in particular our skills, technology, innovations and economic advances—is based on the history of immigrants, people coming from all parts of the world, melting together, and exchanging knowledge and ideas. It is this constant flow of different people from different parts of the globe that helps create an American entrepreneurial spirit and sense of innovation and creativity not enjoyed in more static, less dynamic countries.

The first generation of immigrants may not score high on standardized reading tests, because of language differences, but their intellectual resources, hard work and sweat have spearheaded much of our industrial machinery and muscle in the twentieth century and much of our high-tech information in the twenty-first century. They represent a constant stream of innovation and invention—the keystone to the American economic engine. That said, the founders of Google, Yahoo, Intel, eBay, YouTube, Twitter, Sun micro systems and Tesla Motors were immigrants, born in foreign countries. According to a *Huffington Post* article, immigrants who founded Fortune 500 companies employed 3.6 million U.S. workers in 2011 and were responsible for 1.7 trillion dollars in revenues in 2010. Of the 300 Americans who won Nobel prizes since 1901, about 70 were foreign born. Immigrants continue to make up a high proportion of the American economy and inventive spirit.

In the final analysis, geography and history dictate who we are as people and what opportunities we have as individuals. Most Americans can trace their blood and roots elsewhere, where there were minimal opportunities and mobility, minimal equalitarianism and rewards for individual performance. As for my own history, and on a more personal level, I feel the presence of Yevgeny Yevtushenko, who saw himself and his ancestors "persecuted, spat on, and slandered for centuries in Europe." It culminated in his homeland, Mother Russia, with the death of tens of thousands in Belostock (the most violent pogrom) and hundreds of thousands at Babi Yar (a mass murder and mass grave). "Like one long soundless scream… I'm every old man executed here, as I am every child murdered." So few people seem to care, so few people remember, so few people even know about Yevtushenko or Belostock and Babi Yar.

The history of mankind is a history of plunder, rape and random slaughter—civilizations we think of as "civilized" are no exception. Had my ancestors not immigrated from Russia in 1905 and Czechoslovakia in the early 1930s, I would be nothing—and my children and their children would not exist. Does anyone among us know where Auschwitz and Dachau were located? Who can recall or ever knew the name of the pilot (Paul Tibbets) who dropped the A-bomb on Hiroshima—what his thoughts were as he approached the target, or after the carnage and cloud of dust? The U.S. is not innocent, but this is the best that humankind can offer. Here there is a chance, some opportunity and rewards for excellence and some equality to prevail for common people—for the ancestors of peasants, serfs, indentured servants and slaves to rise from rags to riches. Here the gross inequalities of opportunity are erased, at least partially erased, compared to limited opportunities available in other societies.

Reaffirming the Best and Brightest

We live in a society where few educated people in the Western world would dare admit at a cocktail party they never read Dante's *Inferno*, Cervantes's *Don*

Quixote or at least one or two plays by Shakespeare. We also live in an age where many of us are unable to explain the difference between an atom or molecule and a galaxy or solar system. Most distressing, we live in a "dumbed down" society, illustrated by the National Education Association report in 2007 that "the proportion of 17-year-olds who read nothing (unless required to do for school) more than doubled between 1984 and 2004."

At the turn of the twentieth century, the best and brightest were located in the "civilized" world and the dull and low-achieving populace was found in the "uncivilized" world. These two terms were frequently used by well-known imperialists such as President Teddy Roosevelt and Admiral Alfred Mahan in the U.S. and Winston Churchill, historian Arnold Toynbee and novelist Joseph Rudyard Kipling in England to distinguish between industrialized and non-industrialized nations, militarized and non-militarized nations, white and colored nations (except Japan, largely due to the outcome of the 1905 Russo–Japanese War) and rich and poor nations. The uncivilized world was considered inferior, uneducated and politically unstable; economically static and backward places to colonize by the civilized world.

The outcome was degradation, depredation and underdevelopment for two thirds of the world, especially in Latin America, Africa, the Middle East and Southeast Asia. This was keenly illustrated by decades of economic decline and low living standards in what was sometimes called the *nonwestern* world. In fact, during the British rule over Indian soil, the nation (India) that once accounted for 25 percent of the world's industrial output in 1750 produced merely 2 percent by 1900. Bringing events into the twenty-first century, the rise of radical Islam, directed at the Western world, may or may not have its roots in the Crusades and the Inquisition. More likely, because of the proximity of events, it may have more to do with how the "civilized" world—especially the English, French and Germans—carved up the Middle East and undercut tribal and ethnic relationships in the early and mid-twentieth century.

C.P. Snow coined the term "two cultures," some 50 years ago, to illustrate the two worlds of Western society—consisting of humanities and literary scholars as one group and scientists as the second group. Both worlds were characterized by a "gulf of mutual incomprehension," each with their own databases and research methods. His analyses of both groups were not subtle or vague. Like his English predecessor Herbert Spencer, Snow put his faith in science and believed scientists represented the future, while the former group of intellectuals "wished the future did not exist."

Although literary scholars had produced great works, they were morally flawed: Fredrich Nietzsche and Richard Wagner believed in the superman race. Ezra Pound and William Butler Yeats were closet fascists. All of them, in their own way, contributed to the rise of Hitler and brought us that much closer to the Holocaust. Snow believed that science could improve society and shape the thoughts of future generations. He maintained that only the scientist can save the world through invention and innovation—and by doing so, according to this author, the scientist could reduce the wealth gap between rich and poor nations and subsequently reduce instability around the world.

Snow recommended that the Western world send scientists and technicians to the undeveloped parts of the world to help industrialize those nations and improve the standard of living of their people. Only by erasing the gap between rich and poor nations, between the scientific and unscientific world, could the West be assured of international stability and their way of life. Otherwise, the world of guns, drugs and lawlessness, if I may update Snow, could eventually bring down the West. When people live in absolute poverty, as do one third to half of the world (depending on our definitions), grievances fester and violence is close at hand. Likewise, instability flourishes; given increased globalization, everyone is at risk—the entire world population—in one form or another.

Some 1.5 billion people marginally exist on less than $2 a day and another 1.5 to 2 billion people earn between $2 and $3.50 a day. According to Allan Ornstein, in *Wealth vs. Work*, the bottom half of the world's population owned 1 percent of the globe's wealth; while the U.S. (with 4 percent of the world's population) produced 25 percent of the world's resources. The typical person of the world whose wealth was at the 50th percentile had assets worth $2,200, while the average American had a net worth of $144,000. This kind of inequality tends to increase resentment toward the U.S. and adds to a wide set of threats that we must face. Indeed, we have sufficient first-hand knowledge that more than half the world resents our arrogance, hubris and role as global cop—and would like to bring us down one or two notches. Our critics ask: Who gave us the right to continuously intervene in foreign countries and tell people how to live and how to conduct their domestic affairs? Who gave us the right to insist that people in other parts of the world adapt to our beliefs and way of life? Does a peasant farmer in Afghanistan, or a goat herder in Somalia, or a factory worker in Bangladesh understand why U.S. jets are flying over his nation's air space?

Of course, Snow never imagined that the West, especially the United States, would become more dependent on Asian-rim scientists and engineers, and other foreign-born talented students. Today, they help prop up our economy and maintain our technological edge—and the subsequent flow of wealth and jobs. How could Snow imagine this tilt in the earth, from West to the East, given that English-speaking and Teutonic people during his life were still considered masters of the world with a mission to establish order (and "civilize" the masses) where chaos reigned?

Charles Murray introduces a different twist to the record of human history and why Western nations have advanced more rapidly than other civilizations. Murray was coauthor of *The Bell Curve* in 1994, which relied on statistical data to make a case for innate and inherited intelligences as the crucial factor for success in society and the reason why different racial and ethnic groups think differently (some are more verbal, mathematical or abstract). In his new book ten years later, called *Human Accomplishment*, he ranks geniuses throughout the ages (the last three thousand years). He identifies 4,002 influential scientists and artists, using a method that he claims allows him to rank individuals from numerous fields and different cultures.

Murray concludes that Western culture has contributed most to the arts and sciences. What the human condition is today and what the human species has accomplished is largely due to people who hail from Western Europe in a half-dozen centuries. Sure to fire up the critics, as he did with his earlier book, he makes it clear that white males have been more creative and innovative than minorities and women. Whereas many people consider science and religion to be in opposition, he argues that cultures girded by Christianity have been more productive than cultures bolstered by other religions.

Among the top-ranked, most creative, innovative and influential people, according to Murray, are Galileo, Darwin and Einstein in science and Aristotle, Plato and Confucius in philosophy. Michelangelo is the greatest artist and Shakespeare is the greatest writer. Murray marvels that his conclusions coincide with current opinion. Pompous thinking comes easy to Murray, if I may editorialize. He asserts the people must be right because his research gives them (not him) *face validity*. Murray cares little about opinion, or whether history or philosophy agrees with his conclusions, because his analysis is based on *quantifiable* methods and the opinions of others are based on *qualitative* thought.

Allow me a short aside. If one was a betting man and had been asked to choose in the medieval period which part of the world would dominate the others in knowledge and the arts for much of the coming millennia, a person who was culturally neutral would most likely have put their money on the Islamic world—not Western Europe. For centuries the leading scientists, mathematicians and intellectuals came from this part of the world, and it was the Islamic world that created the first global market, linking Europe with Asia through trade. How Europe and America rose to preeminence after the Middle Ages is for many historians and philosophers a puzzle. Some say it had something to do with the birth of the Renaissance; others refer to the Enlightenment and Age of Reason. William McNeill, Professor of History at the University of Chicago, credits Europe's ascent to its warlike prowess, navigational skills and resistance to disease.

Rodney Stark, a Catholic historian at Baylor University, argues in *The Victory of Reason* that the rise of the West is linked to the spread of Christianity, with its emphasis on preserving manuscripts and embracing the intellect and reason in advancing the faith. Whereas other religions looked to the past for spiritual guidance, Christianity looked to the future in the coming of the Messiah and thus was more progressive. In Thomistic Roman Catholic theology, faith and reason are complementary and support each other.

The suggestion that Christianity is built on reason and is based on a progressive interpretation of the scriptures and/or open to competing views is considered a fairy tale by secularists. But Murray also associates the West's rise to global dominance with Christianity, as well as its people having a respect for science, technology and invention. For the last five or six centuries, the West has cornered the market in knowledge and the arts because of its intellect and open mind and because its thoughts have had a relation to reality—not faith or Zen—and rejected a rigid ideologue. He also argues (as others have) that Christian doctrine allied itself to Greek and Roman art and philosophy. But it is hard not to sense Murray's patrician and elitist background, as his interpretation of the world order is linked to Social Darwinism: Certain people are smarter than others and thus will rise to the top of the ladder and certain societies are more adaptive than others and thus will grow and prosper more than others, while their counterparts falter or decline.

And now for the bad news! Murray warns that the West has peaked. It has lost its vitality and benchmark for history's highest achievers. A champion of excellence, he asserts: "In another few hundred years," we will be explaining why "some completely different part of the world became the locus of great human accomplishment." Sadly, I don't think we will have to wait that long— not if the international test scores in science and math achievement that compare U.S. students to their industrialized counterparts in Europe and Asia are any barometer of the future and not if the fact that China and India each graduate four to one more scientists and engineers than the United States is an indicator of tomorrow's innovation and invention.

Here it is important to add that while the U.S. is still in a leadership position, and the number one economic engine, there are other points of view, creative ideas and patterns of intellectual excellence emerging in other industrialized and developing countries. The U.S. does not have a monopoly on innovation or entrepreneurship. There is a new level of humility that Western society will have to learn as the twenty-first century unfolds.

The next book on the "best and brightest" is bound to profile an increasing number of scientists, engineers and knowledge producers from the non-Western world, with hundreds of hard-to-pronounce names from China and India, and even from Japan, South Korea and Indonesia. Unless some idiosyncratic quirk occurs, America and its European cousins will lose inventive and innovative ground to the East, based on the world's increased production in scientists and engineers now coming from Asia and becoming assimilated into state-capitalist run enterprises. Once Chinese students were organizing demonstrations for democracy, but now they are seeking economic opportunities and, as David Brooks of the *New York Times* asserts, "chances to get rich and serve the nation." Now Chinese scientists and engineers are becoming assimilated into state-capitalist run enterprises. Mao is no longer the main chant: It's money, money, money. Once there was an "over concentration of government power without checks and balances." Now the wind is blowing in a different direction, and Beijing is slowly allowing progressive reform and improving labor conditions and wages.

Murray is telling a story that Western folks (both from the Old and New World) may not want to hear. But Europe's decline may be more than he imagines. Since the turn of the twenty-first century, and especially since the Great Recession in 2007, the European Union has been burdened by high unemployment (average more than 10 percent a year) and stagnant economic growth. By 2013, the 28 countries of the European Union had a combined gross domestic product (GDP) of $17.3 trillion, superseded by the rise of four Asian countries: China ($9.4 trillion), Japan ($4.9 trillion), India ($1.9 trillion) and South Korea ($1.9), totaling $18.1 trillion. Europe has been losing its power and prestige for the last decade to the extent that it seems to have become irrelevant as a superpower in the new century.

Pope Francis, the first non-European Pope for centuries, seems more willing to describe Europe's decline than his European predecessors. In 2014, he depicted Europe as an "aging grandma, no longer fertile and vibrant." The continent gives the impression as "elderly," "haggard" and sick—"losing relevance, internally and externally" (or around the world). It needs to regain its "spirit" and "vitality." For this author, the continents Shakespearean fall comes at the time in history with the rise of Asia, not only in economic terms, but also in terms of growing military prowess, global influence and technological innovation. The question arises: How does Western society address the racial and ethnic biases embedded in our society toward Asian nations? Many whites may not be racist, but we are part of a system that acts racist toward colored people around the world.

The Global Power City Index (GPCI) tells the tale and helps signify the rise of Asia. The index measures (1) business growth and prosperity, (2) financial influence, (3) investment in research and development, (4) entrepreneurial and innovative performance, (5) airport accessibility and number of international flights, (6) English-language-capable business firms, hospitals and international schools and (7) livability and cultural factors. Of the top ten leading cities in the world in 2014, four were in Asia (Tokyo #4, Singapore #5, Seoul #6 and Hong Kong #9). Expanding the picture to the top 35 leading cities of the world, seven additional Asian cities (not counting Sydney, which is Western in outlook) made the list, totaling 11 as the most influential and powerful cities of the world.

At the home front, according to a 2012 Pew report *The Rise of Asian Americans*, Asian students comprise 5 percent of the public school enrollments, K–12, but represent 9.4 percent of the gifted and talented population. On state-wide tests in 2008, Asians had its highest percentage of "proficient" scores in math: 88 percent in grade 4, 86 percent in grade 8 and 81 percent in high school. They outperformed white students in 29 out of 34 states in math tests at the advanced level, representing a median of 46 percent compared to whites at 36 percent. A significant gap existed between Asian/white students and black/Hispanic students across all grade levels, which has serious implications because the enrollment percent of the latter group should reach 50 percent by 2025. Similarly, Vivek Wadhwa, senior vice president of Timex in India, points out that the percentage of Asian-immigrant-founded companies in the computer industry and semiconductors industry in the U.S. by 2005 was more than triple the percentage of European immigrants: 63 percent vs. 20 percent and 55 percent vs. 15 percent respectively.

A Changing World: Globalization and Technology

As the twenty-first century evolves, the world is changing rapidly, more so now and in the future than it has changed in the past. In fact, for thousands of years, progress was basically static and susceptible to centuries of plunder, medieval agricultural methods and Malthus's theories of starvation. Change now takes two forms: *improvement* of things that we know already work, such as a smaller smartphone with more gigabytes, a more efficient automobile that uses less fuel or new winter gear that is lighter and better insulated than the shirt or coat we are presently wearing. This type of change is easy to explain and understand since we know what it looks like and we either use it or have benchmarks and metrics to analyze and judge progress. It's like going from point a to point b in a chess game or from 1 to 2, as with steps on a ladder. Progress can be measured; the past product can be easily compared with the new product.

Change can also involve something completely *new*, that no one has ever seen or done. For example, think of the phone connected to an electric wire that was replaced by a wireless smartphone; or think of a gasoline-fueled car replaced by an electric battery car (in terms of fuel efficiency and reduced carbon imprint). In both cases, a game-changing or revolutionary product has been introduced to the market, leading to major progress. These types of changes are harder to imagine and require thinking and doing something no one has previously done. It often involves a major leap—what I call moving from point 1 (previously known) to point x (previously unknown), or 1 to x.

In the first case, when we talk about improvement, it is much easier to copy, and the Japanese in the 1950s and 1960s and the Chinese now have been adroit in copying American products and mass-producing them because of cheaper labor costs. The second case is harder to copy, but once the product is reverse engineered it can be copied. In both cases, technology and large sums of capital are used to improve the way things are done.

Although it can be argued that the age of technology is rooted in the Industrial Revolution and invention of the steam engine, the current period of technology, along with rapid change, started in the 1950s with the coming of the knowledge and information society and swiftly accelerated in the 1990s with the rise of the Internet. However, when we think of progress today, we must include not only technology, but also globalization. This trend started in the post World War II era, first in the United States as the major world exporter and then with other industrialized countries in Europe, Japan and South Korea. It rapidly increased in the 1990s with the rise of emerging nations such as China, India, Indonesia and Brazil.

Both globalization and technology, the age we currently live in, have created new sources of wealth for people with appropriate entrepreneurial and technical skills. In a highly significant book, *Zero to One*, written by Peter Thiel in 2014, the billionaire and inventor of PayPal maintains that globalization and technology connote different rates of progress. Technology and not globalization is the key to transformative acts of creativity and growth. Globalization leads to slow and steady progress and helps close the gap between the industrialized world and emerging nations. But technology has the potential to revolutionize and reshape the world; it can lead to breakthroughs currently unknown today. Without globalization, growth and productivity would slow down and political instability would probably increase. But without technology, society stagnates and human extinction becomes a possibility through nuclear disaster, biological contagions and/or climate change.

The world must either adapt, a Darwinist approach to life, or face the possibility of Armageddon. "If nothing about society changes for the next 100 years, the future is over 100 years away," Thiel warns. New gadgets or increased competition, as reflected in globalization, will not suffice. Major technological improvements are required which "can make the 21st century more peaceful and prosperous than the 20th."

Beyond the scope of *Zero to One*, if a nation cannot adapt to change, namely globalization and technology, it will likely face decades of economic decline along with the underutilization of its talented and skilled populace. In turn, this will lead to the export of a nation's STEM populace to other places in the world, adding to further the decline of that nation.

Americans are not used to declining living standards because growth in the twentieth century was the norm for industrialized nations, at least so long as they were not at war. Globalization grew rapidly among industrialized nations after World War II. The U.S. was at its economic height, king of the mountain top, the chief exporter in the world; hence, the American workforce (along with unions) prospered, compared with few parallels in history. In the last 25 years, however, globalization led to large trade adjustments with the rise of China and other emerging nations. Many Americans were simply not ready for the new global standard built around cheap labor and products that often ignored high standards of workmanship. To be sure, there is a global shift in economic power which U.S. workers have not realized or accepted: 2.2 to 2.5 billion new working- and middle-class consumers in the next 10 to 20 years, coming first to Asia and then to Africa.

As emerging nations grow in influence, the American workforce (along with unions) has found itself handicapped and unable to compete because manufacturers seek cheap labor and have several places to go—China, India, Mexico, etc.—and for extra cheap, cheap labor there are places like Cambodia, Laos and Vietnam. In this climate, skilled factory workers are not necessarily rewarded; they are exploited. You would think that intellectual piracy, government fines of multinational corporations (totaling in the hundreds of millions) designed to limit competition on foreign soil, and the great firewall that restricts Internet and high-tech companies like Google and Facebook in China (and elsewhere) would slow down corporations from expanding outside the U.S. and Europe, but new markets (billions of potential customers) and short-term profits drive the industrialization of emerging nations.

Announcements about globalization slowing down and going in reverse (back to the U.S.) are hard to prove, and more like a trickle or a raindrop on a summer day. Dozens of companies like Apple, Cisco, and GE talk about new jobs in America, but at the same time move their corporate office outside the U.S. to save taxes and open new plants in emerging countries as they hunt for new markets. Any new manufacturing in the U.S. and other industrialized nations will be capital intensive and require sophisticated tech knowledge that relies on STEM skill sets and few factory workers or the need for unionized workers.

Take note that unions help offset the growing power of corporations; they act as a counter balance or equalizing force for working people and ordinary people against the powerful voice of big business. As unions diminish in power and influence, an increasing number of Americans find they work in an *unorganized economy* with fewer job rights and safe working conditions. In the meantime, with increasing globalization, large multinational corporations have amassed more power to define the conditions of employment. One would think there is a point where cheap labor and minimal benefits lead to other firms raiding the workforce of culprit U.S. companies. There is some validity to this argument, but a vast amount of working people in the U.S. are already living at poverty or near poverty levels. Taxpayers wind up subsidizing Walmart workers. In places like China and India, the result is upward pressure on prices of products, and the subsequent search for cheaper labor markets in Southeast Asia and Africa.

On the other hand, technological change demands special talent in math, science and engineering, as illustrated by the new "rock stars" flocking to Silicon Valley along the Californian coast, as well as in other parts of the U.S. such as the "Golden Triangle," Boston-Cambridge, Dayton, Madison, Salt Lake City, Seattle-Tacoma and Washington D.C.-Arlington areas—what I call "technological pockets." Hence, a new form of talent and reward system is emerging in the U.S. and other major cities of the world, from Bangalore, Hong Kong, Shanghai, Seoul and Tokyo in the East to Berlin, Helsinki, Stockholm, Stuttgart and Tel Aviv in the West.

Housing in small cities and technological hubs around the world have become a new source of conflict as newly arrived "techies" with salaries much higher than local residents' drive up rental and real estate prices and force out people who have lived in the neighborhoods for decades. A new form of inequality has taken shape in many countries as start-up companies attract tens of thousands of global tech citizens to urban areas. Tensions between STEM workers and local citizens is a new phenomenon, between these committed to individual performance and meritocracy against old families, old neighborhoods and old proponents of egalitarianism.

Technology is attracting some of the world's best and brightest with new skill sets in computers, creativity and collaboration that the older generation of workers (35+ years) are unfamiliar with and therefore unable to compete with. In this new technological age, employees with faded jeans, bright red sneakers and hoodies are becoming millionaires and others who understand and can apply computer and digital skills are fast becoming the new middle managers of new corporations and institutions.

Many of these new rock stars can be classified as former "nerds" and "geeks"; kids who were ostracized by their "cooler" classmates in high school and bullied in junior high school. Now mainstream America accepts and respects them, and it's the nerds and geeks who are now in demand and spearheading tech society. "Never before has the boundary between geek culture and mainstream culture been so porous," writes Noam Cohen, a media writer for the *New York Times*. In fact, mainstream America has to catch up to the skill sets of the nerds and geeks. Not to embrace the newest technology, one that the geeky culture uses in its social networks and video games, suggests being out of the mainstream. Although intelligence is widely distributed among all classes and groups, there seems to be an oversupply of smart techies among the nerds and geeks who did not always have the opportunity to exhibit their ability when they were in school. Comfort with being labeled a nerd or geek appears to be characteristic among millennials (18–34 years).

Those who are unable to function in this technological world are handicapped in the new white-collar world. Concrete thinkers and low-achieving students, and that encompasses about half the bell curve, will most likely be relegated to blue-collar and low-paying service jobs. Only those with a special talent or gift— hitting a baseball 400 feet like Barry Bonds or Mike McGuire, singing like Jay Z or Carrie Underwood, or dancing like Madonna—will be able to avoid this employment trap. Companies that are able to hire, develop and retain STEM workers have an advantage. Although unemployment among college-educated workers remains relatively high, companies claim they are unable to find the right people with the right skills for their vacancies. The challenge for the future is to find, hire and motivate talented people who can function in a culture of innovation and invention, or put in simple terms—*How Google Works*, a new book, coauthored by the chairman Eric Schmidt.

Brain Drain Counts

Duke University researchers conclude that approximately 25 percent of science, engineering and technology companies started in the U.S. from 1995 to 2005 had at least one senior executive or founder born outside the United States. The Duke study also found that foreign-born inventors living in the U.S. without citizenship accounted for 24 percent of the patent filings in 2005, compared to 7 percent in 1998. Another study found immigrants contributed more than half the international patents filed by the multinational corporations in 2011. An estimated 7,300 U.S. research and tech start-ups were founded by immigrants, and 26 percent have Indian surnames. Another estimate is that the information and technology sector, founded by foreigners living in the U.S., has accounted for half of the nation's economic growth since 2000.

Other studies reported by the *Economist* show of all the firms in Silicon Valley, about 25 percent were founded by Chinese and Indians entrepreneurs. A 2013 *Huffington Post* piece concludes that immigrants as a group are more than twice as likely to start their own business as a U.S.-born citizen; they accounted for 28 percent of all new U.S. businesses in 2011. For every foreigner given an H-1B visa, five new jobs are created for Americans. Immigrant-run businesses in 2011 employed 10 percent of the U.S. workforce. To be sure, the combination of globalization and technology has transformed how goods and services are made and sold, what jobs are important for economic growth, and what kind of talent (science and math) needs to be supported at the college and university level.

The new wave of scientific and technological knowledge is coming from Asia, given existing education and economic trends. There is also a shift in traditional brain power from the East to the West, commonly called "brain drain," as foreign students leave, or decline to attend, first-rate U.S. institutions of higher learning and follow the lure of economic opportunity, slowing down in the West and routed back to East. Not only has the number of foreign student enrollments in U.S. colleges and universities dropped since 9/11, down from 583,000 to 565,000, fewer students are opting to come to the United States, even after being accepted. In the meantime, between 2003 and 2010, the number of students from China and India enrolled in Australian and Canadian universities increased four- to five-fold because of an immigration "point system" that puts a premium on education. Furthermore, the European Union is in the process of issuing "blue cards" that will give talented people in science and technology a "fast track" to EU citizenship.

As for the U.S., the number of Chinese and Indian students, totaling 25 percent of all foreign students in 2010, has declined because of improved economies and opportunities in these two countries. The booming economies of emerging nations around the world are welcoming the return of their own talent that it was once taken for granted would get educated and then remain in the U.S. The world is opening up to ambitious and educated foreigners at precisely the same time the U.S. is closing down. The outcome is, we are beginning to lose our competitive edge, as most of these students were enrolled in science, math and technological fields and would once have remained in the United States.

The more graduate students in science and engineering we attract from Asia, the larger our pool of human capital that may wind up in Silicon Valley, North Carolina's Golden Triangle, and other high-tech and innovative centers. "Brain workers" migrate to "brain working" centers. Given the rapid increase in globalization and the Internet, brain-based jobs are highly mobile. U.S. immigration policies must attract innovative and technological talent, not repel it by making it difficult to obtain student visas or science/engineering work visas. But Congress has not significantly revised the visa rules for the last 20 years, and has added more restrictions since 9/11.

Miriam Jordan, writing for the *Wall Street Journal*, points out that since 2013 demand for skilled worker visas, known as H-1Bs, usually exceeds the entire year's supply (limited to 65,000) in the first or second week that companies are allowed to file applications. Demand for foreign nationals with advanced degrees from U.S. universities also exceeds supply (limited to 20,000) in a few days. H-1Bs are presently granted for three years and can be renewed for a total of six years.

Hence, there are many brilliant minds who try to get into the U.S. and go elsewhere. Like it or not, the nation's competitiveness and wealth is tied to brain drain, which is now being reversed. In making immigration laws, the U.S. Congress tends to cater to big business's demands for cheap labor to fill the ranks of agribusiness, hotel and restaurant industries, and sweatshop manufacturing, while short-changing high-tech, high-wage industries and ignoring the economic advantages of human capital. For example, an estimated 75 percent of the agricultural workforce is here illegally. The result is that the U.S. immigration policy brings us more unskilled than skilled immigrants and thereby fosters more competition and pressure on low- and middle-income workers. This squeeze on low-income workers is compounded by a minimum wage that does not keep up with inflation or U.S. productivity. The trend is a pro-capitalist, anti-labor attitude filtering through the American political and corporate system, which hinders the bottom half of the U.S. populace from moving up and prospering.

The fact is, foreign student graduates earn a significant percentage of the nation's degrees in science and engineering. For example, in 2009 the U.S. Department of Education reported that 27 percent of the science/technology and 39 percent of the engineering masters degrees and 44 percent of the science/technology and 63 percent of the engineering doctorate degrees were granted to foreign students. Immigrants make up two thirds of the nation's supply of such workers (science, technology and engineers), and it is estimated to be 75 percent by 2015. Their role in innovative and economic growth is obvious, and the more we attract talented immigrants, the more likely new ideas will flourish and turn into future jobs and national wealth. Congress is supposed to revise the student visa rules, currently capped at 85,000 per year and requiring foreigners to wait six years or more for a green card.

Immigrants tend to study in the field of science, technology, engineering and math (STEM). Studying STEM in U.S. classrooms does not necessarily require proficiency in English; values of hard work, achievement and future gratification seem more important than facility in English, as indicated by the large number of foreign students in these classrooms. For many immigrants, they get one chance to succeed; they have no backup or other viable options since the majority come from poor villages and cities around the world. Their only opportunity is to come to the U.S., invest their time and intellect, and succeed in U.S. schools and colleges. They get one chance at the golden ring and some find that ring. To be sure, the immigrant story is the American story, often referred to as the American dream. We sometimes forget that the U.S. is a nation of many nations. It's

American diversity—people with different blood flowing through their veins, different mindsets and ways of thinking—that helps create the talent pool and a system where young people from different parts of the world can go as far as their ability and sweat can take them, despite their initial lack of money and privilege.

Tens of thousands of workers in the tech industries were born overseas and educated in the United States. They are, however, in bureaucratic limbo while they wait for a green card. Nearly half of all engineering graduate students at American universities are from other countries. Tech companies like Facebook, Microsoft and Google want to hire them and continue to lobby for them to get permanent residency, only to encounter Congressional bickering. Employment-based visas were capped at 140,000 per year in 2012 (but only 29 percent were priority workers with advanced degrees). To be sure, many of these talented students and skilled workers are being lost to the Unites States—the nation that educated them. What the U.S. needs to do is to maintain the flow of "brain drain" from other countries by creating an immigration policy that slashes the influx of unskilled immigrants and rewards human capital with a point system modeled after Canada and Australia.

According to Somini Sengupta, a writer for the *New York Times*, a new billboard looms over U.S. 101, the highway in California that runs through the tech industry. It reads "Pivot to Canada," directed at the thousands of foreigners having trouble getting working visas in the U.S. Canada's new "start-up visas" guarantee quick residency for skilled foreign workers and entrepreneurs. England and Australia offer the same advantages to skilled immigrants. Chile is even offering immigrants seed money to come to Santiago and get their start-ups off the ground.

STEM immigrants don't need special visas to be entrepreneurial. It is common knowledge, says Sengupta, they are far more likely than native-born Americans to start science- or tech-related businesses. Immigrant preference is still Silicon Valley over Ottawa, London or Sydney; it's like being in Florence during the Renaissance era: But our industrialized competitors are making it very easy for foreign entrepreneurs to immigrate to their countries while the U.S. Congress argues how to fix its immigration laws.

Instead of trying to lift H-1B visa caps, to allow more foreign and talented students into the country, there are politicians seeking to reduce the number of these visas in order to ensure jobs for Americans. This kind of thinking is counterproductive to our economic health and vitality. It also fails to consider that job openings in science, engineering and technology are increasing and we lack American-born graduates with degrees in these subjects. Not only is American human capital slipping in these fields, we are taking mulligans on international tests in these areas of knowledge. In terms of the future, we are in high-tech decline. Given the U.S. cold shoulder toward immigrants since 9/11 and the status of U.S. education—both underfunding in math and science education and providing almost nothing for gifted and talented students (the top 3–4 percent) because they lack minority status and organized advocates—both trends combine to create the perfect "gathering storm." In fact, the rise of Asia's human capital and potential for innovation can be analyzed in Cold War terms—a "silent Sputnik."

Economists think of knowledge professions, unlike physical goods, as noncompetitive and nonrival. Ideas and innovation by one person do not preclude use by others. The knowledge industry is not a zero sum game, in fact the common argument is one good innovation leads to another innovation; knowledge leads to more knowledge. All well and good. But directing a talented mathematician into engineering or Wall Street is a zero sum game, since the number of skilled mathematicians is limited in the U.S. For every mathematician or potential engineer who chooses a career in finance, the nation loses about five other knowledge and technological jobs. We need to rethink paying "rookie" Wall Street players $250,000 to $350,000 (including bonuses) and "freshman" scientists and engineers $50,000 to $60,000. Eventually, this kind of thinking—where a company considers a Wall Street person a "profit" item or moneymaker and scientists or engineers as a "cost" item—is leading us into a technological and economic hole and hobbles us into decline.

While countless experts call for more STEM courses and greater attention to STEM students, Norman Eng, in a 2015 article on demographics and STEM knowledge, raises the point that STEM jobs account for 5 percent of all U.S. jobs and suggests prudent allocation of education resources. "Do all students need STEM education" to function in the twenty-first century or should resources "be focused primarily on the mathematically and scientifically inclined students?" What are the implications for the majority of students in the U.S. who are not STEM inclined? Given the notion of the whole child and a well-rounded student, plus the advocates of liberal arts (including music, art and physical education), how much more money should the nation devote to science, technology, math, engineering, etc.? Is that the best way to remain competitive? The same questions were raised during the Cold War and Sputnik era by progressive educators in criticism of recommendations by conservative educators such as Arthur Bestor and James Conant, as well as Admiral Hyman Rickover, who urged more math and science courses to compete with the Soviets.

Some social scientists today warn that the U.S. has peaked and the decline of GM, once the largest corporation in the world, is symbolic of the U.S. status. Nonetheless, American universities are still highly regarded; its national character welcomes immigrants and the nation's economy is dynamic, inventive and tech driven. Hence, it does not have to advertise or make special efforts to attract talented foreigners. In order to minimize its fall and maintain its competitive character, the U.S. needs to expand the supply of visas and make it easier for talented foreigners to obtain citizenship. What we need to understand is that migration today is not only about poor people moving to rich countries for opportunities. People from rich countries are now moving all over the world, chasing jobs that are being outsourced from rich to emerging countries. More important, skilled and educated immigrants have come to the realization that emerging countries are growing faster than the U.S. and the European Union; talented workers are following jobs where there are opportunities. As a result, "brain drain" is being reversed—away from the U.S.

All these new shifts in world population need to be recognized if we are to retain American knowledge, innovation and wealth. But we need to also take note that smaller, developing nations are hurt when their talented students and skilled workers emigrate to the U.S. or to other industrialized countries. To some extent, the richer and developed countries of the world are contributing to an economic cycle that promotes suffering and stagnation in poor countries. Of course, true believers of unfettered capitalism or survival of the fittest view the entire world migration policy as the triumph of the strong and smart from the clutches of the weak and backward nations of the world.

The U.S. is still considered the top country in generating new ideas and adopting them quickly, as well as encouraging start-up/innovative companies, according to the major European business school, INSEAD, based near Paris. But other studies by the World Bank rated the U.S. third in terms of innovation, behind Singapore and New Zealand. The U.N. World Intellectual Agency ranks the U.S. fifth in innovativeness behind a number of small countries. For its size, however, nothing comes close to the U.S. But there are warnings on the horizon. Innovation and creativity seem to be in slow decline since the mid-1990s, as reflected by American students' results on the Torrance creativity test, coupled with the recent interest of emerging countries to build a culture of innovation through their own schools.

Tech Companies and Tech Workers

In the last decade, the number of U.S. patent applications has increased by more than 50 percent to more than 540,000 in 2011. Microsoft has filed 21,000 patents since 2000, Apple has filed 4,000 and Google has filed some 2,700. The idea for filing is to secure ownership of an *idea*, even though there is no related *product*, and to use the patent against competitors even though the infringements are vague and fuzzy.

Legal warfare over technology patents has become a huge impediment to innovation. Tens of billions of dollars have been spent in the last ten years in the computer software, tablet and smartphone industries. Patent lawsuits now exceed spending on research and development. Often large companies sue start-up companies and small companies to exhaust their finances and to curtail competition. The larger companies are able to stifle small companies because patents in the computer and Internet industries grant ownership to vague concepts and methods, rather than specific products. This allows the original patent holder to claim wide ownership of unrelated products built by others.

The most publicized patent warfare has involved two giant tech companies— Apple and Samsung. Competition in the global market has led to 50+ lawsuits in ten countries involving billions of dollars in claims concerning the design of smartphones and tablet computers between 2011 and 2013. The disputes are largely aimed to limit the rival companies' market share in selected countries and to put the rival companies on the defensive. In 2014–2015, Ericsson also sued Apple for supposedly infringing on 41 of its patents, used for iPhones and iPads, and for transmitting data between cellular devices. In short, Apple was sued for misuse of Ericsson's intellectual property.

Often smaller companies are sued for violating patents they never knew existed or thought would not apply to their idea or invention—a cost that often threatens the financial existence of the target company. For larger companies, like Microsoft, Apple and Google, the intent is to sue partially for defensive reasons and partially to eliminate competition. Roughly 25 to 35 tech companies continuously buy and sell patents; they also stockpile them in order to sue other companies. The patent lawyers, along with the tech giants, are the winners—at the expense of talented individuals, small companies and consumers who wind up paying more for the products. The dysfunctional consequences of these lawsuits are that job growth and economic productivity are affected for the worst.

Part of its reason for patent dispute is that the computer software industry operates by its own rules. It allows a very broad and lax standard of invention, whereby the person or company applying for the patent does not have to explain how the invention works: The idea alone suffices, without explaining how the product works. The consequence is that the vague standard has encouraged what *Fortune* magazine in 2014 called "patent trolls": People or companies that hold patents which yield no products, bring patent infringement suits against companies that make products. These lawsuits are an extremely profitable business, since individuals or companies usually settle out of court rather than pay for the cost of a lawsuit. Such an approach to software patents only drives up the cost of the final product.

Tech companies also conspire to hoard talent and curb their best engineers, graphic designers, artists, technical editors, analysts and programmers from being recruited by other competitors. The result was a class action suit in 2014 involving 64,000 skilled workers seeking billions in damages against some of the most innovative U.S. companies such as Apple, Adobe, Intel, eBay, Palm, Pixar and Google. We are talking about the "best and the brightest" personnel who built and implemented the hardware and software that have become the lifeblood of the tech industry.

Almost a dozen companies were involved in these unwritten, "handshake" deals, agreeing not to recruit someone else's talented and innovative workers: no soliciting, no cold calling and no hiring of other companies' tech employees. These secret agreements, spearheaded by Steve Jobs when he was alive and Eric Schmidt of Google, checked the negotiating powers and limited the amount of money these highly skilled workers could earn. In short, competition of tech employees was less than what it would have been under normal market conditions.

Ironically *Fortune* magazine ranked Apple as the most admired company in 2014 and Google as third, ranked just below Amazon (as ranked by 800 surveyed executives). These "no poaching practices" prevented companies from cold calling another's employees and thus curtailed bidding wars and economic warfare among the companies for talented workers. Although the "agreement" was unfair to employees, the company executives felt it was essential to maintain peace, prevent intellectual transfer of ideas and curtail potential litigation over patents.

In 2014, the court rendered a decision that awarded $20 million (and another $45 million still pending) to the plaintiffs—not much money given the deep pockets of the companies involved. On the bright side, however, the decision sends a message against anticompetitive agreements and encourages companies to pay more attention to employee rights. Most importantly, the industry-wide agreements to limit talent competition and meritocracy have hopefully come to an end.

That said, it seems flippant to take the position that does David Kappos, the director of the U.S. Patent and Trademark Office: "Litigation is a...sign of economic health" in the smartphone and apps industry. Litigation involving tech patents is high profile, involving major firms, and in more than 80 percent of the cases, the original patents have been upheld as valid, according to Kappos. "It is both natural and reasonable that in a fast growing, competitive market innovators seek to protect their breakthroughs using our patent system." That's another way of condoning or winking at lawsuits among innovators, overlooking the fact that litigation can stifle innovation, inhibit new and small market entrants, and drive up the cost of new products for which the consumer must pay.

The irony or overall problem with the patent system is best described in Lawrence Goldstone's book *Birdmen*, about the famous Wright Brothers who were constantly in the courts to "protect their idea" and curb competition. Without patent protection, a competitor can easily duplicate an invention and undercut the inventor's price since there is no research and development cost in the replication process; hence, the incentive to invent and be innovative is stifled. But if the next person cannot build on previous knowledge and the progress of others without paying exorbitantly, the incentive to innovate and create is also inhibited. It stifles the next generation's ability to build on and improve previous information and innovations.

Talented Workers and Big Data

While people should not assume there is always a market for their special talent, corporate executives in all fields should continuously ask themselves whether they provide sufficient opportunities for varied talented employees. If you are going to engage the "best and the brightest" and retain them, says Don Knauss, the CEO of the Clorox Company, "they'd better think you care more about them than you care about yourself." It should not be about them making the top administrators or job creators look good. In the long run, it is about making them (the employees) successful and paying them what the market dictates or at least what's fair. You can run an organization based on control and fear only for a short time. Good morale and trust are a much more sustainable method for running an organization; nurturing and rewarding talent pays huge dividends for any company in the long run.

The only question is how much more do we pay for talented individuals (in any industry) and at what cost to labor or ordinary personnel. In order to pay extra money for talent an organization or company must "take from Peter to give to Paul"; that is, limit its pay scale for average talent. As in life, there are no silver bullets in making decisions about what talented individuals are worth. In a capitalistic society, supply–demand factors usually determine prices and salaries. With specially talented individuals other factors are mixed into the equation, including the person's name or brand, profitability, impact and potential customers.

Since people in the workplace understand that high-performing individuals and overachievers are usually paid more or promoted faster than average or below-average peers, a significant number or critical mass of workers often undermine or victimize those who outperform them. It's OK to run slightly ahead of your colleagues at work, but if you leave them in the dust they will often conspire and combine together to undercut or bully the high-achiever. (The author has sufficient experience in this workplace dynamic.) Some high-performing workers learn the corporate or institutional ethos and compensate by not excelling or working too far above the average performance of their peers. They recognize that if they do they will threaten their colleagues and therefore get their "wings clipped" by their fellow workers.

Jaclyn Jensen's study of office personnel was summarized in a 2014 *Barron's* article, "Workplace Jungle." She found that the greater the performance gap, the rougher the undermining process. Colleagues exclude go-getters and high-achievers from social activities, withhold work information and resources, accuse them of lacking team effort, assign them to menial tasks or tasks that involve excessive traveling, sabotage their work or claim their work is irrelevant to the goals of the organization. Most of these acts of aggression are covert and below the office radar. Nonetheless, this is the way lagging coworkers alleviate their feelings of envy or inferiority. When confronted, savvy workers deny their culpability and, if I may add, claim the overachieving individual is imagining things. Being hostile to highly productive workers seems irrational, unless the goal is to drive them out of the organization, to undercut their performance so it comes closer to the organization's median performance, or to find methods for reducing or masking their merit. Like it or not, most high-achievers in the workplace must learn to deal with this type of covert hostility, otherwise, it will interfere with their own performance—or worse, they will feel harassed to the point of leaving the organization.

Recent advances for storing and analyzing data, then predicting events and/or behaviors, shape modern society. Vast amounts of data generated from our smartphones, iPods, computers, credit card transactions and social networks (Facebook, Twitter, Yelp, etc.) allow us to improve "idea flow" and leads to a new system for tracking the habits of people and dealing with larger health, educational and socio-psychological issues. Not only does this trend, sometimes called "big data," need grounding in philosophy, but we may also need to develop a new social science that can cope with the growing, all-encompassing digital world we live in.

Moving to another aspect of the workplace, affecting a larger share of the workforce, is the rise of "big data." Analytical data platforms, applications and related services help companies make decisions as they get to know what they want to do with all this new information. But there is a downside: Emphasis on big data may hinder experimental and innovative behavior. As we gain the ability to predict events, we may curtail risk-related and venturesome decisions. We may become reluctant to make mental leaps in our thinking or rely on intuitive thinking, which often fosters creativity and new ideas.

Patrick Tucker, in *The Naked Future*, raises several issues about "what happens in a world that anticipates your every move." We may opt not to have a Facebook or LinkedIn account, not to use e-mail or have a website, not to have a credit card or cell phone, not to have any online activity. Under these conditions, we think we can avoid being tracked. But such defiance is probably impossible if you want to function effectively in our environment today. In the future, the less-educated segments of society will have difficulty functioning in this digitally connected world, comprised of online activity, social networks and data flow.

We need to recognize, however, that people who understand this new digital world, and how to make use of big data, will be more valuable to organizations and more capable of finding new jobs. Those who wish to excel in their chosen professions will need to understand and analyze data flow. With so much predictive power, those who are capable of applying these new data-gathering sources will be qualified for a wider range of jobs. Of course, all this depends upon the kind of job (tech vs. nontech, skilled vs. unskilled) and the degree of expertise or talent involved.

To be sure, the digital world is exploding and impacting on all of us—whether we want to accept it or not. The professional and business world are now aware of the potential of big data, which is becoming bigger and bigger. Machines and applications now talk to one another. More than 90 percent of all data in the world has been created since 2010, according to *Fortune* magazine. The need to store and analyze information has led to huge investments in data centers around the globe. There are 3 million so-called server farms in the U.S. and thousands more are popping up in Hong Kong, Rio, New Delhi, Tokyo and other densely populated hubs. Cloud computing is expected to quadruple from 2012 to 2017. Another huge driver of petabytes are the appliances and machines we use. According to one research firm, there are more than 25 billion connected devices transmitting data, that are not PCs, iPads or cell phones. To handle this massive amount of data, a whole new section of the economy is being developed with the potential of hiring tens of millions of people around the globe—but it will take the right skills to handle this kind of data.

As a side note, if you're not tech savvy—just simply stupid or unlucky—there is a good chance you are about to be mined and scanned for valuable information by a "black hat" or "cracker" (short for a computer hacker). Your identity is soon to be stolen and forged. It's just a matter of time, almost a statistical certainty. Every digital act we engage in—e-mail, Facebook, Twitter, credit cards, ATM, etc.—leaves an electronic footprint that can be swiped, stored and used by hackers. Every time we pay a toll with an E-Z Pass, register at a hotel, use our credit card to pay for gasoline, pay our bills online or shop online (for a movie, song, a pair of gloves or shoes), we are leaving clues behind about who we are (and where we are) that can be stolen by others. Want to avoid being victimized? For starters, change your password every month, set limits on your ATM and credit cards, and pay cash at brick-and-mortar stores. This might not stop a seasoned hacker, but it will reduce unauthorized access into your computer files by a large number of computer criminals. Actually, what is needed is for banks, credit card agencies and corporations to digitally protect the personal data of their customers by implementing multiple layers of identity authorization and other means that protect the public and the "non-techies" of the world.

At a time when every nation must make the most of its human resources and technological knowledge, it is unwise that we resign ourselves to the waste of human or technological potential. We want individuals to fulfill their aptitudes and abilities, but we do not want to encourage criminal behavior. We wish to develop a reward system within the framework of what is rational, just and moral. But we should not encourage or reward dysfunctional values or goals that promote unruliness, greed or lawlessness. We wish to promote intellectual, creative and emotional growth among our citizens, but we do not wish to ignore criminality, regardless of whether it is pre-digital or post-digital, overt or opaque, violent or subtle.

The New American Dream

Today, our workforce (50+ years old) is considered the most educated in the world, largely reflecting a prior immigration trend (pre-1980s) in which most workers came from Western Europe. Immigration trends are now overwhelmingly nonwhite and many are unskilled and uneducated. Hence, our younger workers are in the middle of the global education index and our international test scores indicate we are below average compared to other industrialized countries. The test scores reflect a future in which the American workforce will no longer be on top of the global education level—and somewhat handicapped and unable to compete in a technical and global market. What we have done is to convince ourselves "that our traditional global edge in entrepreneurship and innovation can compensate for our decline in educational achievement." It cannot—and in the long term we are deceiving ourselves.

For most of us who still believe in the American dream, you don't need an IQ of 150 or need to be super talented to achieve beyond our expectations. It's not all about being smart or talented; it takes a certain personality, hard work and luck—someone willing to step up and act, practice or study, and sometimes reach more than once or twice for the golden ring. Few of us are Cinderella and can rise from rags to riches, or like Dorothy—live in Kansas and find the Wizard of Oz. But someone with an IQ of 150 can give away 40 or 45 points and still make it big in America. A lot of "average" people hit the jackpot because of good choices or luck—taking a gamble, making the right decision at a crossroad, being in the right place at the right time, or meeting someone who helps push them up the totem pole. All of us need to learn that we have choices and decisions in life—all which have downsides and upsides. The problem is the downsides usually have greater impact than the upsides. Two or three bad choices can often have a grave effect on most of us, which cannot easily be overcome or corrected. Of course, those who are born with trust funds can absorb more shocks or setbacks before they feel the effects of a bumpy road.

Now a problem occurs when people feel the game is rigged—when they are working harder than ever and getting nowhere, or even going backwards because of lack of opportunity and increasing inequality. To be sure, most jobs created since the recovery pay less than the jobs that were lost during the 2007 recession. A lot has to do with globalization, technology and mass media. But the consequence of lost hope and lost dreams is that people feel frustrated and get angry. That's when ideology, extremism and fringe movements take shape and surface. That's when partisanship trumps compromise, when college graduates find themselves unemployed and underemployed, and when the middle class (however it is defined) begins to shrink. That's when a lot of smart and talented people don't achieve their potential, and look elsewhere, outside the U.S., for opportunities.

Sadly, this seems to be the new America. Moreover, we cannot expect prosperity or economic growth to trickle down from the top. A rising tide does not necessarily lift all people in the same way; in fact, the increasing trend toward income inequality illustrates that prosperity is not evenly shared among people. We should not deceive ourselves in believing that rising inequality is a necessary byproduct of competition, meritocracy or talent. To be sure, inequality leads to fissures and hostilities within society, leaving those at the bottom of the pyramid frustrated and disenfranchised.

In a conservative world, spearheaded by the philosophy of Ayn Rand and Jamie Dimon of Chase Bank, a handful of heroic bankers and business people are responsible for all economic growth, while the rest of us ordinary people are here just for the ride. Or, in the words of Mitt Romney, nearly half of us (47 percent) are "moochers," seeking government handouts and entitlements. On the liberal side of the world, are those who contend that the educated elite and talented deserve whatever they earn, and meritocracy is an achievable concept in a democratic society that fosters entrepreneurship and economic growth.

In both worlds, the average person and the ordinary worker are left out of the equation, a small person in a big arena. In the first case, those who take risks and build a business are entitled to their money and success. In the second case, those with special abilities or talent are rewarded because they are in demand and those with advanced education are entitled to a high-paying job and a high level of prestige. In both cases the "worker," regardless of how hard he or she works, is taken for granted and easily replaceable—meaning the vast majority of us; it's hard to pretend that what is left over in terms of pay for ordinary families (the average hourly working wage was $24.30 in 2014) is enough or that their children will have equal opportunities, compared to children of millionaires and billionaires. For the time being forget the super-rich! Can a child of a wage earner making $972 a week (24.30 x 40 hours), less 50 percent for state and federal tax, social security and Medicare (or health insurance) compete with a child whose household income is $10,000 or more a week?

Put in different terms, from 1979 to 2010, Nina Easton of *Fortune* asserts that after-tax real income of the top 1 percent of Americans increased 300 percent, but middle-class households saw after-tax income gains of 40 percent. The middle- and working-income families have failed to share in the nation's growth and prosperity. Social mobility over the same 30 years has dropped; it's harder to move ahead than it was during the 1950s to 1970s, when incomes were more equal and when working-class people could obtain middle-class incomes on the auto and manufacturing assembly line. Likewise, the tech world we live in today limits middle-class jobs while investment groups chase new start-up tech companies with limited jobs. The best example is Facebook paying $19 billion in 2014 for WhatsApp with a total of 55 employees.

The problem is, most people in the U.S. are not concerned with growing inequality. They are more concerned about their jobs and health—or whether they can pay their bills. Older voters tend to also be worried about their pensions (or whether they will live a dignified retirement) and whether their grandchildren can afford college (and how much debt they may have to incur). Inequality and matters of opportunity and mobility may stir the liberal base in the U.S. (and in other parts of the world), but immigration and cultural issues such as abortion or the definition of marriage rile up the conservative base—and at the expense of the working populace who vote against their own economic interests. Inequality, and corresponding matters of limited opportunity and mobility, are not major considerations for the majority of people who care more about whether there is food on the table, whether the rent or mortgage can be paid, and whether there is heat and hot water in the winter. They don't seem to care that some people make tens of millions (or Apple stock split 7:1 and is now selling for more than $100 or Google stock is selling for more than $1,000) so long as they earn enough to live a decent life (brunch at IHOP or Denny's, a movie at the local cinema, and a week's vacation at the lake).

Centers of Creativity

New knowledge in the United States doubles about every 15 or 20 years. In many third-world countries the mule and horse are the main mode of transportation, and the local economy is mainly picking berries, dragging banana trees to market, or having children clean out goat intestines that can be turned into leather. This is the real China and India, Myanmar (formerly Burma), parts of Pakistan, and the African continent—the rural hinterland—possibly representative of nearly half of the world. This is not to deny these countries don't have a corporate mentality and a class of people that remind us of both old-fashioned industrialists and a new brand of technocrats who are versed in computer software, media and other high-tech and electronic ventures.

What is less clear is the extent to which this new economic growth and human capital trickles down to the masses who live in poverty, or near poverty, in the countryside, or in urban squalor, far away from the "new economy" which deals with the exchange of knowledge and ideas. In this new, global economy old and new ideas and values collide, East meets West and high-tech meets low-tech—causing a cultural rift and the makings of revolution. Here we envision old catchphrases that divide people into "winners" and "losers," societies of widening disparities and growing inequality because of lack of social justice or lack of fair laws. Here in the U.S. we call it the gap between "rich" and "poor." Asians and Africans call it "light" and "darkness." Call it what you want. Extreme disparities and huge inequities hinder mobility around the world, distort markets and detrimentally affect the stability and growth of the economy.

Anyone familiar with New York City, Chicago or Los Angeles understands these cities, as well as smaller cities like Austin, Boston and Seattle, or even smaller cities like Eugene, OR, Madison, WI, or Champaign, IL, house people from a vast assortment of countries with different knowledge, ideas and values. The old patrician class has always disrespected and discriminated against these people, but the quest for economic opportunity and the dynamic factors that drove great numbers of these people to migrate to America have managed to overcome some of the patrician forces, customs and laws that have tried to stifle newcomers to these cities. The cities mentioned, both large and small, not only welcome a large pool of immigrants, but also house major universities and attract a large number of intellectuals and artists, as well as gay and lesbian people.

After several decades of "depopulation," exodus from cities to the suburbs, the cities have been growing in people and productivity—not just with young millennials, but also with new immigrants and retirees. The influx of young, educated people into the cities is the main part of the story. Vishaan Chakrabarti, author of *A Country of Cities*, points out the children of baby boomers comprise 25 percent of the population. Once, only a small percentage of young college-educated people wanted to move into cities; now about two thirds do; and when they get married they no longer flee the cities. The uppies, along with the guppies (gray-hair professionals) no longer move to the suburbs. Crime in cities is at an all-time low and the schools and parks in many cities have improved. It's easier to rent an apartment in the city (with the exceptions of New York City, Washington, D.C. and San Francisco) or buy a condo, and take a subway, bus or bike to work than commute from the suburbs or small surrounding towns.

A whopping 90 percent of our gross domestic product and 86 percent of our new jobs are produced in 3 percent of the geographical area of the U.S., namely, in our cities, according to Chakrabarti. The cities have become the place to climb the ladder of opportunity and for special talent (in the arts, fashion, news and media, sports, acting and dancing) to be recognized, nurtured and rewarded. If I may add, the cities have become the place, since the early days of immigration, where a full range of talents can be explored and developed, as opposed to the suburbs and small towns of America where there is a tyrannical and bigoted narrowing of talent. Tradition, custom and ill feelings toward immigrants, minorities, gay and/or artistic people often impact people who look or act differently, or have special talents or high creative ability. It boils down to the homogenization process that characterizes the suburban and small-town ethos.

Unfortunately, our federal and state governments discriminate against cities. The major cities of the U.S., especially in the Northeast and Midwest, send billions of dollars more in tax revenues to the suburbs and rural parts of the country. With the city taxes being sent to the state hinterlands, the infrastructure of many cities as well housing and schools, remain old and dilapidated. We fail to recognize that we need to diminish the wealth transfer from cities to suburbs and small towns—and thus increase U.S. productivity, reduce fossil fuel emissions (suburban rush-hour driving vs. city transportation) and enhance social mobility.

Far from "celebrating" their particular ethnic or religious identities, most urban dwellers have contact with different people from various parts of the global village and become more "hip," "sophisticated" or "cosmopolitan" than their nonurban counterparts. Even kids who come from the backwaters of the world, say from rice paddies of Vietnam or the mountains of Montenegro, quickly become enculturated into the American environment, especially if they settle in U.S. cities and they step out of their parents' culture and historical isolation. The computer and cell phone may increase our ability to communicate with people from around the world, but there is still a limitation on exposure to new thoughts without actual contact and verbal intercourse among different people.

Our thinking in America is shaped not only by our home environment and community, but also by diverse people we come in contact with who reshape and expand our thinking and imagination. Those who come in contact with people from around the world assimilate more information than those who remain trapped in urban ghettos, rural villages or towns, mountains or islands. To be sure, you can live in most parts of Nebraska and Wyoming, safe from people who have funny-sounding names, different customs and strange folklore, but you are not going to have the same opportunity to expand your thinking and creative juices.

If, on the other hand, you live your life in a melting-pot area, you will more likely to be tolerant, pursue novel ideas and resist large-scale bureaucracy and routine jobs. The point is that human creativity is the ultimate economic resource and link to national wealth. The chances are, also, that the creative mind will raise productivity, earn more money, and enjoy his or her job compared to a close-minded and convergent-thinking individual who is insulted from different people with different ideas and different ways of thinking—and more than likely works on an assembly line and performs routine tasks.

Change is accelerating more rapidly than ever, and complexity is exploding. The world looks very different now than it did ten years ago, even three years ago. The web, social networks and mobile phones are reshaping how people work, think, sleep and interact. Those people who understand and apply these forces faster than their counterparts and competitors from other parts of the digital nation have a better chance for top jobs, as well as to develop and foster their talent and abilities. To learn what works and what is relevant in today's global world, and to test different experiences to see what performs best, is enhanced by coming into contact with different people who have diverse ideas. If we don't pay attention and comprehend what is happening today, we will fall to the wayside. Young people, college-educated people, and creative and imaginative people bring more ideas to the table, as do people from different parts of the world simply through their diverse experiences. These people tend to live in the cities—not the suburbs, not in small towns, and not in ethnic enclaves. The innovative and imaginative spirit is not on the plains, not in the mountains, and not in the jungles. It's in the cities of the world: where cognitive and social action is happening, and where change and complexity move at ever-increasing speed.

If you want to be economically successful, it pays to be an immigrant. Statistics show that Americans born abroad who eventually acquire citizenship get better grades in college, earn more and marry at higher rates than native Americans. In the Northeast cities of the U.S., American-borns are better educated than in red-voting states and better able to keep up with foreign-borns. Anand Giridharadas, author of *The True American*, points out that for every dollar earned by a household of first-generation Americans, native-borns in the ten poorest states, called "Walmart America," earn 84 cents compared to 97 cents for native-borns in the richest states (mostly coastal). In the poorest states, foreign-borns are one third less likely than native-borns to live in poverty and about one sixth less likely in wealthier states. As for graduate and professional degrees, foreign-borns are three times more likely than native-borns to have one of these degrees. It is no accident. Immigrants coming to the U.S. are driven to succeed, and often it is a matter of family honor. They have harder lives than American-born citizens; moreover, the kinds of people who are willing to emigrate and start over have the self-reliance, motivation and wits to succeed. To start life over in another land—to leave home, friends and relatives behind—takes a special person with a special personality and will to succeed.

And where do most "successful" and "well-known" people come from, as selected by Wikipedia? There were some 150,000 Americans in 2014 deemed important enough to be profiled by the editors of Wikipedia; the selection process is of course biased, tending to emphasize those people in entertainment, sports, politics, business and technology—and in that order. Although there is geographic variation in the likelihood of being selected by Wikipedia, your chance of notability correlates with where you were born and grew up.

Overwhelmingly, many notables come from college towns, like Ann Arbor, MI, Chapel Hill, NC or Iowa City, IA, and/or from highly integrated cities like Los Angeles, San Francisco, Miami and New York City. Not only are all the people in those areas more tolerant, and accept diversity in color, gender preference and thought, but also the cities tend to attract a large percentage of our immigrant population. Writing about "The Geography of Fame," Seth Stephens-Davidowitz of the *New York Times* argues that suburban and rural towns are under-represented by Wikipedia notables compared to their city counterparts unless they contain a major college (i.e., Bloomington, IN, Boone, MO, and Athens, GA). If two places have similar urban and college populations, the one with the largest percentage of immigrants yields the most notable Americans. In fact, children of immigrants (such as Steve Jobs, Oliver Stone and Sandra Bullock) are three times more likely to achieve Wikipedia status than the national average.

Three major variables—universities, urbanization and immigration—are associated with various talent and the notion of diverse and innovative ideas. The three factors interact and teach children how to strive and make it in America and on a global basis. Want to be noted in Wikipedia? It helps to be born and grow up in the right place next to the right people. You have a better chance by growing up in Boston than Beloit, WI or Boise, ID; Los Angeles than Lenexa, MO or Lincoln, NE; or Houston than Huntsville or Hartley, TX.

Conclusion

The "Founding Fathers" who built this nation—despite all the liberal bashing that they were white, Eurocentric, male, and some even slaveholders—gave their descendants something very special, peculiar and seemingly implausible, if history were to gauge the success of the experiment. They built a sort of perpetual, ever-increasing, rich, multiethnic, multi-religious stew. They provided a massive dose of super-strength vitamins, to move people from a sense of uniqueness to a sense of belonging, from a harsh to a compassionate breed of Americans. This is why this nation has been able to grow and prosper more than any other civilization and why it continues to attract talented people from around the world. It is a remarkable story, but there is another side to it—one about which Americans need to be reminded.

As a nation, we all need to learn from the lessons of the global village, about people with different customs, folklore and languages, or else we will decline as a civilization. Our decline will have little to do with the loss of Christian values, faith and ideals; rather, it will have more to do with the inability of the Western world to fuse with the Asian, African and Latin American world and the inability of whites to understand, respect and appreciate people of color. Living in an isolated town in Wyoming or Montana, where the deer and the antelope still roam, a throwback to the American pioneer, doesn't work today and breeds intolerance and disrespect for the people of color around the world. If you still hunt deer in Wyoming or ride on the range in Montana, you probably will not accept the analysis that isolation breeds intolerance and limits creative and divergent thinking.

The esoteric abstraction of upper-class "Yankees" living in small secluded villages and towns—still hanging on to the old ways—is a covert, dangerous sentiment, the last flurry of American isolation and hypocrisy. These old families and communities need to open their doors to the world; their children cannot hold back the non-Western and multiethnic storm, the mixed blood swirling at their gates and fences. There are many forks in the road to assimilation, and the themes of melting pot, mosaic, stew and tossed salad to describe American society are as varied as its people. The exact word or concept is not as crucial as some of us would like to think. It matters little what label we use to describe the process of immigration, diversity, demographics—and new patterns of thinking that come with change. Globalization is a fact of life. It's no longer all about the U.S. or Western society. Ability and achievement, innovation and invention, are not byproducts of one culture, one religion or one society.

Much of America's innovation depends on the upward mobility of minority groups, immigrant groups and poor whites, which in turn reflects whether a particular group becomes homogenized or accepted as American or holds on to its separate identity. If, however, the group perceives itself as "oppressed" or "victimized" by the system, with common historic grievances toward the larger society, then the American concepts of equality, opportunity and mobility still need to be reformulated.

If the themes of oppression and victimization, or class warfare dominate, there is no satisfying that particular group; moreover, the nation's rate of innovation and economic prosperity will suffer. On the other hand, more and more Americans are beginning to say that race, religion, ethnicity and class should not be descriptions for categorizing people in any form or shape. We are reminded of Martin Luther King's dream that children "should be judged by the content of their character," not by caste or class; it would be nice if some day we could achieve this goal. To be sure, talent comes in all shapes, sizes and colors. Part of the problem boils down to money—where it comes from, how it gets distributed and whether there is real opportunity and mobility to move up among American castes and classes.

2

EXCELLENCE, EQUALITY AND EDUCATION

No country has taken the idea of *equality* more seriously than the United States. Politically, the idea is rooted in the Declaration of Independence and the Constitution. We have fought two wars over the definition of equality: the American Revolution and the Civil War. Starting in the 1960s, first with the War on Poverty and then the civil rights movement, protest and the language of progressive thought became associated with inequality. The concern focused on poor and minority rights, including women.

Inequality in today's world deals with the growing gap in income and wealth between the rich and the rest of us, the top 1 to 10 percent and the bottom 90 to 99 percent. The difference in percentages is the function of the author's social lens and what point they are trying to delineate. If the discussion is political, ideological or about a small zip code such as Greenwich, CT, Fisher Island, FL or the Hamptons in New York, the discussion can be limited to the top 1 percent. If the discussion is about a city's (or state's) economic and social mobility, it can focus on a broader population, and the top 10 percent suffice.

The notion of *excellence* is a recent concept, first introduced by the British sociologist Michael Young in 1958 in his book *The Rise of the Meritocracy*, in which the process of advancement by merit is outlined. The best and highest-paid positions in society are obtained on the basis of individual performance, rather than positions being allocated at random, by group characteristics such as race or gender, by heredity or bloodline, or by patronage or nepotism. Advancement in the political and social system is based on cognitive abilities or talent and measured by standardized exams and personal achievement in a particular field or profession. But there is a catch. Without special consideration or provisions for the less fortunate (the slow, weak, disabled, etc.), an oligarchy is bound to be formed on the basis of merit over generations because smart people tend to intermarry and have smart children. Of course, some realism must temper the analysis. If making money or rising to the top of an organization were strictly a function of brains and education, the whole world would be run by 30-year-old MBAs and PhDs. Experience, judgment and social skills all enter into the picture, not to mention several family-based variables related to heredity and privilege.

It's sort of a stretch according to this author, to rely solely on a meritocracy, because other factors weigh into the mix—some of which are more important than intelligence and education—ranging from trust funds, family business, interpersonal or social skills, special talent and luck. In the United States, John Gardner, the founder of Common Cause, wrote a small pocket-sized book in 1961 called *Excellence: Can We Be Equal and Excellent Too?* In this book, he points out the need for a democratic society to balance excellence and equality. It must reward people for their talent and abilities, but it also needs to make provisions for the less able person. In both books, the authors remind us that family origins should not count as an advantage or handicap in determining economic outcomes. The key to economic success should be attributable to the person's abilities, skills (or training) and job responsibility that, in an ideal world, make the person more valuable to society. Although Gardner was unclear about what provisions should be provided to the less able, I would argue the need to consider equity and morality, as well as safety nets and social programs. Critics would argue the need to reduce entitlements and that the tone of my argument only increases dependency.

Definitions and Labels

Every modern society must deal with the relationship between excellence, equality and education. When society considers *excellence*, it must deal with the division of labor and what it will pay for certain jobs. When 95 percent of the jobs in the U.S. pay less than $100,000 per year, we need to ask why certain other jobs pay a million dollars or more—and whether the benefits and importance (or responsibilities) of the high-paying jobs are worth the cost. If merit is defined in terms of performance, we need to distinguish between performance and credentials. (Having the appropriate education credentials does not necessarily guarantee good performance.) We must also work out definitions or criteria for performance (good, average, poor, etc.), test and evaluation procedures in school and in the workplace for determining merit and rewards—and the notion of excellence and occasional genius.

Society must consider *equality* in terms of power and wealth: which people or groups have more or less political muscle and earn more or less (and how much more or less) than the average person—and why. The more egalitarian or progressive is society, the more safety nets it will provide to help ordinary, slow, unqualified and disabled workers to obtain and pay for essential human goods (such as food and shelter) and services (such as health, education and transportation).

The exact benefits and standards for obtaining the benefits must be worked out politically. Hence, it depends on what political group (liberal or conservative) controls the process. The more benefits available—unemployment insurance, health insurance, pensions and social security for the poor, disabled and aged—the more egalitarian the society.

From its birth in 1776 to the turn of the twentieth century, the United States moved from an agrarian to an industrial society. *Education* and training were important but not crucial factors for increasing opportunity. Farm and industrial societies are primarily based on muscle power and not brain power, so that a good deal of mobility could be achieved without a high school or college diploma. Apprenticeships, training and learning on the job were more important than a formal education for the masses to live a decent life.

As society became more complex and bureaucratic, education became more important. With the coming of the information age and technology-based society at the mid-twentieth century, formal education took on even greater importance for opportunity and mobility. Brain power now substituted muscle power as the crucial factor for productivity and economic advancement. The female liberation movement which started in the 1950s, with its demand for more equality, coincided with the coming information/technological revolution (a de-emphasis on muscle-related jobs), and provided a much easier vehicle for women to obtain middle-class jobs, economic independence and greater equality in just a few decades.

Education, today, is the link between excellence and equality. In a democracy, it is considered essential for promoting a person's opportunity and mobility and for improving the productivity of society. In a society dedicated to the pursuit of social justice, intensive efforts should be devoted to providing the best education for all its citizens and to close the education gaps that exist between the "haves" and "have nots," rich and poor students. It must not write off its disadvantaged populations as "uneducable" or slot them into poorly funded schools and second-rate programs. Our Founding Fathers understood the notion of social justice, although they called it by different names such as "freedom," "liberty" and "natural rights" of man. They wanted the children of the common people to have a fair chance to grow up as equal as possible. Equal opportunity, regardless of parentage, combined with the need for civic responsibility, were the driving forces for schooling in America.

The Early Role of the Schools

The origins of American public schools are also demonstrated by the concept of equal opportunity and the notion of universal and free education. Thomas Jefferson understood that the full development of talent among all classes could and should be developed in the New World, and especially among the common class. "Geniuses will be raked from the rubbish," he wrote in his *Notes on the State of Virginia* in 1782. He added that the common people of America had the opportunity and ability for discussing social and political problems denied to them in the Old World.

When Jefferson introduced "the pursuit of happiness" at the end of Locke's famous statement "life, liberty and property," Jefferson (like Paine and Rush below) was implying that the common man had the natural right for a decent life, for opportunity and success, and to participate in the social progress of the nation. Such an idea stemmed from the humanitarian spirit of the Enlightenment, although it defied 5,000 years of recorded history: Since ordinary people had no rights and no expectations to live beyond poverty or subsistence levels. In arguing for human rights (what he called "natural rights"), Jefferson was implying a legal and moral duty for equality among people, even between the patrician class and plain people. Education was the key to equality.

Writing during the same Revolutionary period, Thomas Paine, who was an unknown recent arrival from England, began publishing several pamphlets including the best-known *Common Sense* and *The Crisis*. As an anti-monarch and pro-democratic pamphleteer, Paine lashed out against the vestiges of the property- and land-holding class. He argued that government had the power to abolish poverty and provide social and economic security by introducing policies and programs for the disabled and aged by imposing inheritance taxes and rents on government land. The idea that inequality could be reduced and social programs could be implemented by government was a revolutionary idea—and rooted in Rousseau's notion of a social contract between government and its citizens.

Paine also believed that the farmers, artisans and mechanics and other plain people had not taken part in the intellectual and artistic life of the colonies (and for that matter in any other previous society) and declared they should have the opportunity for education and culture. He rejected the common notion that education and culture, as well as philosophical and intellectual concepts, were limited to the province of the aristocracy and Church.

Benjamin Rush, a well-known Philadelphian physician and signer of the Declaration of Independence, asserted that the role of education was essential if democracy were to succeed. The youth must be trained in civil and patriotic duties and in practical skills in order to retain their political and economic independence as adults. Writing a short essay, "Of the Mode of Education in a Republic," he argued that the "form of government we have assumed has created a new class of duties for every American." Education was the key for preparing young Americans for public service and jobs. In order for the blessings of liberty and equality to spread in the New World, the education system had to "prepare the principles, morals and manners of [its] citizens" for a new form of government and new pattern of thought.

The American Revolution had opened up a new chapter in human affairs, one that elevated the dignity of the common man and the humbling of the aristocracy—and all the special privileges that tarnish the dignity and equality of humankind. On trying to elevate the national character, Rush warned about the rise of the banking and finance class and that "a nation debased by the love of money is a spectacle far more awful" than the evils of war.

The Common School Movement

Horace Mann also understood the need for schooling, and argued that education was the chief avenue where "humble and ambitious youth" could expect to rise. The rise of the "common school" was spearheaded by Mann in the 1820s. In the words of Columbia University's Lawrence Cremin, in *The Republic and the School*, Mann envisioned the schools as "the great equalizer of the condition of men—the balance wheel of the social machinery." Mann also saw the schools serving a social need; that is, to assimilate immigrants into the American culture. He skillfully rallied public support for the common school by appealing to various segments of the population. To enlist the business community, Mann sought to demonstrate that "education has a market value" with a yield similar to "common bullion." The "aim of industry…and wealth of the country" would be augmented "in proportion to the diffusion of knowledge." Workers would be more diligent and more productive.

Although the pattern for establishing common schools varied among the states, and the quality of education varied as well, the foundation of the American public school was being forged though this system. The schools were common in the sense that they housed youngsters of all socio-economic and religious backgrounds, from age six to 14 or 15, and were jointly owned, cared for and used by the local community. Because a variety of subjects was taught to children of all ages, teachers had to plan as many as 10 to 15 different lessons a day. Teachers also had to try to keep their schoolrooms warm in the winter—a responsibility shared by the older boys, who cut and fetched wood—and cool in the summer. Schoolhouses were often in need of considerable repair and teachers were paid miserably low salaries.

The immigrants and workers saw the schools as a social vehicle for upward mobility, to help their children realize the American dream. Equality of opportunity in this context would not lead to equality of outcomes; this concept did not attempt a classless society. As Stanford Professor David Tyack wrote in *Turning Points in American Educational History*, "For the most part, working men did not seek to pull down the rich"; rather they sought equality of "opportunity for their children, an equal chance at the main chance." Critics would argue, however, that the public schools assimilated immigrants into the industrial complex as cogs in the wheel.

Equality of opportunity in the nineteenth and early twentieth centuries meant an equal start for all children, but the assumption was that some would go farther than others. Differences in backgrounds and abilities, as well as motivation and personality, would create differences in outcomes among individuals, but the school would assure that children born into any class would have the opportunity to achieve status as persons born into other classes. Implicit in the view was that the schools represented the means of achieving the goal of equal chances of success relative to all children in all strata. Again, critics would argue that the schools' treatment of immigrant and poor children, coupled with the distribution of knowledge and tracking students, limited opportunity for a large percentage of disadvantaged students—and that schooling mainly reinforced the effects of class.

The connection with schooling and society was symbolized by the "little red school house" on the prairie and idealized by Horatio Alger's themes in his sentimental books on the self-made man, vision of the American dream, and power of the individual to rise above his social class. The goal of schooling fit into the popular biographies of Andrew Jackson and Abe Lincoln, how they rose from their log cabins on the frontier to become President, and it fit with the words of poet Russell Lowell, that the essence of the American promise was "to lift artificial weights from all shoulders [and] afford all an unfettered start, a fair chance, in the race of life."

In retrospect, the schools did not fully achieve the goal of equal opportunity, because school achievement and economic outcomes are highly related to social class and family background. Had the schools not existed, however, social mobility would have been further reduced. The failure of the common school to provide social mobility raises the question of the role of school in achieving equality—and the question of just what the school can and cannot do to affect cognitive and economic outcomes. Can schooling overcome the effects of class? Such factors as family conditions, peer groups and community surroundings are all components of class and influence learning. The question arises: Just what should the school be expected to accomplish in the few hours each day it has with students who spend more than three fourths of their time with their family, friends and community?

Class is a matter of culture—what educators now call "social capital," the kind of family and community resources available to children. The difference in capital leads to a system of inequality in terms of how students perform in schools and what kinds of jobs they eventually obtain. The question of fairness or equity is how we interpret this inequality. Do middle-class children simply "outcompete" their poor and working-class counterparts in school and therefore land better jobs (a conservative perspective) or is it discrimination and exploitation that ensure the latter group performs poorly in school, and their parents, who clean up offices or hotels or work on assembly plants, earn significantly less than their bosses (a liberal perspective)?

As middle- and upper-class parents jockey for the best schools for their children and hire private tutors and worry about their children's SAT scores, how are less fortunate students supposed to overcome money, power, privilege and political connections? How is education expected to overcome a system of inequality that leads to the rich pressuring the government to reduce their taxes while it cuts services for the poor, and provides them with second-rate schools, second-rate healthcare, and second-rate jobs? Given the free-market pundits who wish to reduce inheritance taxes, how do working- and middle-class students compete against those students who were born on third base (with tens of millions in net worth)? Education is no longer the great equalizer—not when financial capital, rather than education or human capital, determines outcomes (income and wealth) and creates huge gaps of inequality.

The Conservative Perspective

The notion of differences in class and the relationship to heredity has remained in the background in American thought, an idea rooted in the Old World to help explain the success of the property class—and later used by conservative-thinking Americans to explain the rise of the plantation, merchant and banking class in colonial America, and then the capitalist class in the late nineteenth century during the Gilded Age. By the 1880s, Herbert Spencer, the English philosopher, maintained that the poor were "unfit" and should be eliminated through competition and the "survival of the fittest." Because the evolutionary process involved long periods of time, according to laws independent of human behavior, education could never serve as an important factor in social and economic progress. The best the schools could do was to provide basic knowledge that enabled people to adapt and survive within their environment. Actually, Spencer advocated for competitive private schools that sorted out the "fittest" individuals from the "unfit"—kind of a modern-day homogenous ability grouping or a magnet school, charter school or special high school for the gifted. What Spencer failed to grasp is that with an educated mind, the character and speed of evolution for humans change, moving from a traditional and static society to a dynamic and rapidly changing society.

From 1873 (when the Kalamazoo, MI court decision provided for free public schools) to 1900, questions revolved around the school curriculum: What should be taught at the elementary and secondary school? What courses should comprise the curriculum? How should immigrant children be educated or assimilated? Who should attend high school? Should there be separate tracks or programs for smart and slow students? Should the same education be available for all students? Should the high school be considered preparatory for college? What curriculum provisions should be made for terminal students? Who should attend college?

At the turn of the twentieth century, the development of mind and nature of academic work in the high school coincided with the so-called "laws of nature," and that only a very small percentage of students were expected to succeed in high school or go on to college. Most people accepted this argument and social and economic improvement for the masses, based on education opportunity, was exasperatingly slow. The outcome is that by 1900, only 11.5 percent of 14- to 17-year-olds were enrolled in high school, 6.5 percent graduated and 4 percent of 18- to 21-year-olds were enrolled in college. Not too many people were concerned about these figures, since America was still a farm- and factory-based society with plenty of "manly" jobs available for working people who worked with their hands, not their minds, and who could earn a living wage.

During the same period, in his book *The Future in America*, English author H.G. Wells linked peasant immigration to the country with the downfall of America. "I believe that if things go on as they are going, the great mass of them will remain a very low lower class" and the U.S. population "will remain largely illiterate industrial peasants." Today, the debate is couched in terms like "human capital," "brain-drain" and "illegal immigration." Many Americans contend we are attracting low-wage, low-educated tomato and cabbage pickers, hotel workers and landscapers while discouraging the foreign-educated students, scientists and engineers on whom the American economy depends.

Ellwood Cubberley, a former school superintendent and professor of education and dean at Stanford University, and one of the most influential education voices at the turn of the twentieth century, feared the arrival of immigrants from Southern and Eastern Europe. In *Changing Conceptions of Education*, he argued they were slow witted and stupid compared to the Anglo-Teutonic stock of immigrants. The new immigrants were "illiterate, docile, lacking in self-reliance and initiative, and not possessing the Anglo-Teutonic conceptions of law, national stock, and government." Their numbers would "dilute tremendously our national stock and corrupt our civil life." The role of the school was not only to "amalgamate" them, but also to prepare them for vocational pursuits as "common wage concerns." The new immigrant and working-class children had little need for an academic curriculum, according to Cubberley, as they were lacking in mental ability and character; in fact, he insisted the common man demanded vocational training for their children. It was foolhardy to saturate these immigrant and working-class children "with a mass of knowledge that can have little application for their lives."

Charles Eliot, as the Harvard University president at its turn of the century, played a permanent role in shaping schools and colleges. He emphasized different education tracks for bright and below-average students. He divided society into four segments: (1) the upper one, "thin" in numbers and consisting of the "managing, leading, guiding class—the intellectual discoverers, the inventors, the organizers, and the managers"; (2) a "much more numerous class, namely, the highly trained hand-workers, [who function as] skilled manual labor"; (3) a populous "commercial class" consisting of those who engage in "buying, selling, and distributing"; and (4) a large class engaged in "household work, agriculture, mining, quarrying and forestry." Eliot argued for different education programs for bright and below-average students, including vocational and trade schools for the less able student.

The Harvard president was convinced that only the upper class of students (category #1) were capable on a large scale to work with their minds, not with their hands. Later in life, Eliot partially retreated from this "tracking" position, but measurement and conservative advocates picked up on the idea of vocational education, based on testing and sorting secondary students into academic and nonacademic programs. Overwhelmingly, working-class, poor and immigrant students were slotted into the vocational track. Not until the post-civil rights era did educators begin to question vocational education (among the most vocal critics were Jeannie Oakes in *Keeping Track* and Michael Apple in *Teachers and Texts*) as a second-rate program and designed unwittingly to discriminate against low-income and minority students.

Although progressive educators were concerned about the education of poor, working-class and immigrant children, the fact remains that the great change in school enrollment did not occur until just prior to and during the Great Depression. Adolescent students were encouraged to attend high school so as not to compete with adults for jobs. By 1930, as many as 51 percent of 14- to 17-year-olds were attending high school, 29 percent of 17-year-olds graduated, and 12 percent of 18- to 21-year-olds were enrolled in college. The concept of mass education was just beginning to take shape—as America moved from a farm- to industrial-based country.

IQ Testing and Sorting

G. Stanley Hall and E.L. Thorndike, the two most influential psychologists at the turn of the twentieth century, also supported the cult of individual success and the notions that the inequality resulting from competition and differences in talent and abilities reflected heredity and that the outcomes and differences in human behavior were rooted in human nature or the gene pool. No one was responsible for this inequality, and there was no reason to penalize intelligent or superior people for their success. This type of relationship—superior and inferior, smart and dumb—is what some might innocently call a "sorting-out process" or "tracking system" in school, whereas others would label it as discriminatory and as potential "social dynamite." Nonetheless, this conflict becomes increasingly evident when the economic gap between the upper and lower echelons are continuously widened, and when the lower base comprises an overabundance of people who feel trapped or discriminated against.

For Hall and Thorndike, the main criterion for success or fortune was inherited intelligence. The captains of industry during the Gilded Age (1860s–1920s) had forged their own success and accumulated fortunes because of their unique abilities. Their psychological theories not only fit into the business explanation of wealth, but also the religious explanation of stewardship and charity, including all those who used God and his infinite wisdom to support the business buccaneers and property interests of the wealthy class. Although no adequate tests existed at that period for determining the relationship between heredity and environment, and how they affected human traits or behaviors, their ideas led to the development of intelligence tests in 1908 by Alfred Binet, a French psychologist.

For the next 30 years, the IQ test would be used as an instrument to classify bright and slow students, to classify army recruits into designated assignments, to distinguish between officers and non-officers, and to justify Anglo-Saxon superiority while stressing the shortcomings of immigrants from southern and eastern Europe and later an array of different minority groups. Melded with the idea of Darwinism (biological differences) and later Social Darwinism (social and cultural differences), the IQ test was also used to explain the innate mental superiority of the wealthy and the inferiority of the working class.

Similarly, it was argued that people of limited intelligence, who were suitable for farm and simple rural life, had moved to the cities. Along with the new immigrant arrivals from southern and eastern Europe who settled in urban areas, they were unable to deal with the complexities of city life and unsuitable for urban jobs except the lowest ones. The mass immigration melted the families and streets into an ethnic stew. The peasants and laborers arrived in the cities dazed and stunned, carrying their earthly belongings and bundles. Their fingers were callused and arms muscled by years of toil and drudgery, and their pockets lined with soil and fresh hope, seeking a new life and a new identity as working men and women of worth and dignity. But they were immediately marked by custom, language and minimal skills and education. Living in dense areas, and often unemployed, these people of so-called low intelligence were considered responsible for committing crimes and pulling down the general level of American civilization. The difference in their abilities, coupled with their norms and behaviors, only validated the laws of nature, the rise of people with intelligence and drive and the leveling of the masses.

Enrollment in high school continued to increase so that by the mid-century as many as three quarters of eligible students were attending high school. During the Sputnik and Cold War era, James Conant, the Harvard University president wrote two books, *The American High School Today* in 1959 and *Slums and Suburbs* in 1961. In the first book, he argued that in order to stay competitive with the Soviets schools had to pay special attention to the gifted and talented students as well as the above average or top 20 percent, and to encourage them to attend college and major in science, math and foreign languages. The curriculum had to be beefed up with more homework, more testing and more honor and advanced study courses. The average and below-average student was considered more or less as "a postscript" or "nonstudent," someone who could always get a job and contribute to society as part of the working class.

As for the second book, the civil rights movement was just at its infancy stage and Conant sensed the need for greater education and employment opportunities for minority youth. He warned that "social dynamite" was building in the cities because of massive unemployment among black youth and adults. He compared suburban and city schools, and advocated vocational curricula for nonacademic students attending slum schools as a method for providing them with future jobs. Although his reform ideas were accepted by the Establishment, the minority and reform community in later years condemned his views as racist; it was argued that blacks would be slotted in a second-rate curriculum and be limited to vocational and blue-collar jobs. Conant never responded to his critics.

From the 1950s through the 1990s, conservative psychologists, such as William Shockley, Arthur Jensen and Richard Herrnstein, placed heavy emphasis on heredity as the main factor for intelligence—and the reason why the poor remained poor from one generation to the next. Although the arguments were written in educational terms, the implications were political and implied class warfare; and, most disturbing, resulted in a stereotype for explaining mental inferiority among the lower class, especially blacks, thereby explaining the need for vocational programs, and putting blacks on the defensive.

According to Richard Herrnstein, in *IQ in the Meritocracy*, intelligence tests measure both heritable and socially significant factors. Although the exact percentages are unknown, the genetic factor is estimated between 45 to 80 percent, depending on the research cited. But as society succeeds in equalizing opportunity, "the genetic factors likely become relatively more important, simply because the non-genetic factors having been equalized, no longer contribute to the differences among people." To make matters worse, in Western societies, where there are no arranged marriages, and in a democracy, smart people tend to intermarry—making genetic factors more important and contributing to class differences among future generations. These outcomes, Herrnstein claimed, are "lethal to all forms of egalitarianism." However, he failed to understand that more Americans believe human nature is plastic and capable of improvement through improved social environment and opportunity.

The common purpose of intelligence testing is to predict success in school and suitability for various occupations. The correlation between IQ and school success increases through successive years because the skills called on by conventional intelligence tests (as well as aptitude tests such as the Scholastic Aptitude Test or Miller Analogies Test)—vocabulary, reading comprehension, logic, abstract reasoning, general information—coincide with advanced school work. So long as school and college stress verbal and mathematical skills, IQ tests (and various aptitude tests) are predictive of future academic performance. Children with low IQs usually do poorly in school and children with high IQs cover the range from excellent to poor performance. Here noncognitive factors such as motivation, emotional well-being and work ethic play a role. High IQ offers merely the potential for academic success and preparation for professional jobs that call for above-average IQs.

Herrnstein talked a great deal about the backlash and name-calling he experienced as a result of his publication. To a large extent he is right: Barring drastic egalitarian policies the gifted and talented will move to the top of the totem pole and earn the most money. Most of us accept this type of mobility and it is the kind of society that leads to the most productivity in today's world. What Herrnstein fails to recognize is that capable people are often held back and prevented from realizing their potential because of discrimination or finances. In fact, throughout the ages societies have often wasted human talent by denying them social and education opportunities. In today's scientific and technological world, this spells disaster for such a society—and is an important factor in why the vast majority of nations remain undeveloped.

Not until post-World War II, with the G.I. bill, were large numbers of capable students attending college—a new form of equal opportunity legislated by the federal government to expand higher educational opportunities for ordinary Americans. Even then, occupational choices and opportunities did not always reflect IQ potential—rather social circumstances and family and personal expectations. Nevertheless, by the year 2000, more than 15.3 million students were enrolled in degree-granting institutions of higher teaching. Ten years later, the number totaled 21 million, illustrating the perceived need for a college education in order to economically succeed. The fact is, mass education is a major reason that the U.S. is the leading economic engine of the world.

However, one might also make the argument, which some conservative educators do, that half of all children are statistically below the average in IQ and basic achievement, and many just do not belong in college. Writing for the *Wall Street Journal*, Charles Murray, the co-author of *The Bell Curve*, states "if you don't have a lot of *g*," that is general intelligence, "when you enter kindergarten, you are never going to have a lot of it. No change in the educational system will change that hard fact." The most important characteristic of *g* is the general ability to learn new skills and knowledge quickly and easily, as well as to analyze and integrate new ideas—exactly the type of "human capital" that employers seek and reward in this new informational/technological economy.

It just so happens that "smart" people with a high *g* factor tend to go to school longer and get higher grades; it is not the amount of schooling or high test scores that are primarily associated with future earnings, but the *g* factor that leads to more schooling, better test scores and better job performance. Now that is a tough pill to swallow, especially in a society that prides itself in being egalitarian or among school reformers who believe in the importance of education and the opportunities that go along with it. Moreover, the inference is that *g* is a biological or hereditary factor, not environmentally based.

For Murray, the top 25 percent of high school graduates have the abilities to make good use of a college education, and the remaining youth would do better in vocational training. Combine those who are unqualified and those who are qualified but unmotivated, and the majority of college students today are putting a false premium on attending college and looking for something that college was not designed to provide. Few working- and middle-class parents, who are spending tens of thousands of dollars a year on their child's college education, want to hear this analysis—or even worse that perhaps their children should become plumbers or electricians.

Now, it may also be too frightening for the rich and well born to suppose that the reason for their fortunes has little to do with intelligence, but in a longitudinal study of 7,400 Americans between 1979 and 2004, Ohio State's Professor Jay Zagorsky found no meaningful correlation between *wealth* and high IQ scores. "Those with low intelligence should not believe they are handicapped and those with high intelligence should not believe they have an advantage." There was a slight correlation with IQ scores and *income*; each point in IQ scores was associated with about $400 of income a year. Assuming a 10-point spread in IQ and 40 years of work, the difference is only $160,000, which can evaporate in one or two bad financial decisions. The IQ link breaks down with wealth, that is the accumulation of assets, because smart people are just as likely as others to make bad financial choices over their lifetime. One very bad decision can wipe out a lifetime's savings. (Investors of the Madoff ponzi scheme certainly learned this fact of life the hard way.) More important, wealth often takes generations to accumulate and to pass from one generation to the next.

What all this seems to mean is that the sorting-out process between IQ, education and economic outcomes are not easy to separate or pigeonhole into neat predictions. Not only do Americans have multiple chances to succeed, but also you don't have to be an intellectual whiz-kid or a college graduate to succeed. Bill Gates and Steve Jobs never finished college; neither did Alex Rodriguez, Willie Nelson or Lady Gaga. Nine of the top 25 billionaires in the world (as of 2014) either never went to college or dropped out of college (see Chapter 5). We would like to think that the American education system is designed, at least in theory, to enable every youngster to fulfill his human potential, regardless of race, ethnicity, gender or class and regardless of intelligence or creativity. But education, although important, is only one factor to consider in explaining economic mobility and social stratification.

Howard Gardner takes us beyond the traditional method for measuring IQ. In his book, *Frames of Mind*, he argues for a theory of multiple intelligences and contends that there are different mental operations associated with intelligence and many different types of intelligence. Too often (at least in school) we emphasize only the verbal or linguistic factors. He outlines seven types of intelligence: (1) verbal/linguistic, (2) logical/mathematic, (3) visual/spatial, (4) bodily/kinesthetic, (5) musical/rhythmic, (6) interpersonal and (7) intrapersonal. Around 2000, Gardner added an eighth intelligence that he called "the naturalist." This is the person who relates extremely well to nature, perhaps pursuing a career in marine biology, veterinary science and so forth. As for this author, I would prefer calling these forms of intelligence special "talents" or "aptitudes" that need to be nurtured in school in order to give our youth multiple chances to succeed later in life.

In connection with Gardner's ideas, we might conclude that there is a place in school not only for the three Rs, or core academic subjects, but also for music, art, speech and even people skills (winning friends, influencing people, negotiating, and the like). These bodies of knowledge and processes can be considered part of multiple intelligence. They have a place in our "other-directed" society and help people interpret and deal with social situations that can foster economic achievement and success in adulthood.

Subscribing to Gardner's ideas means not only being a cognitivist but also a "positive cognitivist," if we can coin a new term. It means there are many opportunities and chances in life—not just related to academics. Someone who can dance, sing, act or hit a baseball or golfball can rise to the ranks of excellence in various fields. Someone else who is entrepreneurial, willing to take risks and driven to the point of making others feel unpleasant to be around can revolutionize the world and make billions. If encouraged and given a chance, many of our school dropouts would not be wasted. Therefore, those in charge of planning and implementing the school curriculum must expand their vision beyond intellectual and academic pursuits, without creating "soft" subjects or a "watered-down curriculum."

We must nurture all types of intelligence and all types of excellence that contribute to the worth of the individual and society. We must be guided by reason and balance and consider the versatility of children and youth. We need to be aware of their multiple strengths and abilities and the multiple ways of thinking and learning—and that there are multiple ways of reaching Rome or finding the end of the rainbow. Some caution must be noted, however. We live in a knowledge-based, technological society which calls for verbal, mathematical and abstract skills. The vast majority of us need one or more of these skills or measurements of IQ to succeed on the job in the twenty-first century. The chance to support oneself as an artist, dancer or baseball player is probably 1 out of 100,000. The chance to grandiosity, or to change the world by inventing a new telephone or car, or a special gadget, is probably 1 out of 1,000,000. Hence, it might be foolish to put too much emphasis on the notion of "multiple intelligences," unless we at least emphasize in school old-fashioned verbal, mathematical and abstract skills for purpose of future jobs. In this way we guarantee the majority of students the chance to obtain a decent job—bordering on at least a lower-middle-class or middle-class lifestyle. Hence, a college education today has its limits in correlating with future income.

Do Schools Make a Difference?

The modern view of educational equality, which emerged also in the 1950s, goes much further than the old view that was concerned with equal opportunity. In light of this, James Coleman, when he was professor of education at Johns Hopkins University, outlined in the *Harvard Educational Review* five views of inequality of educational opportunity, paralleling liberal philosophy: (1) inequality defined by the same curriculum for all children, with the intent that school facilities be equal; (2) inequality defined in terms of social or racial composition of the schools; (3) inequality defined in terms of such intangible characteristics as teacher morale and teacher expectation of students; (4) inequality based on school consequences or outcomes for students with equal backgrounds and abilities; and (5) inequality based on school consequences for students with unequal backgrounds and abilities.

The first two definitions deal with race and social class; the next definition deals with concepts that are hard to define and hard to change. The fourth and fifth definitions are the most difficult to fix. In today's world, no one wants to hear in public about inequality based on students' intelligence. Given a revisionist (or highly liberal analysis), equality is reached only when the outcomes of schooling are similar for all students—those who are lower class and minority as well as middle class and majority; those who lack basic skills when they start school eventually catch up to those who start with basic skills already acquired. Of course, that is not an easy goal to reach, given the fact that the education gap at the first grade usually widens by 200 to 300 percent by the twelfth grade.

The mid-1960s and early 1970s produced a series of large-scale studies, the biggest in education history, which basically showed that teachers and schools have minimal effect on student achievement. Over the years the data have been ignored or buried by the liberal/minority community, because it lets teachers and schools off the hook, and implies there is little that educators (or society) can do to overcome the effects of poverty on education. In startling contrast to conventional wisdom, the studies by James Coleman and Christopher Jencks concluded that schools have little influence on children's intellectual achievements. The results of these studies are difficult to present concisely, since the analysis includes a host of variables and a large number of subgroups.

The Coleman Report

The Coleman Report, *Equality of Educational Opportunity*, deals with 625,000 children and 4,000 schools, and the report is about 1,300 pages long, including 548 pages of statistics. It is the largest educational research enterprise conducted in the United States, and almost everyone of whatever political persuasion can find something in it to quote. Coleman found that the effects of home environment far outweighed any effects the school program or the teacher had on achievement. The report analyzed the results of testing at the beginning of grades 1, 3, 6, 9 and 12. Achievement of the average Mexican American, Puerto Rican, American Indian and black was much lower than the average Asian American and white student at all grade levels. Moreover, the differences widened at higher grades. The characteristics of teachers and schools had the least impact on black students among all other minority groups; teachers and school characteristics could not account for all the reasons why blacks, who started only six months behind in reading at the first grade, ended up three and a half years behind whites in reading at the twelfth grade.

The general approach used by Coleman sorts 45 school characteristics or variables into correlates and noncorrelates of student achievement. For this purpose, a *correlate* was loosely defined as any school characteristic that correlates 0.2 or better with any one of three achievement measures—reading, mathematics and general information. Of the 45 variables, 19 showed some relationship with at least one of three achievement tests, and 26 failed to do so.

The 19 correlates that tend to be associated with student achievement cluster around *student* and *teacher* characteristics, and especially around students; those are hard-to-change variables. Those that are unassociated with student achievement are by and large school characteristics and easy-to-change variables. In effect, the Coleman Report says that schools in general have little effect on learning. Changes effected by spending extra money—such as teacher experience, teacher turnover and student–teacher ratios, books and materials, reading and tutorial programs and length of school day—are easier to bring about but have little relation to achievement. Thus, the correlation between expenditures per student and learning was essentially zero at each grade level examined.

Coleman's findings raise difficult policy questions for the nation's educators. If increases in student expenditures, higher teacher salaries, reduced classroom sizes and other conventional remedies for low achievement have virtually no effect, what grounds are there to seek increased funds for education? Compensatory education advocates were being told that extra spending basically makes no difference in outcomes because it does not correlate with student achievement. Reform advocates generally are being told that they need to come up with a better idea than increased spending, special programs or special schools.

Even worse, the data led to the conclusion that schools and teachers can do very little to effect changes in student achievement; rather, home characteristics and peer group influences are, in that order, the two major variables associated with achievement. In a subsequent interview by the *Saturday Review*, Coleman put it this way: "All factors considered, the most important variable—in or out of school—in a child's performance remains his family background. The second most important factor is the social-class background of the families of the children in school." Those two elements are much more important than any physical attributes of the school. And, it might be argued that ranking family background better than others is a basic statement or rationale for inequality; hence, a very sensitive issue can stifle frank discussion.

The major criticism leveled against the Coleman Report is that the criterion of academic achievement is almost exclusively a measure of verbal abilities, which are more likely to be the product of the child's home than his or her school experience. Another criticism is that it is difficult to find circumstances where one can measure and account for all the factors that result in student achievement. However, most other studies rely on the same test measurements (reading and math tests) and use similar subgroups (based on class or ethnicity); when the results appear more positive, these so-called bias factors are not mentioned. If Coleman can be criticized for this bias, it follows that almost all other studies on school achievement are also misleading.

Most important, the reanalysis of the Coleman data by other investigators, as well as other large-scale statistical studies of the determinants of student achievement show similar results. A large fraction of the variation in student achievement is accounted for by out-of-school variables, such as the students' community and home characteristics. Another large fraction is attributable to the so-called peer group effect—that is, the characteristics of the students' classmates. The blunt fact is that most student output is directly related to student input: High ability yields high achievement; low ability yields low achievement. If this is the case, if abilities are unequal, then achievement results will be unequal—at least in large samples. A *Newsweek* 2015 report on the "best high schools" in the nation puts the dittie in a slightly different way: "Best in, best out, best school." Later, the report concludes: "Best schools would do best not to get bogged down serving students considered 'unbest.'"

In an earlier related report, *How Effective is Schooling?*, the Rand Corporation concludes: Of the variation that is explained by school factors (usually no more than 17 to 20 percent), only part of this percent can be attributed to teachers (no more than 10 percent). For those who push the notion of equality in lieu of excellence, the 2010 reanalysis of the Coleman Report, by Wisconsin professors Borman and Dowling, suggests that as much as 40 percent of the difference in student achievement can be attributed to differences in teacher and school characteristics. The differences in academic outcomes are explained by the teachers' biases favoring middle-class students and the schools' programs, curriculum content and tracking policies. Of course, critics can make the counter argument that teacher attitudes and behaviors are influenced by student attitudes and behaviors, and schools modify their programs and policies to fit the abilities of their students.

The Jencks Study

Whereas Coleman showed that there was not much schools could do to improve the achievement levels of students, Christopher Jencks went one step further and indicated the differences in school achievement as well as economic attainment are related more to socio-economic origin than to schooling. In his four-year study of the reanalysis of the U.S. Census, the Coleman Report, Project Talent (a study of more than 100 high schools) and several smaller studies, Jencks concluded, in his book entitled *Inequality: A Reassessment of the Effect of Family and Schooling in America*:

1. The schools do almost nothing to close the gap between the rich and poor, the disadvantaged or advantaged learner.
2. The quality of education has little effect on what happens to the students (with regard to future income) after they graduate.
3. School achievement depends largely on a single input—that is, the family characteristics of the students—and all other variables are either secondary or irrelevant.

4. About 45 percent of IQ is determined by heredity, 35 percent by environment and 20 percent by a covariance or interaction factor.
5. There is no evidence that school reform (such as compensatory spending or integration) can substantially reduce the cognitive inequality that exists among students.

Whether we are inclined to accept the data of Coleman, Rand or Borman and Dowling, the really important variables in education are not found in classrooms or schools. The important dependent variables are located outside the schools— within (and among) families, peers, communities and SES (socio-economic status) in general. Our testing and education processes tend to ignore these factors.

These are hard-to-swallow conclusions, and a number of social scientists and reformers would rather discard them; the inference is that equality of outcomes is not possible. But committed to total egalitarianism, Jencks concluded that it would require actual redistribution of income to achieve complete economic equality regardless of ability. Since we cannot equalize hereditary or family, we are inclined to put the emphasis on economic equality. Given this rationale, most people might object to income equality, and argue that economic inequality reflects genetic, family and cultural differences among groups. Most people would rather not discuss these differences in public. But considering the period, it was a major shift in thinking—from equal opportunity to equal results. Given the world we live in, it is hard to talk about increased or progressive taxation, or any other "Robin Hood" theory that takes from the rich and gives to the poor. Conservative pundits would argue: Stop talking about redistribution and taxing the rich and put your emphasis on increasing productivity and expanding the economic pie for everyone.

The main policy implications of these findings are that schools cannot contribute significantly to equality. Jencks maintains that educators at all levels of instruction are not improving the lives of students, but this is not really their fault; rather, the problem lies with the children's social class and other home characteristics. Economic equality in U.S. society will have to be achieved by changing not the schools but the economic institutions. School reform failed because policymakers tried to effect changes that were not feasible.

Jencks's positions on heredity and environment, his support of standardized tests for predicting school success and measuring academic skills, his belief that schooling is without significant value and his espousal of income redistribution, regardless of differences between those who are smart and ambitious or dumb and lazy, aroused criticism from the political Left and Right alike. The *Harvard Education Review* devoted a feature issue to the study. In trying to answer his critics, Jencks strongly responded that those who are politically oriented or are advocating a specific position will "deplore anything that undercuts [their] arguments." He said that sufficient criticism had been leveled at the book so that educators, laypeople and policymakers "feel free to accept or reject its conclusions according to their prejudices." The critics' arguments were unconvincing: "Most of the ideas they raise [were originally] covered in the text…or appendices." This does not necessarily mean that the study's conclusions were correct, but "the assumptions are plausible" and those who reject the data "are under obligation to offer an alternative view of how the world works, along with some empirical evidence that their view is more accurate than ours."

Coleman and Jencks challenge both traditional and revisionist theorists who put more stock on the influence of education. Whereas the traditionalists today argue that education is the main avenue of opportunity, and teacher effectiveness and school reform are crucial, the revisionists criticize it as a vehicle by which inequality is perpetuated by a "dominant" group that discriminates against and imposes tracking and testing barriers against the "subordinate" group. Both theorist groups probably overstate their cases as to the influence of education, but the latter argument dominates college course work in philosophy, sociology and education.

For those who have trouble accepting Coleman and Jencks, and seek another explanation why disadvantaged groups have difficulty in school, or why there is such inequality of academic outcomes, another explanation is needed. To say, for example, that there are correctable inequalities suggests that we haven't worked hard enough to increase educational opportunity for all students. It might also mean that schools and society do not reward certain qualities or characteristics that they should, or that they favor certain abilities and gifts that some groups do not take steps to enhance within the family or community.

The general idea is that children should not fail in school, but the attempt to diminish competition and differential achievement among groups often results in the dilution of standards or the scramble to put the blame on everyone except students. All of us do not have equal levels of ability. The idea is for teachers and schools, as well as society in general, to accept (and not reject) differences and then reduce tensions, bind students and offer appropriate opportunities for those who are not going to college.

The Duncan Model

It's important to note that the correlations among occupation, income and education are based on averages. The spread around the mean is considerable, which reduces the real predictability for each occupational and income group. That said, in a classic study on *The American Occupational Structure*, involving economic mobility of over 20,000 male Americans, Peter Blau and Otis Duncan show that the direct correlation between schooling and occupational status is a modest 0.32, but that when all variables are considered, education accounts for only 10 percent of the variation in occupational status. Obviously, no one in education wants to hear this kind of news, especially dedicated teachers who expect to make a difference; likewise, most textbook publishers put pressure on authors to screen out this kind of research because it is too negative and may even affect textbook sales. It is considered prudent to kill off this kind of messenger, although Coleman and Jencks can be gingerly tolerated because of their stature and influence.

Blau and Duncan further explain the relationship. A high school graduate, on average, has a lower occupational status than a man who has attended college. However, a considerable number of high school graduates have better jobs than do those who leave college before graduating as well as those who finish, and one third do as well as those who do graduate work. At the other end of the scale, half the men who did not complete high school are doing as well as those who completed high school, although as an entire group the high school graduate earns more than the high school dropout.

In a related research project entitled *Socio-Economic Background and Achievement*, Duncan found that education is only one of several variables influencing a person's occupational status and income later in life. What accounts for the assumed relationship between education and occupation and income are a number of underlying variables related to education, such as family origin, family education, inherited IQ and socio-economic class. For example, parents with high incomes are able to provide more education for their children, just as they spend more on food and housing, and therefore the children of the affluent attend better schools and obtain more education and go on to higher-paying jobs. Parents with high educational levels themselves are more likely to expect and to motivate their children to continue further in schooling. There is also a relationship between social class and intelligence of parents and, in turn, the inherited IQ and education of children; thus, those with higher measured IQ scores are more likely to attain higher levels of education.

Duncan synthesizes the relationships between intelligence, socio-economic position, education, occupation and income in what is called a path-analysis diagram—indicated below in words:

1. Family origin or socio-economic class is correlated with IQ, but the correlation is low, indicating that IQ is a result of other nonmeasured environmental or heredity variables.
2. A person's IQ has a direct influence on how much education he or she gets. Independent of education, IQ also has some direct influence on the status of occupation and income.
3. The socio-economic status of a family has its main influence on education; it has some direct influence on occupational status and income.
4. Education is highly correlated with occupational status (or type of job) and therefore has an indirect influence on income.
5. The main determinant of how much money a person earns is the status of his or her occupation. Education and IQ have less important direct effects on income; family origin has a greater impact.

The Unaccounted Factors: Luck

In the previously mentioned and highly controversial research project on education and social mobility, entitled *Inequality*, Christopher Jencks also studied the effect on income for the following variables: (1) father's occupational status, (2) father's years of schooling, (3) father's IQ, (4) respondent's IQ at age 11, (5) respondent's Armed Forces aptitude test, (6) respondent's years of schooling, (7) respondent's occupational status and (8) respondent's income. Jencks found that the number of years of school does not significantly predict income. For white males with the same family background and initial ability, an additional year of elementary or secondary education increases future income about 4 percent; an additional year of college, about 7 percent; and an additional year of graduate school, 4 percent. Controlling for IQ, the top fifth of the population earns seven times as much as the bottom fifth, whereas it should only account for 1.4 times as much; this suggests that other factors are related to inequality of income.

All the eight variables (including education and IQ) combined explain only 25 percent of the existing differences in income. This means that if everyone had the same family origin, if everyone had the same IQ and education, and if everyone had the same occupational status, most of the existing differences would remain. Jencks calls this luck. If, by "luck," one means all those variables not included in the Duncan model and not accounted for by Jencks (or for any research study), then Jencks is correct.

To call all these variables luck, however, is not a very good choice of words, because it implies that people have little control over their economic fates. Moreover, most of us in the business of education find it hard to accept that luck, or factors unrelated to schooling, has much influence (actually more influence than schooling) in the outcomes of life. To believe such a thought would mean that our intelligence and efforts are somewhat meaningless. More important, all our reform efforts have limited value. Jencks argues that two brothers who are brought up in the same family and who have approximately the same IQ and years of schooling may earn considerably different incomes. One becomes a surgeon who earns $500,000 a year; the other becomes a college professor who earns $100,000 a year (my example, my figures). There is considerable difference in their incomes, but this difference could be the result of other personal decisions or psychological/emotional factors over which both brothers had full control.

Rather than conclude that individual success is largely based on luck, it might make more sense to say that economic success is only partly related to family origin, ability or education, and there are many other intangible factors—such as motivation, disposition, drive and overall personality and people skills—influencing income differences among individuals. Of course, education cannot neutralize the wealth or political connections of the Rockefeller, Kennedy or Bush families, nor can it neutralize the possibility that someone might inherit Daddy's franchise business consisting of 15 McDonald's restaurants or five

Walmart-anchored retail centers. The list of factors is not endless, but it goes way beyond teaching and schooling. It is important for educators to understand and accept that there are limitations of what schools can do to bring about equality, despite the philosophy of Horace Mann and John Dewey, despite the faith all of us have in schools as the instrument of equality, and despite the additional billions we spend annually on compensatory programs for low-income/minority students.

Although many may disagree with Jencks's reference to the unexplained variance of income as luck, he may be right in concluding that equalizing opportunity or equalizing education will not reduce inequality. Jencks, who is a revisionist, argues for the redistribution of income—taxing the upper-middle and upper classes and distributing revenues to the poor. Now, if that sounds un-American, or like some "Commie plot," then we have two other options to further the goals of equality: (1) quicken the pace of affirmative action and related requirements of quotas and (2) turn back the repeal of estate tax and increase taxes for the super-rich, which is even more difficult since the accumulation of wealth is sanctioned by religious scripture, folklore, a host of conservative economists and pundits and those in political power who write the laws. Of course, we can always take the position that if the poor get poorer, so what, they can eat cake. If they keep their noses clean, live good lives (meaning don't cause trouble or challenge the system), and believe in Christ, Muhammad or Buddha (or hope, faith and charity), they will be rewarded in the hereafter. I guess that is one way of sedating the poor. It has worked in the past, at least for the last 2,000 years.

Suppose luck could be broken down and analyzed, although I would argue it is fuzzy and nuanced. Part of luck is being in the *right place at the right time*: then understanding the potential, seizing the opportunity and making the most of the moment, etc. How do people get in the right place at the right time—and know this is the time to act? Perhaps it is the *personality* factor. Some people act—others do not.

Why is it that some people do great things: constantly outperform their competitors, build a major company from the bottom up, earn not 2x or 3x more than colleagues in the same field but 10x or 25x more? Jim Collins and Morten Hansen, in their 2011 bestseller book *Great by Choice: Uncertainty, Chaos, and Luck,* refer to "luck events"—in terms of good or bad luck, the timing of luck and size or impact of the luck. The key point is not "are you lucky"—we all have the potential for good and bad luck—but the "returns on luck" or making the most of our luck.

Bill Gates was more than lucky. Yes, he was born at the right time and place. Had he been born ten years earlier or later, or in another country, he would have missed the PC electronic age. But he wasn't the only whiz-kid in math who attended Harvard. Thousands of other smart people could have done the same thing at the same time but did not. The difference was his personality—and his ability to produce a huge return on his luck.

We all have our share of good and bad luck. Some people give up or get knocked out of the box for good. Others learn from mistakes, deepen their commitment, increase discipline and persist. They just keep going, pushing, marching, working and making the most of their chances. Collins and Hansen would call it "return on luck." I would just say a tiny percentage of us are super lucky, and fall into the third deviation of the bell-shaped curve. But most of us fall somewhere in the middle of the curve. It's a matter of simple statistics. There is little room in space available at the third deviation of the curve.

Aptitude vs. Achievement

By the turn of the twenty-first century, the debate continued about the influence of schooling and improved cognitive test scores and whether academic outcomes affect economic earnings. Schooling explained only a modest amount of the variation related to academic achievement, highlighted by James Coleman; and academic achievement explained a modest amount of the variation related to income, highlighted by Christopher Jencks and Otis Duncan. Although employers value what students learn in school and are willing to pay for it, they also value other skills.

Most of the variation in economic outcomes can be attributed to noncognitive factors such as special talent, physical characteristics, personality, motivation, reliability, social and group skills, decision-making skills, honesty and creativity. Since social scientists have spent little effort analyzing these characteristics, the cognitive factors remain masked (by noncognitive factors) and for the time being appear to have less impact on jobs, productivity and wages (or income) than what educators would like to hear.

The best analyses of education and earnings since Coleman, Jencks and Duncan are by Susan Mayer (formerly part of the Jencks's team) and Paul Peterson (a Harvard professor); those by David Grissmer and his colleagues at the Rand Corporation; and the publications of the Brookings Institution, and the Urban Institute. In general, these reports do not repudiate Coleman and Jencks, or the Duncan model, or the unaccounted variances related to economic outcomes (what Jencks calls luck). We are told that schools help promote intergenerational mobility, although they do not themselves provide sufficient opportunity to break the general socio-economic class structure. Given our information age, in which knowledge is crucial, formal education should increase mobility; however, we cannot dismiss growing economic inequality when students are completing more school years. Students at the bottom of the social order tend to be "frozen" in their parents' status; but for the small percentage who can rise above low status, the schools are the chief route to success.

Statistical reality tends to mask the effects of school reform (smaller classes, better teachers, early child education, etc.). Common sense tells us that the amount and quality of education has a greater impact on low-income students and low-achieving students than their middle-class counterparts because of regression factors to the mean. Since low-income and low-achieving students usually start school far below the mean, they have the greatest potential for improvement. Statistically, if someone starts at the 20th percentile on standardized tests or family income, they have a greater chance to show upward movement or gains, that is to score closer to the mean (50th percentile), on future tests and income rankings than someone who started at the 80th percentile. Statistically the middle-class group has a greater chance to regress to the mean than they do to improve and score above the 80th percentile on future tests and future rankings of family income. It's a side note worth considering, given the volume of the school reform literature.

Now Mayer and Peterson in *Earning and Learning* argue that both aptitude and achievement result in adult success, but aptitude is more important because people who learn more quickly are more useful to their employers than people who learn slowly or with difficulty. Their model also assumes that "the entire school curriculum is a prolonged aptitude test, and that the specific skills and knowledge taught in school have no economic value" because people who easily learn Latin also easily learn algebra, computer skills or financial banking skills.

Most educators and policymakers prefer the achievement model, arguing that academic outcomes and schooling count, and what you know counts more than how hard you need to study to learn it—or what potential you have for quickly learning new knowledge or solving problems. For this group, outcomes count more than the learning process. Math or verbal scores count because employers seek someone with math or verbal skills, not because the scores indicate the worker's ability to learn other skills. Mayer and Peterson ask us to imagine two groups of adults with similar math (or verbal) scores: one with less math training but high aptitude and the other with better math training but low aptitude. According to the achievement model, the two groups have an equal earning potential. But the aptitude model assumes that the high-aptitude group with less math training can learn more than the low-aptitude group with better math training. Most people have no problem with this analysis until they realize that aptitude is a form of g and suggests heredity.

Mayer and Peterson further maintain that schools can exert considerable influence on the child's experiences, and these experiences affect achievement. In general, each additional year of schooling beyond high school increases wages 2 to 4 percent, not considering the effect of aptitude or intelligence. However, in *Class Counts*, Allan Ornstein argues that "most of the variation in occupational status and salaries has little to do with education and is not measured by conventional tests. Employers seek reliable, creative, honest, and socially skilled persons." Pedigree, nepotism, parental social contacts and how someone talks and dresses also affect economic outcomes. "But social scientists have devoted little time and effort to measuring the effects of these characteristics." That said, before we alter the classroom and students' instructional experiences, we need to know how much achievement would vary if we treated all children alike and how assigning children with different aptitudes to different environments would alter the variance of achievement. In this way we could determine (in theory) which changes have the most influence and how our resources can be earmarked to improve achievement.

A slight variation to the aptitude–achievement model is the idea presented by Tiger Tyagarajan, the CEO of Genpact, a technology management company. The most important characteristic he looks for in hiring personnel is the desire to learn (as opposed to the ability to learn). Are you curious? If so, then you learn. If not, then you won't learn. Curiosity leads to questioning more and the likelihood that you will work hard to learn. "In today's world, if you're not curious, you're dead, because every day is so different from yesterday." Hence, curiosity and the willingness to learn is the key, not just aptitude or ability.

Grissmer, in *Improving Student Achievement*, takes us to the final step in the debate about family and school characteristics, and their effect on achievement. He speaks in terms of family capital and social capital. *Family capital* refers to characteristics within the family passed from parent to child, the family's quality and quantity of resources, and the allocation of these resources toward the child's education and socialization. *Social capital* refers to long-term capacities within the community and school district that affect achievement—for example, peer group, parents' involvement in the community, the community's safety and support structure and the community's ability to support and pay for schools and social institutions (community centers, theaters, libraries, athletic clubs, children agencies and events, etc.).

Grissmer infers that family capital is more important than social capital, and this author agrees because family characteristics are relatively static (or slow to change), while the school and community can easily change (simply by the family's moving); moreover, the child's earliest experiences (which are essential for growth and development) are rooted in the family. However, Grissmer points out that family and social capital are not independent, or randomly distributed, but are grouped together because of economics. "More social capital arises in communities and states having higher income and more educated families. Thus achievement scores across schools, communities and states differ partly because their families differ in their internal capacity to produce achievement and partially because families with similar characteristics are grouped in communities and states creating different levels of social capital." In other words, high-income families tend to cluster in high-income communities that spend more on schooling and have smaller classes and better paid, and more experienced teachers.

Do school characteristics by themselves shape academic outcomes? No. Family and social capital differences lead to academic differences. For instance a review of the National Assessment of Educational Progress (NAEP) results, which now test students in 44 states and are considered the best indicators of national achievement, shows that achievement levels are directly related to family and social characteristics across states and only a tiny portion of test results is related to what schools do. Moreover, it is difficult to discern which school policies succeed, because so many of the measures concerning school spending, classroom size, teacher education levels and so on are related to family and social capital. There is some indication that changes in school spending and classroom size count, but these results are "inconsistent and unstable...to guide policy" and sometimes even based on "noncredible estimates."

James Heckman's 2011 article in *American Educator* points out the value of equalizing educational opportunity and achievement in order to improve the workforce and increase economic productivity. His emphasis is on the quality of early childhood programs yielding the best results for individuals and society, and economic productivity in general. Undeveloped human potential detrimentally impacts our economy, maintains the Chicago economics professor. Although equity (fairness) and efficiency are often constructed as competing goals, there are times when they are compatible—stimulating investment (which benefits rich and poor alike) or early childhood programs (in an attempt to equalize the disadvantaged child's potential for economic success which benefits society as a whole).

He agrees that cognitive and psychological factors influence education and life success, and these factors stem from family differences in income, mental health, emotional support and child-rearing practices—and whether the family unit is a one-headed or two-headed household, broken or intact. Good parenting (providing security, love, support, proper stimuli and modeling, etc.) is more important than socio-economic status. While higher income correlates with good parenting, it does not guarantee it. All things being equal single parents are at a disadvantage because of added stress and the high cost of living. That makes quality parenting difficult. We are never going to have all children raised in two-headed households; in fact, the trend towards a single mother has rapidly increased in the last 20 years. To that extent, according to the 2010 census, only 25 percent of the U.S. households consist of a nuclear family—a mom and dad. Society is not going to dwell on whether families are socially or psychologically equal or unequal. That is too controversial. But in this day and age, American society needs to recognize this problem and make proper social and economic investments to fill this household gap by focusing on nursery, family and school programs.

The net result of Heckman's data is he affirms the Coleman/Jencks research that family characteristics are more important than teacher or school factors. Again, this may be a hard pill for single parents, teachers and reformers to digest, but it's a trend that cannot be ignored if society wishes to deal with the problem of educating all of its students—and providing equal educational opportunities. The need is to pay closer attention to the role of the family and the relationship it has toward nurturing the child and working in conjunction with the school and community. To ignore the family factor is to dilute the chances for educational opportunity among disadvantaged groups.

In their best-selling book, *The Triple Package*, Amy Chua and her husband Jed Rubenfeld have entered the cultural and racial minefield by examining family values and behaviors among eight "superior groups" or minority groups of people in the U.S. As measured by test scores, college admissions, occupational status and income, these ethnic and religious groups do much better than others in the U.S. economic and social pyramid. Chinese mothers make the best mothers, we are told, and have more successful children than other groups. They are "tiger moms"—pushing their children in school to outperform and get higher grades than their classmates, and pushing their children on the job to be better than their colleagues. The two Yale law professors, branded as "racists," claim successful family groups share three characteristics: a *superiority* complex, that is, thinking they are better than others; a sense of *insecurity*, that what you do is never good enough; and the need for *impulse control*, meaning to curb instant gratification. This "triple package" yields an excessive drive to achieve. America used to represent this "triple package culture," but it has lost its way (some 50 years ago) and succumbed to instant gratification.

That is probably the period when David Riesman of Harvard University wrote *The Lonely Crowd* in 1953. He formulated three major classifications of society in terms of how people think and behave: traditional (a bygone era in the U.S.), inner, and other directed. The prevailing values of *inner-directed society* are highlighted by hard work, individualism, achievement and merit, saving, respect for adult authority (teachers, police, clergy, etc). *Other directness* is the emerging character of the American family and society, evolving since post-World War II and heightened by social media. It is a trend that encourages group activities and group integration, organizational behavior, conspicuous consumption, plastic debt, keeping up with the Joneses and being accepted by peers. In fact, conformity is extracted from peers as well as by the mass media in the "Pepsi generation" and the "Gap world," Calvin Klein and Victoria's Secret ads and now the hip-hop generation. Nontraditional and highly provocative models are popularized—all of which are anti-education and anti-authority—Dennis Rodman, Lady Gaga, Jay Z, etc. It is this new type of family structure and society that Chua rejects—the one Riesman described as emerging more than 60 years ago.

Most Americans are not ready for a world in which all behavior, worthy or unworthy, superior or unsuperior, is conceived to be culturally or genetically based. The more one believes in equality of outcomes, the more one must consider the role of government intervention. The more one believes that hard work, delayed gratification and honor for the family affect the outcomes, the more one is inclined to accept the inequality of outcomes. The more one accepts Chua's notion of "Chinese tiger mothers," the likelihood is that the Coleman–Jencks family variable is the acceptable sorting-out model. Family is crucial. The more one is reluctant to put emphasis on personal responsibility, hard work and individual differences of achievement or ignore family life as a factor in determining school and occupational success, the more one is likely to degrade excellence and high standards, and emphasize an anti-intellectual, anti-subject, anti-testing, anti-teacher argument.

Education and Economic Opportunity

All these reports and policy implications may be hard for the reader to follow, so let me sum up. The easiest and most explicit way is to rely on the *New York Times* Op writer David Brooks's ditty: "Liberals emphasize inequality... Conservatives believe inequality is acceptable so long as there is opportunity." Now let me advance one step further. Most communities in the U.S. are stratified by income, and public schooling cannot compensate for tremendous variations in wealth and status. But within the community, the people spend about the same amount of money on each student and are inclined to let the best student go to Harvard or Yale and the best person to win in economic matters.

When great economic divides exist, the solutions are unclear and open to more debate. New York City, for example, with 8 million people has roughly 700,000 residents worth a million dollars or more and another 1.5 million residents living in poverty. How can education, or for that matter any policy short of redistribution of wealth, rectify this gap, the inequality between the rich and poor? The public generally accepts wide discrepancies in achievement and reward, partially because of the notion of the "self-made man" and the American dream. Nonetheless, it should be opposed to excess or extremes at both ends of the scale—and without critics stifling debate by using labels such as "socialist" or "redistribution" in a derogatory and divisive way.

When inequality is defined in terms of unequal outcomes (both cognitive and economic), we start comparing racial, ethnic and religious groups. In a heterogeneous society like ours, this results in some hotly debated issues, including how much to invest in human capital and schools, how to determine the cost effectiveness of social and educational programs, who should be taxed and how much, to what extent we are to handicap our brightest and most talented minds (the swift runners) to enable those who are slow to catch up, and whether affirmative action policies should be continued or whether they lead to reverse discrimination. Indeed, we cannot treat these issues lightly, because they affect most of us in one way or another and lead to questions over which wars have been fought in the past.

In a more homogenous society, such as Japan, South Korea, Norway or Germany, the discussion of race, ethnicity or religion would not deserve special attention nor require judicial measures. Although it is doubtful if increased spending in big-city schools (where poor and minority students are concentrated) would dramatically affect educational outcomes, poor and minority students still deserve equal education spending—better-paid teachers, small class sizes, high-tech resources, new textbooks and clean bathrooms—as in affluent suburbs where expenditures often are twice or more the amount in adjacent cities.

Students deserve equality of expenditures simply on the basis that schools are public institutions, not private. But it does not ensure equal academic outcomes among students. In a democracy, citizens and their children are entitled to similar treatment, especially because intellectual capital is a national concern, not designed for the benefit of one class or group of students nor the exclusion of another group. It can also be argued that the poor are entitled to special treatment, actually more money, because in the long run the health and vitality of the nation are at stake. Sadly, in comparison to other industrialized nations, the U.S. enrolls the largest percentage of poor students, approximately 24 to 25 percent. Since school performance reflects the social and economic system, this high percentage of poverty explains why, among other factors, the U.S. students on international tests score consistently behind their industrialized counterparts.

There is no question that other factors arise that prevent equal school spending that are not simply symptoms of racism or class prejudice. They deal with the notion of social and moral values and the rights of people: the preservation of neighborhood schools, concern about big government and state-imposed policies directed at the local level, fear of increased taxation and why someone should have to pay for someone else's child's education, and the inability of politicians to curtail well-to-do parents supporting their own neighborhood schools and property values. The question is how much education equality should we strive for? We can have greater equality by lowering standards or tracking bright students into heterogeneous classes. We can have more equality by handicapping bright students (as in affirmative action) or by providing an enormous amount of additional resources for low-performing students (as in compensatory funding and early school and family programs). But eventually we come to a slippery slope and ask: How much money? Who is to pay for it? Who is to be handicapped or overlooked? How can society improve family structure—or should it be ignored as too controversial or politically incorrect?

If we stop and meditate a little, how both sides of the political aisle embrace the vision of America and how the "meritocrats" and "egalitarians" of society phrase their words in the public arena, we can get a better feel for how divided the American people are on the issue of opportunity and mobility. The Republicans during the Bush administration cut the tax rates of the rich at the same time as they were amassing huge fortunes and while the gap between wealth and working people was widening. The Democrats during the Obama administration tried to protect safety nets and entitlements, despite the fact there were insufficient revenues to meet these obligations. In addition, the Democrats seem married to a system of affirmative action that judges people on the basis of race—not merit—and are less inclined to embrace standardized tests for schools and colleges or jobs that result in making decisions based on performance.

The assumption is, however, more people would be willing to accept some kind of affirmative action program based on income and thus widen the idea of equality for more Americans. Of course, self-help and personal responsibility are crucial. The goal is not to bury test scores, nor provide a free ride for slow runners or less-deserving candidates. But the goal should not be "survival of the fittest." Some kind of balancing act is needed, one that provides additional help for those who need it while rewarding various forms of excellence for those who exhibit it.

While consideration for efficiency and objectivity are good reasons for relying on standardized tests, they should not be allowed to distort or limit our notion of talent. There are many different forms of talent—creative, artistic, athletic, etc.—that don't correlate with or rely on academic emphasis, nor are measured by standardized tests. The demand for talent is crucial in a bureaucratic and complex society, but the importance of formal education is not always paramount for nurturing special skills and special kinds of talent. Special skills and talent can be developed outside of schooling, often requiring specialized or one-to-one training, apprenticeships or the willingness to take unusual risks—or to pursue an idea or product in the midst of people criticizing or making fun.

There are not only talented physicians and engineers to nurture, but we need also to recognize talented plumbers and talented chefs. While we need to reward different forms or types of talents, society needs to be realistic and discourage negative talents like the ability to pick pockets or de-emphasize esoteric talents such as the ability to read lips or stand on your head. A democratic society must recognize multiple talents, and not only talents based on academic or cognitive intelligence. That is the genius of a progressive and democratic society.

Allow me to throw one more factor into the mix. The question of talent and rewards go hand in hand and lead to results related to inequality—and in turn the values of society. What rewards should highly talented individuals earn? When someone is paid tens of millions of dollars because of a special talent related to the entertainment, fashion or sports industry, we need to consider how these earnings contribute to inequality, as well as the emotional consequences felt by professional and middle-income people who have college degrees and play by the rulebook and can barely keep up with payment of their bills. We need to consider whether the rewards, especially if excessive, contribute to the common good and needs of society, to what extent extraordinarily high salaries or earnings lead to inequality, and how they affect the standard of living of ordinary working people who comprise the foundation of American democracy. Since services and goods are limited, people with vast amounts of income drive up the prices of homes, autos, college tuition and even baseball tickets.

For example, today, the average cost for attending a baseball game for a family of four, including burgers and Cokes, parking, and tickets in the second tier between third base and left field in the mezzanine now costs between $500 and $750. This amount is more than the weekly take-home pay of the average worker in America. Of course Yankee Stadium has history and is located in the "Big Apple," where prices are often sky high. A box seat at the stadium runs $2,500—available only for Wall Street players and global high-flying capitalists, perceived now by 99 percent as the *bastards* and *plunderers* of the world, but for blue bloods and aspiring MBA's *heroes* and *superstars* to emulate. (You might want to know that Madoff's season box seats at Yankee Stadium were auctioned off.)

Conclusion

Essential good services—housing, education, health, etc. (as well as leisure activities such as watching a baseball game)—have increased far more than the median wages of workers ($36,000 annually) or household incomes ($50,000) as of 2012 (both about the same they were in 1980, after considering inflation). It now takes two spouses to work in order to live a "middle class" lifestyle, when 50 years ago, it took one working spouse to live a similar lifestyle—portrayed in *Ozzie and Harriet, Father Knows Best,* and *I Love Lucy.* For the time being this middle-class lifestyle seems to work for a married couple, both of whom are college educated and working. The model breaks down in one-head family households or when one of the two spouses loses their job or stays home to raise children.

If you want to feel even less optimistic, consider that most U.S. politicians seem committed to protecting the rights of the rich and super-rich via a tax code that favors wealth over work and wages. The dominance of capital and investments over income and salaries not only reduces the importance of education, but it also favors those children who start from a position of hereditary privilege that schooling cannot easily, if at all, overcome—and in turn reduces social and economic opportunities and mobility.

Given this scenario, the notion of intelligence, and the policy reports discussed in the chapter, it's possible that both Michael Young and John Gardner (who were introduced in the beginning pages of this chapter), along with multiple reformers, have overstated the effects of education (more so for working- and middle-class children than those from the lower class or from households of the bottom 20 percentile of income). The major concern is that education cannot fully neutralize the effects of privileged birth status. The American dream still exists but not in the same manner or frequency we would like to think. We would rather not have to admit to these new "realities," but that's the way of the world.

We must also recognize that plenty of dull, dim-witted, slow and uneducated people will somehow rise to the upper class, and plenty of bright, capable, creative and educated people will somehow fall to the bottom of the socio-economic ladder. There are sufficient numbers of unaccounted-for and unpredictable factors such as motivation, drive, character, personality, social skills and dumb luck that undermine the sorting-out process based solely on merit and talent. Nonetheless, those involved in education—our parents, teachers and principals— must ask themselves how to promote *equal* educational opportunities for less privileged children and youth as well as for individuals of varied degrees of ability, as well as *excellence* in education. Both goals are essential for a fair and just society, as well as an efficient and productive society.

3

SOCIO-ECONOMIC CLASS AND MOBILITY

Social scientists study social mobility in order to ascertain the relative openness or fluidity of a society. They are interested in the difficulties different persons or groups experience in acquiring the goods and services that are valued in the culture and may be acquired through unequal contributions. In *ascriptive* societies, the stratification system is closed to individual mobility because status and prestige are determined at birth. One's education, occupational status, income and lifestyle cannot be easily changed. In an *open-class* society, although people start with different advantages, opportunities are available for them to change their initial class positions. The life chances of a welfare recipient's child born in the slums differ considerably from those of a banker's child born in the suburbs, but in an achievement-oriented society the former can still achieve as much as or more than the latter.

The emphasis on vertical social mobility in the American social structure is one of the more striking features of our class system. Kurt Mayer, in a classic sociology text, maintains that the United States puts emphasis on social mobility, more than any other nation in modern times: "Americans have firmly proclaimed the idea of equality and freedom of achievement and have acclaimed the large numbers of individuals who have risen from humble origins to positions of prominence and affluence." Indeed, the belief in opportunity is so strongly entrenched in the culture that most Americans feel not only that each individual has the "right to succeed but that it is his duty to do so." Thus, we look with disapproval upon those who make little or no attempt to better themselves—or who become "welfare junkies."

There is historical evidence of considerable social mobility in the United States. Studies of *intergenerational mobility*—the occupational career patterns of individuals in terms of their mobility between jobs and occupations during their lifetimes—reveal that a very large proportion of American men in the past have worked in different communities, different occupations and different jobs. Nonetheless, there are certain limits to the variety of such experiences; most notably, occupational mobility is confined primarily to either side of a dividing line between manual and nonmanual occupations and between nontechnical/ nonprofessional and technical/professional jobs; little permanent mobility takes place across this basic blue–white-collar line. Increasingly, now, little mobility takes place across class lines.

There are powerful conservative interests who support the rich and super-rich—based on a platform that includes reduced taxes for the rich, favorable estate planning to pass wealth to the next generation, small government and minimal government regulation. These people accept growing inequality as proof that capitalism works. There is no shame in being successful or making lots of money based on achievement and hard work. They believe America is the land of opportunity where people can still get ahead based on ability and motivation, etc. So long as individuals can move up, they are willing to accept inequality. In fact, there is nothing wrong with greed, materialism or conspicuous consumption. This is the fuel that drives the economy. Liberals claim mobility in the U.S. is limited today—in fact, more limited than in many other countries. They see ordinary people, common people, the majority populace, etc. as victims, sometimes as oppressed, and doubt whether most individuals can climb up the ladder of success without government assistance and social programs.

Conservatives are willing to acknowledge the playing field is tilted in favor of the rich and that opportunities are not equal. But they argue that although people start with different opportunities, with education, effort and commitment, people can overcome their disadvantages. Liberals counterclaim that anyone who takes this position must be wearing blinders or earplugs, because income has been stagnant for several decades (after considering inflation) for the poor, working- and middle-class populace. Mobility has been frozen and present tax policies add to limits on mobility since labor is taxed at a higher rate than capital. The notion of "rags to riches" or even "riches to rags" are rare incidents in the lives of Americans (or anyone around the world). The worst thing is to get used to minimal mobility or accept it as a way of life.

The idea that differences in social status are due to differences in hereditary factors or genetic superiority has been rejected, and replaced by the belief that inequalities between individuals are due to social inequalities but not necessarily lack of opportunity. Those weighing the evidence prefer today to claim environment is much more important than heredity. But they often fail to recognize that opportunity and mobility are increasingly becoming limited as income and wealth becomes more concentrated in the hands of a few. What it all boils down to is what Milton Friedman once extolled: Researchers and pundits tend to resolve conflicting ideas and outcomes in favor of their own ideology and pet theories. If they look hard enough, they can find proofs of their theories wherever they look even if they analyze the same data.

Measures of Inequality

Once we were called a classless society. Class, today, is blurred by dress and credit card debt (permitting people to buy more than they can afford). Most Americans charge and borrow. As a nation, we owe more than $1 trillion in revolving plastic debt, a six-fold increase from 20 years ago. In recent years, the personal savings rate fell below zero for the first time since the Depression, an indication of the nation's growing debt, which exceeded $18 trillion in 2015. Under the guise of "democratizing credit" and making things more accessible to moderate-earning Americans, the credit card industry is sealing the fate of the bottom half and possibly the bottom two thirds of Americans; they will remain buried in their lower-income quartiles or classes and not have the capacity to get out of debt. It's a ticking time bomb that few people realize and it is bound to affect consumer spending and the economy.

Given the fact that we all have a different gene pool, and grew up in a different environment and our family heritages are varied, we should expect and accept some inequality. However, the major reason for economic inequality has less to do with ability or talent, and more to do with our socio-economic roots. For some of us, our ancestors were slaves with no ability to accumulate and pass on wealth. Others are descendants of peasants and refugees who came to America with little more than the shirts on their backs, a few suitcases of clothing and family trinkets. On the other side of the divide are descendants of wealthy parents and grandparents who have provided their children with investment trust funds and stocks, as well as fine art, a family business and large homes, including beach homes on the Cape or in the Hamptons and still others in West Palm Beach and the coast of Newport Beach.

Most of us in the U.S. are the children of parents who can be classified somewhere in between rich and poor, with a mom and/or dad who managed to earn a living as a laborer, factory worker or government bureaucrat. We grew up in apartments or row houses in the cities, and others grew up in steel towns and mining towns, small suburban and rural towns. Our parents did not earn enough to accumulate wealth; rather they provided us with love, hope and motivation to go to school and to work hard. As students, we grew up with our own dreams, and our aptitudes and performance were measured in school and predicted from early grades. More than three fourths of us graduate from high school, about one third from college; hence, we would expect less imbalance and less stratification than what presently exists.

So long as people are able to keep their bellies full and attend to their basic needs, they are more likely to tolerate differences in income and wealth. So long as the system is perceived as fair, most Americans feel the super-rich are entitled to their bundles. (Actually, there is a false belief that the system is fair when in reality it is unfair.) It comes pretty close to Orwellian logic or *doublethink*: Forget facts that are inconvenient; draw it back from oblivion for just as long as it is needed, to deny the existence of the reality which it denies.

Given the real world, the question of race should be considered. The history of slavery in the U.S., followed by Jim Crow laws, Ku Klux activities and convict labor policies (leasing black convicts to companies as nonpaid laborers) well into the twentieth century, has prevented blacks from competing for many good-paying jobs and accumulating wealth. Inequality is further aggravated by job and housing discrimination, as well as *de facto* school segregation. Hence it is estimated that the average black household income is 2005 was 40 percent lower than that of whites and wealth accumulated was 90 percent lower. Uncomfortable questions arise. Are whites still supposed to feel guilty? Are they required to make perpetual apologies? Should the "blame game" be transferred into reparation payments or reverse discrimination? What special provisions, if any, is society obligated to make up for past-discriminated groups? Many societies in Asia, Africa and Latin America have the same dilemma, given their history of tribal, religious and/or ethnic conflict. Does social justice require special compensatory provisions for its disadvantaged groups?

Other questions arise: What safety nets should exist for the majority of people? What should be done, if anything, to limit or restrict the smart and swift? How do we balance entitlements, opportunity and redistribution of revenues derived from tax dollars? How do we ensure that too many entitlements don't lead to hindering advancement and merit, or even worse creating a culture of poverty. The answers have very little to do with a game well played, as the very rich do not play by the same rules as the common people do. They have a host of advantages and clout, of which the average person is unaware.

Sadly, most people who play by the rules still believe in the "dream" but get nowhere; they are barely treading water and staying afloat—trying not to accumulate too much debt and go under. One wrong choice, a stroke of bad luck or an uncontrollable event often leads to millions of Americans each year heading to the poverty line or hovering around it. This is not a great testimony for the world's largest democracy, which once led people to claim there was gold to be found in the streets, for those who were willing to work hard—and follow the rules. Of course, if you are born in the "right household," with Ivy League and corporate legacies and a trust amounting to millions, you get more than one wrong choice, more than one stroke of bad luck—and you still get the chance to succeed. But what provisions should a rich society make, if any, for all the children and youth born to a single mother—working on a factory line or at Walmart? Only a handful of these kids manage to overcome the long odds against them; so much talent and creativity are wasted away in all societies because of lack of access to equal opportunity.

A Just Society

Harvard philosophy professor John Rawls (now deceased) examines the notion of equality and inequality in what he calls a "just and fair society," one which is grounded in liberal and democratic principles of political rights—and, if I may add, significant educational and economic opportunities. He provides four reasons for a society to regulate economic and social equality, and to limit inequality.

1. In the absence of special circumstances (such as war, disease, economic depression), it is wrong for the least advantaged group(s) to suffer personal *hardship*, not to mention hunger and treatable illness. In a fair society, *basic needs* for everyone should not go unfilled, while "less urgent ones of others are satisfied."
2. Political equality is essential to prevent one part of society from dominating the other. One group should not have the ability to pursue its political or economic interests at the expense of another group, or to extract a legal system or economy, or to make "many peoples' lives less good than they might otherwise be."
3. Equality of opportunity is essential so as not to "encourage those of lower status to be viewed by themselves or by others as *inferior*." Such an arrangement fosters arrogance, exploitation and deprivation.
4. A just society must avoid the conditions of *monopoly*, not only because it reduces equality but also because it leads to inefficiency and permits the dominance of a wealthy few at the expense of the remaining populace.

These four elements help comprise what Rawls calls "democratic equality," and they should exist if society is to be just and fair, if there is to be "social cooperation between free and equal citizens," and if there is to be consideration for the common public good. In short, in a just society, "everyone as a citizen should gain from its policies." Moreover, we might add that the gains should not be overly lopsided in favor of the rich, such that the least advantaged groups get minimal benefits and cannot dig out of their unfortunate circumstances. No person who works full time should make so little that he or she is still categorized as poor or near poor. No point on the economic curve should exist where the gap is too wide to overcome by education and/or hard work, thereby curtailing mobility.

In other words, there should be a floor and ceiling in determining income and wealth. Just where this point lies on the economic curve, and how to regulate or achieve this point, is debatable and makes for liberal and conservative discussion. As the distance from the floor and ceiling grows, so does the gap in income and wealth increases among people. If the gap between the floor and ceiling is reduced, then inequality is reduced. In the world we have inherited, the entertainment and sports industries, along with the corporate elite, are leaving middle- and upper-middle-class Americans behind—eventually leading to a small group of winners and a huge group of losers. Today the lines are blurring in Western society, the U.S. and Europe, between the middle class, the working poor and those who are unemployed or underemployed, especially as well-paying jobs seemingly disappear and are replaced by low-wage jobs with minimal benefits. Most of us would like to deny this socio-economic trend exists, especially among those who are driven by competitive desire to be excellent at something and manage to succeed. We fail to grasp that for every person who grabs the golden ring, there are thousands who fail to do so. Statistically the chance to succeed, to move from a modest family background to the top income quartile (80 percent plus) is fast becoming folklore.

Here I would add two other reasons for enhancing equality and reducing inequality. First, there must be *equality of opportunity*, whereby the least advantaged groups feel they have some chance to succeed; otherwise, they will grow frustrated and cynical and retreat from the larger society, forming a subculture of their own and rejecting the values of the larger society, possibly engaging in criminal and deviant behavior and affecting almost everyone in the larger society except the very wealthy, who can insulate themselves or create buffers.

Second, for people to be committed to society they must lead a decent life, with a minimum socio-economic level that meets their basic needs. Everyone in a democratic (and humane) society is owed at least this much; moreover, it is politically prudent to diminish the potential for political instability, civil strife and violence. The concept of minimum level is vague because guidelines and definitions fluctuate, depending on the views of pundits and the political and moral views of those in power. Nonetheless, there is practical interest to prevent social unrest.

Similarly, profits among large corporations and financial institutions should not continue to grow at the expense of workers. The outcome is monopoly power of big business, whereby the common people are left behind. Put in mathematical terms, according to Scott DeCarlo of *Fortune*, productivity is at an all-time high for the 500 top companies in the U.S.; every employee generates $1.2 million in annual revenue. That being the case, you would think that large corporations could increase employee compensation and benefits. But the idea of "inclusive capitalism," "trickle-down economics" or "profit-sharing" with employees is more a dream than reality. American capitalism, and global capitalism as well, has always been characterized by economic disparity. Very few working people get rich.

The policies of a democratic (and humane) society must try to maximize the prospects of the least fortunate and avoid a "culture of poverty," passed from one generation to the next, that in turn will sap the health and vitality of society. When referring to a culture of poverty, no one whatsoever should single out one racial or ethnic group—a code word in the U.S. for "them," or what really means Hispanics, blacks, immigrants, etc. Poverty cuts across all ethnic groups, in both the inner cities and rural parts of America, whereby people are often scapegoated as "lazy," "genetically inferior," or they are considered a product of a stunted culture. By engaging in these assumptions, we deflect the features that help perpetuate poverty from generation to generation, such as low wages, poor schools, lack of nutrition, over-crowded housing, gangs and drugs, large-scale imprisonment, and discrimination—all of which limit opportunity.

Developing a social and economic floor or minimum level must include, today, *educational opportunity* for the most disadvantaged populace. In this way, ability and talent can be nurtured and not lost at the expense of the individual and society. John Goodlad, former professor of education at the University of Washington, reminds us that "millions have fallen far short of their potential by the simple fact of their birth." These millions serve as a reminder that we are not the nation we think we are. We still have a way to go in terms of humanity, opportunity and prosperity for all. If not for all, at least for the majority of the populace.

Social cooperation and commitment, or a *common good*, whereby those in political power work with leaders of social institutions to formulate prudent public policy, must exist. If, however, self-interest or ignorance dictates policy, if the robber barons are not curtailed, if Ayn Rand's idea that business excess and greed are good for growth and productivity overrides basic checks and balances; or, if Milton Friedman's unregulated capitalism overshadows the notion of justice and fairness, then by inference the common good will be shoved to second place. Here I am reminded of the graphic words of Jay Gould, the ultimate capitalist and robber baron. Bragging he could break any strike, he said in 1886, "I can hire one half of the working class to kill the other half." In 2014, 128 years later, several Wall Street CEOs received $25 and $50 million annual bonuses, a form of lunacy given the fact that 23 million Americans were unemployed or underemployed and most wages of labor (including recent college graduates) were stagnant for the last 30 years, and worsened within the last ten years. What we have is a whole new generation of forgotten Americans, left behind, a deepening inequality, in the midst of a growing economy which benefits a tiny percentage at the top of the pyramid.

The question is, when is enough enough? How much money does someone have to earn before someone says, "I earn enough"? A 4 percent tax increase, from 33 to 37 percent, of the richest 1 percent raises about $20 billion of revenue over five years. A tax increase to 50 percent on the same group of people would raise approximately $150 to $200 billion, enough to bolster programs like Social Security and Medicare. If we started to phase out government subsidies for special interest groups (i.e., farm subsidies cost the tax payer $20 billion per year) and funnel it to the least advantaged groups in terms of food, housing, health and education, then inequalities would be further diminished.

But government programs, once created, become virtually immortal, and no government official wants to incur the bad publicity of taking something from anyone. Government officials fail to recognize that a democracy consists of a government by and for the people, and that big government should not bend to the whims of power and money. Together they (power and money) work against the common good. On the flip side of the coin, is there a point when too many entitlements curtail motivation and inner drive to succeed, thus fostering personal laziness and irresponsibility as well as minimal effort and low productivity within society? Proponents of equality may be so concerned about unequal outcomes and growing inequality they may overlook or stifle performance based on ability, aspiration and hard work. Critics argue a government that redistributes from "makers" and "risk takers" to "takers" and "moochers" winds up swindling taxpayers and rewarding those who don't want to work.

A major feature for dealing with various levels of ability and aspiration is for society to provide different jobs with different skill levels. The more opportunities provided to the working population and the more chances to succeed, the easier it is for people to discover themselves, and to feel worthwhile and successful. Ideally no one should feel he or she is limited in opportunity or facing a last chance to achieve or secure a decent job. It is not only late bloomers who benefit from various job opportunities and multiple chances, but also society, which needs a competent workforce to grow and expand—and to support its aging and disabled population.

While U.S. unemployment in 2015 was relatively low (near 5.5 percent), the percentage of American workers actually in the workforce was at its lowest levels (about 63 percent) in more than 35 years and is likely to persist. The newspaper *Barron's* considers it to be a *structural* problem, linked to changing values of "beating the system," working off the books and collecting disability insurance or unemployment insurance. Charles Murray, a fellow at the American Enterprise Institute, asserts that men in their prime who did not work were once scorned as "bums." Now they brag about exiting the workforce and receiving government tax-free money. This trend has nothing to do with lack of job opportunities, rather how federal programs can cause disincentives to work.

The result is that disability rolls among prime age groups (25–54 years) have increased from 1.4 percent in 1970 to 3.3 percent in 2013. This increase comes at a time when health and safety laws in work environments have increased, when the percentage of dangerous jobs has decreased and the general population has gotten healthier. The gap of 1.9 percent, the increase from 1.4 percent to 3.3 percent, accounts for an additional 1.2 million people claiming disability who might otherwise be working. The share of men ages 55 to 64 collecting disability has skyrocketed from 7.1 percent to 12.5 percent since 1970, resulting in 1 million additional people on disability.

During periods of recession and/or slow economic growth, pundits tend to focus on unemployment. This issue is usually temporary and reflects the changing economy. Rising disability is more of a structural issue, reflecting social and moral issues. Most of these people don't want to work or lack appropriate skills to obtain decent jobs. In both cases, government policies are not going to help. The issue revolves around the individual's attitude toward work and society—and deeper ideas about the common good and the need to provide proper rewards for work and proper disincentives for preventing people from becoming an unfair burden on others. For a nation to prosper, people must care. There must be some sense of interdependence, a feeling of "we" and a sense of community and nationhood. The individual must be willing to give something back to family, community and nation.

Another structural problem is that while older workers (over 50) are likely to be laid off during hard times, they are about half as likely to be rehired. Moreover, the prospects for older workers being rehired deteriorate sharply the longer they are unemployed. These people, unlike the disabled, want to work. The old adage, "If you work hard, opportunities will come along and success [recognition, reward, etc.] will follow," doesn't apply to the older workforce. This is hard to admit, especially if you're a team player or believe in the American dream. But millions of older workers have been disconnected from the economy and possibly even from the larger society. If not reconnected into the workforce, a great deal of skilled labor, talent and expertise is lost to society, which in turn affects the political instability and economic productivity of that society. Retraining programs rarely seem to work. In the U.S., older, displaced workers who lose their jobs on average go back to work at half to two thirds their original wages.

We must take note, however, that people who graduate from high school and college are not a homogenous group—all wanting to work, all driven by ambition and opportunity. Some of us, because of poor decisions, lousy luck or limited choices—or just lack of ability or ambition—wind up aimless and are forced to look in the mirror and face our own inadequacies. It should be understood that those who lose the competitive race in a *capitalistic* society have a worse image of themselves compared to those born to a *stratified* society. In the later situation, it is easier to explain your failure to corrupt government officials or to traditional rules and rituals that restrict mobility. In a competitive society, where everyone is supposed to have some opportunity, losing the race has more detrimental effects on one's self-identity and image.

Power, Privilege and Elite Institutions

The Ivy League colleges were built on the premise of educating the children of the elite class, originally when young men graduated from the Latin School in New England colonies and into the mid-twentieth century when they graduated from private academies like Groton, Choate and Exeter, which are modern "knockoffs" of the old Latin School. Presidents Franklin Roosevelt, John Kennedy and both Bush presidents were graduates of these private academies and moved easily to Harvard and Yale, despite their "so-so" academic achievement.

Up to the 1930s, most people who applied to Harvard and Yale, and other places like Princeton and Dartmouth, were admitted because people who were not from the proper social class did not bother applying, as they knew better than to waste their time. The history of admission into these elite colleges is the history of the conflict between merit and privilege. The voices of reform began to conflict with the voice of tradition over what kind of applicants to accept and to what extent should class, alumni status and social connection trump academic ability and scholarship. According to Jerome Karabel, a sociologist from Berkeley, it was not until the Jews began to apply—students who prized scholarships, academic achievement and high test scores—that the Ivy League colleges faced a dilemma.

Slowly and grudgingly, the Ivy League colleges modified their anti-Semitic policies and allowed a small number of Jews into their institutions, although the number was restricted. Embodied by the spirit of the American dream, so characteristic of all immigrant groups, these striving Jews were merely seeking bits and pieces of the opportunity that their parents had been denied in Europe. For readers who fail to grasp the historical and contextual meaning, the story is played out in *Chariots of Fire*, some 35 years ago. Although the movie takes place at Cambridge University in England, all the reader needs to understand is that Harvard, Yale, Princeton, etc. are forged on the basis of Oxford and Cambridge universities.

Despite the shocked reaction of the Protestant establishment, the genie had been released from the bottle by aspiring Jews and once freed it paved the way for other high-achieving immigrant groups to apply; and, later, minority groups wanted the American dream. In a way, the admissions processes at Harvard and Yale, among other Ivy League colleges, provide a valuable preview of the coming civil rights movement that was to soon explode, where the democratic forces of fairness, equality and equity were pitted against the traditional forces of protection and privilege. (You can say that this battle has been waged since Jefferson crossed swords with Hamilton, or as far back as the Greeks who tried to forge their theories of democracy in the town squares of Athens and Delphi, the latter of which was considered by the Greeks as the center of the world.)

Given the beginning of the cold war in the late 1940s and early 1950s, and the need to produce scientists and engineers to defend against Soviet expansion, the faculties at Ivy League colleges slowly began to stress academics. At the same time, James Conant was president of Harvard. He was the most influential educator of the mid-century, and when he spoke the educational establishment listened. Conant urged that American schools and colleges add academic rigor to the curriculum, upgrade teacher training, test and measure students' achievement and devote more resources for the education of the top academic 20 percent, especially the gifted and talented students.

The Boston Brahmin's idea of "The Harvard Man" was much more progressive than "The Yale Man," as perceived by Yale's president Alfred Griswold, who, in 1950, reassured the Protestant establishment and Yale alumni that the future graduate would not be a "beetle-browed, highly specialized intellectual, but a well-rounded man." Well-rounded, of course, implied you could lack academic credentials, so long as you were well connected or from the right patrician family. Your chances of admission were just fine.

The injustices that were once imposed on over-achieving Jewish students are now directed at over-achieving Asians. To get into an Ivy League school, Asian students need about 120 to 140 points more than whites on SAT tests. They comprise about 15 to 20 percent of the Ivy League enrollments, but make up about 50 percent of the applicants with the highest SAT scores, according to one Harvard professor. Today, the excuses for capping Asian students range from a need to balance the racial/ethnic student body, the desire to recruit other minority students, and to recruit other students with leadership potential and/or strong "extra-curricular" backgrounds. Some of these traits sound vague and are purposely designed to help nonAsian students—other minorities and whites—and to limit a true meritocracy. Indeed, the decision to admit various groups of students, and just how many in each group, has political, social and moral tradeoffs. Who gets to go to an Ivy League school has an impact on future opportunities and competitive success. Do we make excellence the chief criteria? What form of excellence? And who decided the form it should take? Are there other considerations? Like who would make the most of their education? Who would most likely become a future leader? Who would most benefit the larger society? There are no right answers, only various beliefs based on human bias.

The conflict between meritocracy versus the well-rounded student persists today by nuance—by putting as much emphasis or more on "character" than academics. Academic merit is but one of many criteria used to judge applicants, along with social skills, leadership skills and creative/artistic skills. All these sets of skills, along with alumni linkage, are designed to allow sufficient flexibility to preserve the status quo and power of these institutions, to ensure that "well-rounded" students are sought and accepted. The balance between academic *mediocrity* and *merit* has permitted and still permits children of the rich and powerful to be admitted because of hereditary privilege. Today, family legacy determines about 20 to 30 percent of Ivy League admissions; that is, about four to five times the overall admission rate.

At Princeton, it is estimated by Michael Hurwitz in the *Economics of Education Review* that legacy is equivalent to 160 additional points on the applicant's SAT score. To be sure, the deck is still stacked in favor of the rich at Ivy League schools. Despite the rise of a new educated class, men and women of high academic caliber who were unable to go to Harvard or Yale, or the likes of Princeton and Dartmouth, had to "settle" for the University of Michigan, University of Wisconsin or University of Illinois—all top-notch colleges, but not part of the cultural and financial elite, not part of the Protestant and corporate establishment. Most people still believe that a college education is the key to remaining in the middle or upper class or rising from a lower to higher class. However, they now worry about rising costs of tuition. One method for choking the opportunity of students from a modest background is to limit financial scholarships and the government funding of Pell Grants.

In context with today's sorting and selection process and notion of "success," the elite institutions are "churning out drones," who are lining up to get jobs in finance and corporate America, according to William Deresiewicz's book *Excellent Sheep*. He probes the "miseducation" of America's elite students. We've created a generation of "polite, striving,…[and] grade-grubbing nonentities, who just want to make money." Ivy league education has been perverted, the ex-Yale professor claims, turning out students who are afraid to follow their dreams, and instead obsess about tests and grades and extracurricular activities in order to attend Harvard, Yale, etc., and work for J.P. Morgan and Goldman Sachs. Colleges encourage this funneling process, lining up future donors a generation in advance. Those students who go into public service, the arts or not-for-profit agencies are considered "do gooders" and are tolerated as moral balancing wheels; someone possibly for alumni to remember and brag about.

We all know students whose growth and learning can be explained in terms of motivation, curiosity and creativity—and a desire to write, compose or invent. In general, the students at Harvard, Yale, etc. have a different type of ambition— to make money or wield power. Their talent and inner drive is highly focused at the expense of ignoring other gifts and abilities. Their notion of excellence has little to do with serving the common "good" or helping others; it is limited to reinforcing their sense of superiority and privilege. Talking about climate change, organic farms or the Boy Scouts is a way of fooling others at neighborhood parties or soccer fields; that is, letting themselves off the hook, or portraying a socially sensitive façade.

It is sufficient to add one more wrinkle to the equation. While overt racial and religious discrimination has been eliminated from the college admission process, as have overt quotas based on affirmative action which discriminate in general against white candidates, race remains a qualification for college admission and job applications. Under the guise of diversity, it is important for colleges and corporations to display a "sufficient" number of minorities. It's not necessarily based on the need to compensate for past injustices, as was the original intent, rather now to generate diverse thinking and experiences on college campuses and to expand business markets and serve clients among customers who prefer to work with members of their own race. Indeed, the racial factor is slippery but widely used, so we need to make sure that it doesn't block opportunities for ordinary white candidates who have their own disadvantages based on class. Reasonable people may disagree on affirmative action policies, but in an age of meritocracy it is harder to explain why children of Ivy League alumni, usually rich children, should have this advantage, which is nothing more than a heredity-based privilege. All it does is reinforce inequality and reduce educational opportunity for bright students.

For example, if we compare high school and college students with the same standardized test scores who come from different socio-economic backgrounds, we find that their educational outcomes reflect their parents' income, not test results. Students from lower and moderate family incomes who want a college education run into a host of problems along the way, and many never get their degrees. Nearly 45 percent of U.S. students who start at four-year colleges haven't earned their degrees after six years. This trend correlates with one major variable— how much their parents earn.

As wages for the working class and middle class remain nearly frozen and college costs continue to spike, higher education opportunity has become increasingly limited and stratified. Every year college students from moderate family incomes are more likely to attend community colleges, where tuition costs average about $5,000 or less per semester, or 20 percent of the tuition of elite private colleges. But graduation rates at community colleges are considerably lower than at selective institutions, and those who graduate are much less likely (about 3 percent) to attend elite colleges, where nearly everyone graduates and has a chance at competitive success.

The promise of social and economic mobility in the U.S. and elsewhere depends on devising appropriate solutions. One method is to reduce the rewards of competitive success and the costs of mediocrity. Instead of trying to make more people good at the job, one option is to provide safety nets that ensure a minimum reward level for a particular geographical area (state or province) with an agreed minimum standard of living. It's easier, however, to make selective colleges more accessible to working- and middle-income students and provide greater transfer links from community colleges and selective colleges. This method should be acceptable to people who are concerned with and oppose limiting the rewards for hard work, sustained effort and differential performance.

If the upper class seizes the benefits of an education (say by directing their children into private schools or by spending in public schools twice or three times as much money in property taxes on their children as low-income children and by ensuring their children are admitted to Ivy League schools), and seizes the gains of national productivity, as they have in past decades, we have a situation where the advantaged group "ruthlessly exploits its position to ensure the dominance of its class." Surprisingly, these are the words of David Brooks, the *New York Times* columnist and the liberal's favorite conservative. He continues, members of the upper class are more likely to intermarry, which "is really a ceaseless effort to refortify class and solidarity and magnify social isolation," and thus perpetuate their dominant position.

Given his conservative views, Brooks, surprisingly and whimsically, urges "uneducated workers of the world [to] unite…You have nothing to lose but your chains." He concludes: "I don't agree with everything in Karl's manifesto, because I don't believe in incessant struggle, but I have to admit, he makes some good points." Brooks has a sense of humor, but he is making a serious point. For the last three decades, the winds of big business have been whipsawing and blowing strong, from coast to coast and through the heartland, financially breaking the lives of many ordinary people, creating a rising scourge of debt, decline and despair among working- and middle-class America, and leaving everyone behind except the high-end and wealthy elite. To be sure, this is not the America most of us grew up in nor envision and believe in. For the sake of our children and their children, we all hope this is not the America we know when we take our last breath and make peace with the Almighty.

Adding, still, another conservative voice to the mix, in a 2014 *New York Times* article, "Capitalism for the Masses," Arthur Brooks (no relation to David Brooks), the president of the American Enterprise Institute, defends the capitalist system. He does so not on materialistic grounds (because the discussion eventually drifts to inequality), but on a moral and humanitarian basis. Capitalism can be analyzed on the basis of helping the majority of people become self-sufficient. It can also be measured on whether people enjoy their job or feel their job helps other people. (In this way a nurse or teacher can feel fulfilled and that their work amounts to something worthwhile.) Whether people work at odd jobs or on Wall Street, as a plumber or professional ballplayer, the important thing is that people feel a sense of achievement and/or success. The fact is in the last 30 years, the percentage of the world population earning $1 a day, after considering inflation, and the number of malnourished children in the world, have dramatically declined. The primary reason, according to Brooks, is related to globalization and capitalism.

A Change in Meritocracy

The phrase "postindustrial society," coined by Harvard's Daniel Bell, describes the scientific-technological societies evolving in developed countries in the second half of the twentieth century. The singular feature of this society is the importance of scientific and technical knowledge as the source of production, innovation and policy formulation. Emerging from the older economic systems in both advanced capitalistic and socialistic countries is a knowledge society based on preeminence of professionals and managers. In the United States during the 1950s and 1960s, Bell notes in *The Coming of Post-Industrial Society*, "this group outpaced...all others in rate of growth, which was...seven times more than the overall rate for workers."

In the 1990s, computer and high-tech sectors outpaced the entire economy, reflected by a soaring NASDAQ market whose bubble burst in 2000. Today, the stratification structure of this new society produces a highly trained knowledge-based elite, which is supported by a large scientific and technical staff and which has become the economic engine for the new century. Moreover, it is the only part of society that has successfully competed with the patrician (super-rich) society, at least up to the point where the "blue bloods" have taken notice of who is being admitted into Stanford or MIT and who is working on Wall Street, as well as in Silicon Valley. In this connection, some of the nation's tech giants are bolstering the talent pipeline in math and science education at the middle school and high school level with hundreds of millions in funding. Apple, Microsoft, Intel and Facebook are making broad efforts in sponsoring programs that teach technical skills with an emphasis to increase the talent pool of women and minorities.

The basis of achievement in the postindustrial society is education and high academic expectations. Merit and differentials in status, power and income are awarded to highly educated and trained experts with credentials; they are seen as the decision makers who will inherit the power structure in business, government and even politics. Achievement and mobility are also related to entrepreneurship and the risk taking: what Ben Franklin would call hard work and *Forbes* magazine might call "making money the old-fashioned way." Paul Fussell, a University of Pennsylvania sociologist, labeled these postindustrial "knowledge workers" as the "X class." C. Wright Mills said the middle-class person was "always somebody's man," whereas the X person is nobody's. X people are highly independent, educated, and achievement oriented: "retirement being a concept meaningful only to hired personnel or wage slaves who despise their hard work."

This trend toward a meritocracy of the intellectual elite has aggravated inequalities. The majority of people in a democratic society accept this form of inequality, because it is based on individual talent and achievement—not inherited privilege or rank—and because this form of meritocracy is designed, at least in theory, to benefit the common good. Because of socio-economic deprivation and limited education, a significant percentage of poor and minority groups are unable to compete successfully in a society based on educational credentials and educational achievement. Without the appropriate certificates they are not needed by the economy; not necessarily exploited, but underpaid for their services; not necessarily discriminated against, but not in demand.

Excellence vs. Equality

In his classic book on excellence and equality, John Gardner in *Excellence: Can We Be Equal and Excellent Too?* points out that, in a democracy, the differences among groups cannot be dwelled on and we go out of the way to ignore them. He describes the dilemma: "Extreme equalitarianism…which ignores differences in native capacity and achievement, has not served democracy well. Carried far enough, it means…the end of that striving for excellence which has produced mankind's greatest achievements." Gardner also asserts that "no democracy can give itself over to emphasize extreme individual performance and retain its democratic principles—or extreme equalitarianism and retain its vitality." Our society should seek to develop "all potentialities at all levels. It takes more than educated elite to run a complex, technological society." Every modern society, as well as every ancient society, has learned this hard lesson, some only after tremendous bloodshed and loss of life.

Every efficient and innovative society has also learned to recognize and reward various abilities, talents and creative endeavors. In school, and other aspects of American society, the chief instrument for identifying ability and talent is a standardized test. It is not surprising, according to Gardner, that such tests are the object of criticism and hostility, because they encourage the sorting and selecting of students into special tracks and programs. The fact is, "the tests are designed to do an unpopular job." They are designed to measure what a person knows or how well a person can perform particular tasks; the data can be used to compare people and make decisions—such as who gets into what college and who gets selected for various jobs. Tests are also used for applying standards to determine quality—and who gets ahead in schools and society.

Although in our society, unlike most other societies, we are given multiple chances to succeed, the search for talent and the importance of education in our knowledge-based and high-tech society leads to increasing inequality among educated and uneducated individuals, and among those who can digitally communicate and those who can only communicate on a limited basis, among those who can work with multiple data systems and databases and those who cannot, among those who understand what is going on in their companies at any given moment and those who are limited to specific tasks (usually low level or rote) because of lack of ability to retrieve, understand or apply digital information.

Without doubt predictive analytics is the next big force in the tech world, leading to many new jobs and determining the economic value of an individual on the job. This conception is independent of education; it involves special talent, adaptability and creativeness. With adequate knowledge of past events, human characteristics such as age, weight, gender—all of which can be captured as data and statistically analyzed—and other influencing factors, we will be able to estimate outcomes or probability. Giant corporations are now able to assess a customer's previous behavior in order to predict patterns and preferences. Never before has artificial intelligence been available to so many institutions and companies to predict behaviors and outcomes. "We are in the early stages of a data science revolution," according to the founder and CEO Marc Benioff of Salesforce. There is "a huge amount of data than ever before." The challenge is to understand, make sense of it and use it to make appropriate decisions. What's needed is "a new generation of [managers and] executives who can understand and organize" their business around the data.

It's the difference, say in baseball, illustrated by the movie *Moneyball*. The movie chronicles how the Oakland 'A's were able to predict the odds in identifying the best players for a particular position, using a statistical-driven method in lieu of traditional scouting methods and judgments of coaches and managers. It's now happening in medicine, Wall Street and various types of innovative research, whereby risk factors are assessed and numerous variables are analyzed on a laptop to determine strategy. It's based on understanding empirical information, what some of us call new information and others call "big data" or the cyber system world.

The issues of performance that Gardner (and test specialists) raises, compounded by the computer-driven world we now inhabit, and the use of statistical data, will not go away, at least not in our democratic and heterogeneous society; they directly affect the social fabric of the country and have echoed loudly since the War on Poverty and the civil rights movement. They lead to heated arguments in the media, often where frank discussion is curtailed; the worst culprits are college campus newspapers and forums—ironically a terrible place for academic freedom if the messenger moves too far to the political Right. While pundits today talk about difference between excellence and equality, and the need to achieve some balance in a democratic society, we can also distinguish between equality and equity.

Equality has to do with similarity in opportunity or results, but equity (or fairness) deals with a person's or group's effort and the reward (or outcomes) for that effort. Inequality occurs when a person or group works harder but achieves little reward or, in reverse, when a person or group works less and receives most of the rewards. Inequity involves lack of opportunity, whereby the laws and/or social intuitions discriminate against certain people or groups based on a perceived characteristic; henceforth, those people will be disadvantaged in society. It is important to consider the characteristics and design of society: Whether there is equal opportunity or unequal opportunity will determine what happens to people in education, jobs, healthcare, housing, etc.; how income and wealth will be distributed among people, and who will be taxed and to what extent. (For example, top earners today pay lower tax rates than working people because they have tax loopholes that protect their income and profits.)

Here we are not attempting to achieve an equal result, which ignores the concept of effort or ability and assumes that everyone is entitled to equal rewards, regardless of effort or ability. Such an assumption has more to do with affirmative action and quotas. With equity, we are seeking some sort of fairness, what Harvard professor John Rawls in *Justice as Fairness* would refer to as a just society. We want to avoid a stacked deck, the existence of inequality and inequity— when no matter what their effort or ability some people will always be discriminated against. The potential effects of such discrimination are more than just economic; the outcomes have social, political and emotional consequences, resulting in feelings of inferiority, anger, hatred of others, producing pathological and delinquent behavior (in terms of crime, delinquency and drugs), and detrimentally affect the productivity and vitality of that nation. If a person cannot find viable work, if the deck is always stacked against a person, the argument can be made: Why go to school? Why try to find a job? The system is unfair and unjust; it is easier to drop out.

Educational Opportunity and Mobility

In a market where long-term unemployment and underemployment become the new norm, people lose valuable job skills and experience over time, and become less committed to the workforce. Given the post-recession period of employment to population ratio, policymakers may have to accept that low employment is the new norm, and fewer opportunities for college graduates is the new reality. We don't even know for sure how many people have just stopped looking for a job, and are no longer part of the unemployment figures. What we do know is that the long-term trend of more high school graduates going on to college has come to an end, reaching its peak in 2005, just before the Great Recession, at 69 percent, and is now leveling off. Falling college enrollment figures means that upward mobility among poor and working-class students will probably become more difficult in the future; inequality will continue to grow.

It is likely that some students who fall into this category would have exceeded academically had it not been for socio-economic factors. But there are many children and youth whose academic outcomes cannot be traced to family or socio-economic limitations. It would be silly to reduce college standards so a greater percentage of college-age students can attend. What we need, ideally, is some form of continued education, vocational training or apprenticeships that produce worthwhile learning and growth. The fact is, a large percentage of U.S. students are concrete thinkers, neither abstract nor divergent, and limited in cognitive processing. Given wide human capacities, society must offer alternative paths to enhance personal and economic success. By emphasizing college as the main prerequisite to success, we have put enormous pressure on many students and their parents to attend college who do not benefit from it. In short, academic achievement or attending college should not be confused with human dignity or human worth.

When we talk about equal opportunity, eventually the question arises as to whether everyone should have the right to go to college. If everyone has the right to get a high school education, why not college? But the pool of abilities and talent varies, and there are many children whose academic limitations cannot be traced to poverty or deprivation. Children who come from upper-class homes have the advantage of social capital, and have parents who have the ability to move to a successful school district—where schools are cleaner and more modern, where teachers are better paid and generally have more education and experience, and the school climate is more conducive to learning. But others who are less fortunate start out on a less than equal footing and continue to experience family, school, peer group and community handicaps that only increase their disadvantages—and thus are often doomed to disappointment.

Despite ability or talent, children who come from advantaged homes have parents with political and social connections that help get their children into Ivy League colleges and high-paying jobs. Brian Barry, in *Why Social Justice Matters*, points out that competition for good jobs requires that you get into the *right* university, not just a university. Some 35 percent of undergraduates at Princeton are "from non-sectarian schools [rich kids]: over 20 times their 1.7 percent in the school population." You don't have to be a rocket scientist to get into Yale or Harvard or to work on Wall Street, and many people who accumulate the usual clutch of mansions, fancy cars and millionaire baubles possess lesser abilities and are "C" students. Ironically, the business world is depressingly full of millionaires, who ignore their head start in life and equate their net worth with brains; that is, wealthy boys and girls born on third base who think they hold the major league record for triples.

Differences are further aggravated by those who through brains, perspiration, drive or just sheer luck—such as the right decision at the right time or meeting someone at a convention or party—believe everyone else has the same opportunities to make it in America or anywhere on the globe. Smart people recognize the element of luck and that there are uncontrollable factors in life—or that their parents' legacy, name or social connections helped them succeed. Narcissistic and hubristic people are prone to blame others for their lack of success. For example, they allude to someone else's lack of intelligence or initiative, ignoring all the other elements that lead to the outcomes of life.

Economic Opportunity: Old Ideas, New Ideas

You would hope that we have come a long way from the robber baron days of the nineteenth century, when business tycoons amassed fortunes by trampling competition, exploiting workers and fleecing the public. All you need is to be reminded that big business, in the spirit of Jay Gould, is today ready and willing to hire illegal immigrants at $7 or $8 an hour and replace American laborers who expect $20 or $25 an hour for the same work. What does $20 an hour mean? Considering an eight-hour day, five-day workweek, and 50-week wage, this amounts to $40,000—not much more than today's average American annual wage. (More precisely, in 2014, the average working wage was $805 a week.) Also consider that nearly all the major multinational companies in America are outsourcing jobs for approximately one third to one fourth the American wage. Sadly, the American workforce has become a disposable workforce, under the guise of competition, efficiency and global supply–demand curves. Here in the U.S., we will never be able to compete with Bangladesh or Mexico in labor costs; what we need is to find ways to attract new businesses by offering good infrastructure and transportation links, a skilled workforce and attractive tax codes.

Economically there is little difference in the outcome caused by the tactics of Gould and the robber barons of nineteenth-century industry and the tactics of many twenty-first-century business CEOs and investment bankers, who move money around the world with a click of a mouse and have little or no concern about the average nine-to-five workers in their companies. You might argue that American labor must learn to trim costs and that outsourcing and global trade is inevitable. That is all well and good, but the only people in our country benefiting from these new trends are the wealthy, who invest capital and not their labor. Whatever the increased productivity or profits gained by hiring illegal immigrants, outsourcing jobs or developing new plants abroad, these are not shared by the vast majority of American people or the American workforce. Moreover, these days business and banking executives seem more interested in short-term profits than building corporate infrastructure for the long haul, more interested in pursuing paper profits through tax arbitrage and relocating to countries that have lower corporate tax rates than producing stuff that people need or want to buy.

The fact that our intellectual capital is also being drained by outsourcing scientific and technological jobs and by development of new manufacturing sites abroad doesn't seem to concern the power brokers and money movers of the American political and economic system. Few political leaders seem concerned that future generations will have trouble finding decent, middle-class jobs. The free marketers and conservative pundits continue to tell us that globalization and unrestricted trade policies are good for the nation. Good for whom? Cheap labor and cheap prices may be good for the consumer now, but in the long run the U.S. worker will be left behind—at a distinct disadvantage, unemployed or underemployed because of global markets and technology. Think of the three forces impacting on American workers (and college graduates): robots, robber barons and corporate outsourcing. The outlook is not bright; the American worker had his day in the sun some 40 or 50 years ago when a larger share of corporate profits were earmarked for workers, and when corporations and unions got along because the U.S. economy was booming.

While robber baron and corporate behavior can be modified by government regulation, robots represent a trend that cannot be easily limited or shaped by government policy. Robots are the seeds for a new revolution which may eliminate muscle-powered jobs and rote jobs and create good jobs for semi-skilled and skilled workers. Or, robots may just eliminate many more jobs than they create. Will doctors be necessary in the future? Will robots perform surgery? Will they prescribe medical treatment or drugs? Vinod Khosla, cofounder of Sun Microsystems, predicts that computers and robots will shortly replace 80 percent of the physicians in the U.S. The point is that algorithms will replace the need for doctors, and many other workers. What about our airplane pilots, autoworkers or any worker engaged in repetitive tasks? Are we mechanizing and computerizing ourselves into obsolescence? Are we going to lose our jobs to a machine and wreck the middle class? Are we reaching the end of labor? Do smart machines threaten our future careers? A number of social scientists and news reporters think it's a real possibility.

In the past technological change has led to increased productivity and new jobs for skilled personnel. On one end of the continuum, the new economy calls for people skilled in abstract thought, intuition, creativity and ability to understand data. On the other side, technology has reduced the need for routine tasks and repetitive work, eliminating many low-skilled jobs. But trends, today, seem to indicate that employment has increased among high-wage earners in managerial and professional jobs and in low-wage occupations that cannot yet be performed by robots, such as in retail, restaurants, landscaping and the hotel industry. But the middle of the labor force is shrinking, as is the middle class. Automation can reduce production costs but also can become a job killer among middle-class workers who do machine-related and/or automated work. In a recent book, *Race Against the Machine*, Erik Brynjolfsson and Andrew McAfee of MIT warn that there is no law that says that technology must benefit most people. It's possible that productivity increases and the economic pie expands, but the benefits go only to a few people. That said, compensation for workers has been flat for the last 30 years, after considering inflation, but corporate profits and economic growth have steadily increased.

To be sure, a growing number of economists and labor union leaders are concerned that technological change will hinder job opportunities for large numbers of people. It's a concern that can be traced to the Luddites, according to Ross Douthat of the *New York Times*. But the growing influence of computers, robots and nanotechnology gives new impetus to the idea that many people of average abilities will no longer find meaningful employment, while those with higher than average abilities (data-crunching capacity) will exhibit high job performance and gain greater income.

Even worse, certain work will slowly disappear and the majority will experience a squeeze on wages and human equality. This type of future is illustrated by Yuval Harari, in his 2015 book *Sapiens: A Brief History of Humankind*. He argues that the global and technological world we live in is creating huge breakthroughs and economic growth, but also new classes and class struggles at the expense of ordinary people. Dislocations are inevitable, as occurred during the Industrial Revolution. The vast majority of working- and middle-class people will either lose their jobs to machines or will gradually see their job opportunities limited.

According to Harari, the most innovative place today is Silicon Valley. Here people are creating "new religions" and "techno-utopian" ideas that will shape the world we live in. Either we learn to adapt, in the words of Darwin, or we find ourselves on the wrong side of the twenty-first century: lost, irrelevant and unable to function effectively within society.

Different Talents, Different Rewards

The nation was conceived by the principles of political liberalism and democratic philosophy: certain natural rights and egalitarian values based on equality, fairness and opportunity, as well as personal responsibility. Capitalism would be encouraged to expand, but there would be no feudal class, no peasant class, no serfs perpetually indentured to the nobility class. There would be genuine social reform in which people engaged in different occupations would come nearer in speaking the same language and having the same opportunities and rights, the same spirit and soul, than anywhere else in the world. That is, the American invention, or what others might refer to as the "American character."

A basic tenet satisfying the principles of democracy is to curtail a reward system based on inherited privilege and power, so that we don't consistently have the same "winners" and "losers" from one generation to the next. This idea is not based on Athenian democracy as some might believe, but rather rooted more in the ideas of John Locke and Jean-Jacques Rousseau, who in turn influenced the liberal wing of our Founding Fathers such as Thomas Paine and Thomas Jefferson.

It is the same ideas expounded more recently by political scientists and philosophers such as Brian Barry, John Gardner and John Rawls (all three of whom recently died). As in a sporting event, the best performer(s) deserve to win, noting that chance and luck are factors and can enter into the final outcome. In a fair society, rewards are distributed on the basis of ability, talent and creativity, and ways are provided to encourage those who have such native endowments to seek education and training to fulfill their potential.

The concept of *meritocracy*, a relatively new idea that coincides with the coming of the knowledge society and information age as well as the growth of a professional middle class in the U.S. and Western Europe in the 1950s and 1960s, is based on rewarding the deserving, as long as their abilities and talents are put to good use—to benefit the larger society and contribute to the good and prosperity of others. Differences in rewards are accepted so long as those people with special endowments serve the common good and do not use them against society or an individual, say in robbing a bank or creating a Ponzi investment scheme. While there is an expectation that a variety of abilities and talents will be recognized and rewarded, it makes no sense to encourage or reward esoteric abilities and talents, such as standing on one's head for an hour, or repeating the names and addresses of all the people under the letter A or B listed in the local telephone book (which few people even use any more) or walking on a tightrope between buildings.

Most people in a democracy accept there will be a difference in rewards for individuals who use their talents for the general good. There is a legitimate expectation that deserving people will share in greater power, honors and income, so long as agreed-upon rules are followed. There is also an expectation that society will establish appropriate institutions such as schools and colleges to nurture those differences in abilities and talents, but it must also provide opportunities for those people who are not as smart or talented. These experiences might include apprenticeships, vocational training, military careers, lower-level government jobs, etc. Otherwise, the discrepancies between high-achieving and low-achieving people will become too large and threaten the principles of democracy. At all costs we need to provide safety nets, second chances and multiple chances for those less able to reach their full potential.

We need to recognize different forms of excellence. If we remain blind sighted to different kinds of abilities and talent, then the principles of democratic equality will be lost under the guise of a restricted form of meritocracy. Not everyone can be a scientist or musician; some of us will be plumbers and truck drivers. Not everyone will get "A"s in school, and we need to ensure that opportunity is provided for the least advantaged groups so that society doesn't lose a critical mass of people because of background or differences in class and status. We also need to recognize that gender is a critical factor in the world, especially in traditional and Muslim orthodox societies. The result is half the human capital never gets an equal chance to succeed or dream the "impossible dream," to fully contribute to the growth and development of that society. When stratification and social hierarchy is based on gender and women are considered "unfit," when their school and job opportunities are limited by custom, religion and/or the norms of society, a great tragedy and loss in productivity occurs within that nation. Similarly, we should not overlook the issue of basic human rights and loss of human potential that can benefit the common purpose.

The more the distribution of rewards is based on inherited wealth and power or gender, the more inefficient and less innovative society is; in the end, it will lose its vitality and possibly become stagnant and corrupt. Existing inequalities should be considered for the purpose of partial *redistribution*, not for entitlement purposes but so as to benefit less privileged groups, to the point that they feel they have some chance to succeed through education and hard work.

The Role of Government

The problem is, despite recent tax increases for the top 1 percent, the average federal tax is relatively low, compared to the last 50 years. Still, nearly half of all Americans believe their income tax is high and the majority also reject the notion of redistribution as a code word for "socialism." Yet most Americans do not want government to cut Social Security, Medicare or education funding. But we have little choice. Either we reduce entitlements and safety nets or we accept larger tax revenues and an expanding role for government.

As for government, we've had this debate before. Teddy Roosevelt expanded the role of government in order to curb the power of large corporations and corporate monopolies. Franklin Roosevelt's New Deal was based on the notion that government had to play a bigger role to ensure America's economic health. President Johnson's War on Poverty and civil rights legislation assumed that government had to play a larger role in order to ensure the social fabric of society and help the poor and minority populace. President Reagan changed the role of government by claiming it was the problem, not the solution to our economic concerns—and the need was to shrink government. Today's Democrats line up with the Roosevelts and Johnson, and Republicans claim Reagan's philosophy as key for America's free market and economic vitality.

Regardless of one's view of the government's role, and our willingness to either cut entitlements and safety nets or increase taxes and redistribute income, real opportunity must exist: Everyone cannot hit home runs, but everyone should get up to bat in a democratic society. What's worse is when some people never get up to bat at all. What's almost as bad is that throughout life someone has always batted last. Eventually, the sandlot ballplayer who always bats last gets the message and drops out. It's no different in school and society. It comes down to what kind of society we want. Do we want one where there is a distinct cleavage, one group always hitting doubles, triples and home runs and another group striking out, or not even getting up to bat, living a half-life, passing time away and doing very little for themselves and society?

The situation being described leads to a large economic underbelly, class antagonism and nationwide decline because a large portion of human potential is curtailed. It's one thing to experience setbacks, react or modify our behavior and learn from our mistakes. Managing the gap between hopes and reality is a lifelong process. But always being exposed to discrimination, failure or the lack of opportunity eventually leads people to recede into silence and from life. What we cannot allow to happen is for failure and frustration to become a way of life or a vehicle for engulfing one's identity, rather than an opportunity to learn and bounce back from. Similarly, we cannot have a tiny group hoarding money and engaging in excess (big houses, big boats and lavish entertainment) and the masses living day to day, on the edge, in debt—and as cogs in the machinery of big government and/or corporate America.

How wealth should be redistributed depends on the leaders in power and their moral fiber and values, their belief in equality and equity (or fairness). There will never be full agreement on this issue, and that is what makes liberals and conservatives debate across the aisles. Ideally we can proclaim that laws and social institutions should be developed that do not lead to unfair advantages for some at the expense of others. Everyone should be working for the common good, rather than their own interests. Some social and economic inequalities are acceptable as a byproduct of capitalism and as an outcome of excellent performance. But the institutions and policies of society must limit major inequalities of opportunity and mobility if society is to work for the common good.

The problem is, benefits are rarely proportioned equally among advantaged and disadvantaged groups, so that the unequal distribution of the economic pie will not have the same benefit for those who are disadvantaged or on the lower end of the totem pole. Similarly, it becomes a quandary to try to agree that someone's success must benefit the common good or the less fortunate. It might be easy to determine how a physician or judge benefits society, but it would not be easy to show how baseball players or rock stars earning $25 to $50 million a year benefit society or less fortunate groups. When all is said and done, most people act on self-interest. In opposition to the philosophy of Herbert Spencer and Ayn Rand, the need is to curtail greed and materialism and to establish laws that restrain powerful people and wealthy people.

Only if inequalities of income and wealth are curtailed can equal opportunities for education, healthcare and work be achieved. Only in a more equal society can disadvantaged groups and ordinary working people hope to succeed in large numbers. By allowing too much wealth in the hands of a few, by distorting financial markets or by creating tax policies that favor the rich and super-rich, we eventually reduce consumer spending and investment in productive endeavors. The outcome is perilous for the economy—eventually hindering investment in infrastructure, education and research and development. Let's be clear about it—the wealthy have not created new wealth for the nation. If so, our gross domestic production would be much greater. They have taken money from others by restricting labor (a better word might be that they hold labor "hostage" by stifling unions), limiting minimum wages and by working with the government to ensure favorable tax policies. The need is for balance: to redistribute wealth so that those who inherit wealth or those with natural abilities or strength do not run away with most of the gold. At the same time, we cannot overtax to the extent that wealthy people move to another country to avoid taxes. The goal is to achieve compassion and charity, to be fair and just, to seek balance in the distribution of income and wealth, to appeal to the better angles of our instincts.

We would like to believe in the image of a person who rose from nothing and who owed nothing to parentage. This part of the American dream and the notion of the self-made person (usually a man) is commonly accepted as part of the norm, and there is just enough truth in these stories, a testimony to American democracy. But given the last 25 to 30 years, the humblest and poorest rarely rise to the top. Statistically the odds do not coincide with popular literature or folklore. For every poor or working-class person who becomes a captain of industry or a super athlete, tens of thousands are doomed to live out their life in the same quintile they started in, or slightly move, an inch or two higher. Given a highly competitive society, life is not a bowl of cherries or a rose garden; sometimes there is more rain than sunshine. All you have to do is listen to the songs of Muddy Waters, A.P. Carter and Johnny Cash—and you hear a prickle or sad story about the human condition and reality of life.

Merit and Achievement

In education terms, what counts today is how the government spends money on intellectual capital—federal support of schools, college scholarships, retraining of labor, etc. Actually, nurturing *intellectual capital* (educated and credentialed professionals and business people) is the key for creating *economic capital*. Should Alexander Hamilton's mob be educated (his view of the common people), and to what extent? In the final analysis, intellectual capital (Thomas Jefferson's position) is more important than economic capital (Hamilton's position) if democracy is to survive and if the country is going to continue to prosper. The irony is, however, inequality is exacerbated by the development of intellectual capital; that is, by an increase of knowledge-based and technical workers. Inequality is greater in cities such as New York, Boston and Los Angeles because knowledge- and tech-based workers easily find work in these cities and earn considerably more than people who engage in routine tasks, or low-tech and low-end jobs. But the other side of the coin is that educated and professional people contribute more to society and therefore deserve to be paid more. In simple economic terms, how much more can we raise the salary of an *expert* janitor—$1/hour, $2/hour? Consider the janitor's raise vis-à-vis the raise for an expert physician, computer programmer, scientist or airplane pilot.

An achievement-oriented society based on academic credentials and standardized tests (which compare individuals in relation to a group score, say on IQ, achievement or aptitude) condemns many people who cannot compete on an intellectual or cognitive level to the low end of the stratification structure. It is a classic problem: The rich (who have more resources for better education) get richer and the poor get poorer; thus gaps between the "haves" and "have nots" have dramatically increased in the last few decades. Put in more precise terms, since the Reagan presidency, one tenth of the population (on the income pyramid) has been improving its prospects while the remaining 90 percent has lagged behind.

It is the top 10 percent, especially the top 1 percent, that has glommed almost all of the economic growth—because of increased globalization, free-market policies and tax revenue policies that favor investments and capital and discriminate against wages and labor. Nicholas Kristof, writing "An Idiot's Guide to Inequality" for the *New York Times*, estimates that the top "1 percent in the U.S. now own more wealth than the bottom 90 percent." Surprisingly, no one has rebelled. The majority has not imposed higher taxes on the wealthy, as it was in the Reagan administration (50 percent), Wilson administration (70 percent) or Eisenhower administration (90 percent); in fact, the opposite has occurred, partially because conservative forces since the Nixon administration have dominated the White House and Congress. The 2013 bump (from 35 to 39.6 percent) in taxes for those earning $400,000 or more is a drop in the bucket, compared to what it was during the previous Republican administrations.

As of 2013, the top 10 percent earned about 50 percent of the nation's income while the top 1 percent earned 22 percent. As for assets accumulated, the top 10 percent had a larger share of the nation's overall wealth than the bottom 90 percent, and the top 1 percent owned slightly more than 40 percent of overall wealth. According to Eduardo Porter of the *New York Times*, this gap in income and wealth tops the inequality index among 32 industrialized countries (except Singapore and Hong Kong). Similarly, nearly 40 percent of the wealthiest 1 percent of the global population are Americans, although this inequality is gradually shifting to China and India. A new study authored by Jonathan Ostry and funded by the International Monetary Fund reveals that economic growth becomes stifled in countries like the U.S. with high levels of income inequality— slowing growth and job creation up to one third of potential. Economic inequality feeds into political and economic instability; the economy stalls or experiences major volatility, which in turn leads to fear and reduces business investments and productivity.

According to Joseph Stiglitz, in *The Price of Inequality*, excessive inequality reduces economic growth. Just as discrimination reduces opportunities for many citizens, inequality of income has a similar effect whereby it leads to inadequate housing and schooling, as well as limited job growth for the majority of the people. The Columbia University economist argues that today's economic policies have weakened labor and strengthened capital—resulting in greater inequality. As inequality grows, society becomes more divisive—leaving those at the bottom marginalized, rejected and disenfranchised—even worse, dysfunctional and a major cost factor and burden for society. The outcome is, we now live in a divided world in which the rich and super-rich live in gated communities and send their children to Ivy League schools while the majority of Americans live in a world marked by second-rate housing and mediocre schools.

We can put the blame for rising inequality on numerous factors. Ineffective political leadership, big government and government regulations, entitlements that create a culture of poverty and a host of "moochers" and "takers," tax policies that favor wealth (assets) over work (labor), a slow-growing economy, lousy schools, incompetent teachers and lazy students, lack of a skilled workforce, the influence of unions, decaying infrastructure which discourages job-producing investments. You can make up your own list. Actually, the number one culprit is the estate tax code which permits intergenerational transfer of capital, property and stocks. Abolish inheritance or tax it at progressively high rates and you eventually end inequality. Abolish birthright inheritance and privilege, and you can end inequality within most countries. Prevent the transfer of titles, money and legacy—thus equalize the playing field for the next generation—and you allow ordinary people greater opportunities.

What's your limit: allowing $1 million, $5 million, $25 million, etc. to be the maximum transmission to the next generation? Or do you allow, as free marketers would argue, sky's the limit, with 99 percent of U.S. citizens and the world population playing the role as subordinates to an oligarchy? If I suggested that the people put a limit on estate transfers, would you call me a Marxist for restraining capital or a Rousseauian who believes that government should have a social contract with the people?

Harvard's Michael Sandel, in his book *What Money Can't Buy*, notes that "democracy does not require perfect equality" (that would be an extreme form of socialism). But it does require that the citizens share in the production of goods and services and employ some moral barometer, some moral limits and some legitimate way to share in the fruits of the nation's economy. Extreme inequality, the path we are on, ultimately shrinks the middle class and destroys the common purpose and common good of society. In such societies, excellence, meritocracy and mobility are meaningless words. The playing field is too far tilted for education, hard work and/or talent to overcome the initial differences at the starting point.

While the potential for individuals to improve their status is essential in a democracy, it is now more limited in the U.S. than it appears to be in earlier periods. Contrary to popular opinion, Timothy Noah's *The Great Divergence* maintains that incomes have become dramatically widened in the U.S. and mobility is more limited than in many other countries. "You'd have to be blind," he writes (and I would add stupid or a complete idiot) "not to see that we are headed in the wrong direction." The worst thing is for people to get used to or just accept it as a way of life. If we stop to pause, lack of mobility along with a nobility class from the Old World has reappeared in the New World with greater disparities than we could have ever imagined.

Merit and Human Capital

Americans now produce fewer and fewer products; however, we produce intellectual property (i.e., pharmaceutical research, computer chips, software, etc.), which has dramatically increased the nation's innovative, information and high-tech economy. This type of intellectual capital has led to millions of new jobs. Bill Gates, who blends Jefferson's politics with Hamilton's economics, is critical of the nation for rationing education on wealthy and suburban children at the expense of low-income and urban children. He has personally committed $1.2 billion for high school reform that would ensure that all students in his funded programs receive a college prep curriculum. Along with Warren Buffett he has created a billionaire's club where people worth a billion or more can pledge half or more of their wealth for the social and medical benefits of global society.

Will the efforts of Bill Gates and other reformers help achieve a more meritorious society? People are human, complicated by a host of flaws including greed and arrogance. If those who advance come to believe they have achieved economic success on their own merits, they may come to believe they are entitled to what they get—and the hell with stupid, slow or lazy people. According to Michael Young, the English scholar and sociologist, those who rise in a meritorious society can become smug, just as smug, if I may add, as people who were born on the more fortunate side of the economic divide and used their parents' economic resources and social connections to rise up the ladder of success. The newcomers to wealth, the academic and professional elite, and the entertainers and sports heroes, may actually come to believe they have morality and justice on their side.

A new form of arrogance can develop by the creation of meritocracy, by the same people who once believed in and exemplified the political theories of Jeffersonian democracy and the stories of Horatio Alger. If true merit becomes associated with heredity or innate ability, as it is often construed, as opposed to the notion of opportunity, than meritocracy becomes less of a virtue and more of a propaganda tool for patricians and conservatives to wave and use against the populace who have fewer opportunities because of their social and economic status.

In a society that prizes merit and achievement, the reward structure is linked to a person's natural ability. In *The Rise of Meritocracy*, Michael Young warned that such a society would put most of its resources in effective programs and schools that favored the academic elite, thus pushing the gifted and talented to the top and the less gifted and talented behind. Even worse, the process would continue over generations because of the assertive and class-based mating patterns and the component of heredity, which people in a democracy prefer not to discuss because of its racial implications. Both bright and slow students (and adults) will continue to compete in school and society, partially fortified by class distinctions (environment) and heredity. Barring drastic government policies, the search for merit and achievement will move capable people to the top and less capable people to the bottom. Although some say this is the most ideal society, as it gives everyone the chance to rise to the top, it has serious implications for average and dull people, and with people who have fewer opportunities because of class. If left unchecked or unregulated, it leads to increasing inequality, and ultimately where one group feels they belong to another species—very high or very low.

It must be said, however, that this entire discussion on talent, ability and meritocracy can be turned upside down by dumb people and smug people who for some reason rise to the top. At this point, Young's theory falls apart. For example, we know that dumb people and socially inept people sometimes rise to the top of the corporate ladder or government bureaucracy because of heredity privilege, politics and/or dumb luck. Unquestionably, there is a host of reasons why unqualified people advance over smart and talented people. Similarly, some people can be over their head on the job and be saved by rank and privilege of class. CEOs, generals and politicians are good examples, especially if the rise to the top had something to do with family connections or family fortunes. Some of us refer to this process as part of the "Peter Principle." We might also call it the "Idiot's Principle," after John Hoover's book, *How to Work for an Idiot*.

His contention is that idiots roam all levels of the workplace. Despite their education, they cause organizational waste and chaos and have a tendency to chew up and eliminate talented people. Most of us are forced to work for idiots for portions of our careers. Just listen to workers (in most professions) in the cafeteria or lounge describe their supervisors; they tend to complain about much more than they compliment their boss. (The problem is further complicated when the idiot is protected by affirmative action or a protected class.) The bad news is a worker's relationship with his or her boss is nearly equal in importance with a spouse's relationship. When it comes to mental health, psychological well-being and work productivity, the data suggest, according to psychologist Willow Lawson, that nearly 50 percent of all workers have a shaky, if not strained, relationship with their boss. It is the chief reason for quitting a job or taking early retirement. All of this contradicts Young's position about smart and talented people rising to the top; in fact, it can be argued that many smart and talented people are kept from being promoted because they have an "idiot" boss. To be sure, all of us have had our share of such bosses if we've worked long enough in an organization.

But organizational imperfections can be modified and enhance leadership. Sarah Barnett, president of SundanceTV, maintains: "As long as we are heading in the right direction, and with the right momentum, then it's OK to not always be perfect as a leader." In some organizations the focus is "sort of trying to be perfect." Sometimes things go wrong; it's important to discuss the issues. "Everybody gets heard [at meetings], and it gives me [Barnett] information that we might use to change strategy." It pays to "create a culture where you can say: 'Hey, maybe I didn't deal very well with you yesterday; this is what I meant to say.'" Indeed, the best organizations care about standards and on the job performance but there is need to make appropriate adjustments that are suitable to a large range of employees at various levels of ability, and that takes leadership to instill within the organization.

In particular, lower-echelon personnel, subordinates and mid-level employees tend to keep their thoughts to themselves at meetings when superiors or middle management are present. They usually have a point of view, but are afraid to say anything until the meeting ends, and then whisper to someone or express their thoughts afterwards to a trusted colleague. It's great to work in an organization that fosters honest dialogue and frank discussion, but don't count on it. You need to get involved at meetings, in the conversation taking place. Only a few, self-assured leaders encourage open dialogue, and treat men and women alike at meetings. Often, women tend to be cooperative in social settings and play down their successes—or not claim their voice at meetings. It's OK to be low keyed or even humble, but women need to own who they are in the professional and business world, and find their voice and seat at the table. Perhaps, we need to accept to some extent that men are from Mars and women are from Venus, or men have Y chromosomes and women have X chromosomes. But all of us should have the confidence to stand out, own who we are and express a "can do" attitude among our colleagues. In the end, all of us have to find our way to succeed—and need the confidence and desire to stand out.

Barney Harford, who is CEO of Orbitz Worldwide, says, "If you rely on executives to spot opportunities, you miss out on so much potential." He prefers "T-shaped individuals—people who can go really deep in their particular area of expertise, and also go really broad and have that kind of curiosity about the overall organization and how their particular piece of the pie fits into it." You want people "who have the curiosity to find out how other parts of the company work." For him, "it's all about creating a culture where you share information." Harford looks at merit based on performance, but acknowledges that there are budget limitations. The wrong approach is to spread "budgets across the organization like peanut butter." You need to learn as a leader to allocate merit "based on peoples' performances and their potential." It's essential to identify the "weak links" and address their performance issues, "by mentoring and coaching." If you can't improve their performance, "you need to find a way to exit them from the organization." The question arises how practical this solution is with laws involving reverse discrimination and protected classes, or whether organizations are willing to invest time to remedy disadvantages that some of us start with.

Trying to figure out the interactions of environment and heredity is a hopeless policy issue; rather the crux of the problem is to deal with disadvantages of a limited environment because class factors at the bottom limit and deform the spirit and lead to the plight of the next generation. We need to find the sweet spot! Some entitlement or safety net that protects the lower classes, which children and parents of various abilities and talents can accept. The issue can be exemplified in reverse—the current period in schooling which de-emphasizes programs for the talented and gifted. This is due to pressure to create heterogeneous classrooms with a wide range of academic abilities, and in the passage of affirmative action legislation. Part of the search for fairness is to adopt an uncompromising commitment to produce more effective schools in lower-class communities—at least fund the schools equally.

Winning at All Costs

The focus on excellence can reach an extreme. In a capitalistic and competitive society, motivation and drive to be number one can turn into an emphasis on destroying your opponents and winning at all costs. In business, the emphasis on excellence can turn into beating the competition in order to win fame or fortune—and becoming arrogant. When the end-goal is winning—on being a super star in sports, highly successful in business or just getting accepted to Harvard or Yale, the difference between being a genius or highly talented and engaging in unethical or criminal behavior can be a fine line. It can be nothing more than a matter of semantics or a distortion of reality. Defying convention, taking excessive risk, or engaging in exhaustive training or preparation is one thing. But breaking the rules, bending the law, or just outright cheating is not what we expect from our heroes and icons, nor from our top students.

In sports, take Lance Armstrong—the poster cancer survival and win-at-all-costs cyclist. For more than 15 years, after hiring doping experts and beating the anti-doping authorities, bribing doctors to look the other way, character witnesses to lie and cycling officials to bury their suspicions, and paying competitors to lose, Armstrong finally admitted in 2013 that he had consistently used performance-enhancing drugs. The evidence had become overwhelming, and he had been caught in many lies. In a nutshell, Armstrong was most proficient at cheating and using chemical technology. He consistently won cycling races by hiring doping experts to boost his energy and to mask pain, and he earned hundreds of millions in prize money, speeches and endorsements. He was ruthless in discarding friends, mentors and teammates and threatened witnesses or anyone who spoke out against him.

Rules didn't apply to Armstrong. A talented cyclist, a ruthless competitor with a desire to win at all costs and to gain fame and fortune, he gamed the system and broke the methods of enforcement to his advantage. His fall from grace is well documented by two recent books: *Cycle of Lies* by Juliet Macur and *Wheelmen* by

Reed Albergotti and Vanessa O'Connell. Everything in his path—the drugs, doctors, expert witnesses, cyclist officials, lawyers, etc.—were obstacles to beat; anything to win. His competitive drive allowed him to push the envelope and ignore the norms and rules of society. To be sure, the desire to win, whatever the price, infects nearly all sports around the world—soccer, swimming, racing, javelin throwing, discus throwing, wrestling, etc.—in which good athletes want to become super athletes. We are talking about thousands of athletes who bend the rules in order to gain a small but critical advantage that makes the difference between winning or finishing second or third. Here in the U.S. baseball has been dramatically changed by a host of athletes who have been caught using performance-enhancing drugs, and suspended from playing up to 50 to 100 games.

There are times when the notion of excellence becomes so tainted or perverted in a desire to be number one in your profession or career, that the idea is to crush your competitors. For those who are driven to succeed at this level, fair competition and rules don't apply. The "wolves" on Wall Street, who fit the Gordon Gekko profile in the movie *Wall Street*, typify this image. The obsession to win at all costs, to be the last person standing in a battle against competitors, has also infected Silicon Valley.

Take Steve Jobs, the cofounder of Apple, who was revered by his tech contemporaries and considered by many tech users today as the number-one inventor of the twenty-first century. Not only did he flaunt the Sherman Anti-Trust Act—that is, restraint of trade—by initiating an anti-poaching pact with other tech companies (see Chapter 1), but also he threatened other tech companies with patent litigation for the sake of financially draining them, unless they agreed not to recruit his employees. According to James Stewart, in a 2014 article in the *New York Times*, Jobs also conspired in price-fixing e-books with the large publishing companies in an unsuccessful effort to topple Amazon. (The publishers paid fines; he escaped prosecution.)

He was consistently in court fighting over patent rights involving iPhones and tablets (involving Samsung) and Internet services (involving Microsoft and Google), sometimes as a defendant and sometimes as a plaintiff. He regularly appealed adverse decisions, settling claims and paying fines in order to show he was a peerless inventor, *numero uno*. Jobs played a major role in backdating options involving hundreds of millions when he was at Apple and Pixar Studios, a computer animation company; and, he was involved in fabricating corporate minutes to cover up his fraudulent behaviors. Although he was never charged, many of his executives settled with federal regulators and others went to jail.

Jobs's behavior, from his early years at Apple, when he was working out of a garage, to the end of his life in 2011, reflects the fine line between genius and criminality. He constantly took risks, flaunted the law and believed (like Armstrong) that rules that apply to ordinary people did not apply to him. He was driven with the obsession to crush his opponents and be the best in Silicon Valley. He had little regard about ethics or the law. In fact, it could be said he thought he was above the law; he could bend it, distort it and violate it. There is no question Jobs pushed the envelope and ignored the norms and rules of society, as did Armstrong. The nice interpretation is that people like Jobs don't care for the status quo and are always on the fringe—pushing boundaries, challenging convention and going where others dare not go. But when does genius turn into obsession and when does obsession turn into defiance of the law? In describing criminal behavior, how much slack should we allow the likes of Steve Jobs? When he was healthy? When he was diagnosed with Stage 4 cancer? The answers we voice should vary among readers, reflecting the clarity and convictions of our own set of principles, sense of ethics and morality, and view of the law.

There are hundreds, if not thousands, of other business people and companies that could be cited for their ruthlessness, competitive drive and desire to achieve at all costs. To name a few, there are the Koch brothers who make billions in gas and oil while they pollute the air and wreck the quality of life on the planet. There is Rupert Murdoch, the global media billionaire—noted for crushing business opponents, bribing politicians and hacking into phone conversations of critics and competitors. There are companies like Enron, which fleeced stockholders and employers of billions; when executives jumped the ship, they were assuring the public and their 25,000+ workers to buy more stock which eventually became worthless.

Then there is Walmart—the largest private employer and revenue leader in America, with an ethos noted for driving out hundreds of small businesses every time they open up a store in the U.S., paying poverty-based wages to workers while top executives earn millions and bribing foreign politicians in order to expand their brand and become the number-one retailer in the world. "If you work hard and play by the rules, you should have the opportunity for a good life," so the folklore goes. That's not how it works at Walmart, for some considered a throwback to the sweatshop factories of the early twentieth century and whose executives remind us of the robber barons of the Gilded Age.

In 2013 Walmart workers were paid an hourly wage between $8.50 and $12.50 with bonuses capped at $1,200. Meanwhile the top ten executives earned several millions and averaged $8 million in bonuses. Comparing the top hourly salary to the earnings of former CEO Michael Duke, it would take 785 years for the average full-time Walmart worker to earn Duke's annual salary ($20.7 million in 2012). You have to ask: Is this difference in pay justified? Is another human being worth tens of thousands more than another human being? Are we inflating the pay for talent beyond a person's potential ability, performance level or actual contributions? More than half of the 2.2 million workers at Walmart must look to food stamps, Medicaid and other forms of public assistance, while the company was the nation's number-one revenue producer of $476 billion and rung up profits of $17 billion in 2013. Less known, the combined net worth of four of the heirs of the Walton family was over $144 billion and they were among the 10 richest people in the United States; two other heirs were in the top 100 richest list. Of course, all this criticism of Walmart may be premature or for naught given the recent rise of Amazon and Google, which appear bent on world domination of the Internet (with only Alibaba left as a rival competitor).

In trying to determine the best and brightest—that is, being committed to superior achievement in your field—Western society has implemented a filtering process that concentrates those with high IQs, vision, strength, motivation and hard work with top jobs and those with low IQs and lack of vision, strength, motivation and hard work at or near the bottom. Does that mean those who are smart, take risks and are driven to succeed get most of the benefits, and those with opposite traits, or who are just plain average, or below average, get mediocre or boring jobs? Should smart bankers who take risks with other peoples' money, and cause havoc to the economy, be given the benefit of the doubt? Should Barry Bonds, Mike McGuire, Melky Cabrera or Alex Rodriguez, given their history with performance-enhancing drugs, be given the benefit of the doubt? Should they be inducted into the baseball Hall of Fame? Should the student who sits next to you and cheats on the final exam be given a "do over"? In the quest for achievement, meritocracy and excellence, where do personal responsibility and acceptable limits enter into the equation?

In the quest for achievement, even for being number 2 or 3, are we to accept extreme or polarizing behavior, cheating, ruthlessness, etc.? No. What we need to do is provide the diverse opportunities and fair treatment that different people with differential abilities require. We need to remember that most of Horatio Alger's heroes did not have college degrees. We need to respect our proponents and competitors, and provide suitable goals for people (youth and adults) to achieve at the maximum level, or their highest potential, in which their ability and ambition will take them. We need to ensure the game is played by the rules—not bent, side tracked or ignored by someone hell-bent on winning and/or wiping out opponents or competitors at any cost.

Conclusion

If we are forced to rely on the wisdom and goodwill of politicians, who are often influenced by corporations and special interest groups, then the working and middle classes (even the mildly affluent) become unknowing victims and duped by the people they trusted. In some ways, then, we are forced to reread the ideas behind a *social contract*, the principles that this country was founded on. Here I am talking about the Age of Enlightenment and the theories of Locke and Rousseau, bolstered by Thomas Hobbes's *Leviathan* and Immanuel Kant's moral doctrines. Once more it comes down to Jefferson's thoughts on the rights of people. Some readers might say the author is putting too much stock in one person, that Washington, Lincoln or Franklin Roosevelt are presidents whom no one in American history rivals. So be it! We all have our own idols, heroes and superstars whom we worship or praise. Where I stand on the political fence, Jefferson was the first American to put the important ideas of equality on paper, and in the right way.

Americans tend to see inequalities as part of the natural order, whereby outcomes and new opportunities cannot be equal. For example, deficit spending is bound to influence the standard of living of our children and grandchildren by limiting entitlements and essential services, as well as raising prices of products and services for those who need them the most and cannot afford them. But reduction of social, health and education spending only increases inequality, because the rich are still able to pay for services they want. Moreover, the fight for essential human services will most likely be tilted in favor of the aging baby boomers at the expense of school spending, because they represent the largest and most consistent block of voters. Education as a social category or variable cannot alone reduce inequality or uplift the masses. To put it in reverse: Only if inequalities of income and wealth are kept within a limited range can education be used as an equalizer. When inequality grows out of proportion, with limited checks or balance, the concepts of excellence, opportunity and mobility become increasingly blurry and then futile, the middle class shrinks and the economy stagnates.

To achieve greater equality and to assist the unfortunate, we need to increase taxes for the wealthy; improve tax compliance; shut down tax loopholes and offshore companies that avoid taxes; regularly audit the tax returns of the wealthy (with annual incomes of more than $500,000 and/or assets of more than $5 million); and limit estate trusts, which currently save taxes from generation to generation and allow the transfer of wealth. The need is to ensure a wealth transfer tax at every generation, especially after the $5 million level. (This level only affects the top 0.5 percent of taxpayers, but such a law would sharply reduce run-away inequality (or the makings of a financial oligarchy).) If we don't address these issues now—that is, put restraints on money moguls—then we are spinning our wheels in debating the relationship between equality and opportunity, between education and mobility, or between excellence and rewards for performance. Hence, we can ask whether the American dream still exists for the majority of Americans, despite what they hope or believe.

Because these measures are not being implemented, we are witnessing a rise of a new aristocratic class, based on wealth and power, far worse than the European model our Founding Fathers sought to curtail. What we need is a set of political, economic and moral principles that are based on our history, philosophy and literature. The author would start with the Hebrews and the *Talmud* and the Greeks, with the "liberties of the ancients" during the time of Pericles, and work his way up to the great books and great minds of humankind. Locke, Rousseau and Jefferson would be high on my recommended list, along with Kant and the current readings of John Rawls and John Gardner. Of course, anyone with a half wit already knows that I favor these voices of reason.

There is no set of recommendations for achieving equality (or excellence) that can please the entire American populace. It involves a balancing act that changes with history—who is in power and to what extent political compromises are made among interest groups. Perhaps someone in a little cabaret in South Texas (a Johnny Cash jingo) or a coffee shop in Hoboken, NJ (a Philip Roth location) or a church in Yoknapatawpha County (William Faulkner's fictional but real place) can figure out a solution, as our leaders and statesmen cannot come to a consensus, and instead regularly engage in partisan politics and negative nabobs. All we can hope for is some balance in society—a sense of fairness, a varied set of parameters in the search for talent and an equitable reward system for achievement. Hopefully, we would recognize unique and diverse talents. At the same time, we would hope for rigorous standards to define excellence, without stereotyping some groups as incapable or making unfair comparisons, and without discriminating against other groups because they are high-achievers and insistently motivated. We should also provide second chances and multiple chances for late bloomers, slow runners and disadvantaged groups. Similarly, we would hope for some equity in the distribution of wealth and reduction of inequality. This assumes you believe that inequality taken to an extreme violates moral principles, hinders the economy and limits the pursuit of excellence (and rewards) to fewer people.

4

INNOVATION AND HUMAN CAPITAL

As a nation, less than 250 years old, the humblest and poorest in America have been able to lift up their heads and face the future with confidence. Since the rise of the common school movement, starting in the 1820s, the majority of Americans have increasingly relied on education as an integral part of this process of becoming. The culture that evolved during the post-Civil War was sanctioned by Darwin's theories of natural selection and perpetual mutability. It fit well into the American faith in the doctrine of progress—where people could shape and improve themselves. Little indeed was considered fixed or static. Here people could rise from their low station in life and move in one generation from an unprivileged class to a middle or privileged class.

The American style of capitalism that emerged permitted the bold, adventurous and more adaptable person to realize profits from the labor and sweat of the working class. It is this unrestrained form of capitalism that continued to enjoy some vogue in the later decades of the nineteenth century and into the early twentieth century, creating the bubble that led to the Great Depression. It is the same free market system, the false belief that the market can correct itself, which led to the bubble bursting again, 75 years later—and the deepest recession most living Americans have ever experienced.

Ordinary people, today, have to work two or more jobs, and married people need two incomes to keep up with a 1950s standard of living. Back then, it took a sociologist (like David Riesman) or psychologist (like Dr. Benjamin Spock) to tell people what they were feeling. Now commentators like Lou Dobbs, Scott Pelley and Diane Sawyer report to Americans how they feel, how they struggle to make ends meet, and, even worse, how our jobs are being exported abroad (85 percent of our retail purchases is now manufactured overseas), which in turn compounds with the imbalance of trade (cheap overseas labor markets exporting goods to the U.S. market). Moreover, the outsourcing of jobs is now affecting middle-class and white-collar employment as such jobs increasingly drive the engines of the knowledge, technological and digital economy.

Outsourcing Middle-Class Jobs

It started with a company named IBM in 2005, when it announced that it would shift 114,000 high-paying, high-tech jobs (paying $75,000 or more) to India at salaries about one fifth of those in the United States and Western Europe. Hewlett-Packard stated the same year it would lay off 19,000 to 25,000 employees earning between $50,000 and $125,000, representing a saving of $605 billion per year, and build a new assembly plant in India. The next year Dell announced it would double the size of its software workforce in India to 20,000; it is also expected to shift tens of thousands of additional jobs once it set up a new manufacturing site in the country.

By 2010, similar announcements had been made by Cisco, Intel and Microsoft, the engines of the technological future, which planned to double and triple their workforces in India. Cisco and Intel each planned to invest more than $1.1 billion in India, and Microsoft is investing $1.7 billion. Apple, Boeing, Ford, GM and Motorola were right behind these high-tech companies, opening up new factories outside the United States, in China and the Asian rim, to save money. Even our old enemy Vietnam is on the radar screen for billion-dollar investments by high-tech firms such as Intel and Hewlett-Packard. Microsoft has also opened up a software center in Canada because of liberal immigration laws which make it easier to recruit qualified people from around the globe. Walmart is the worst culprit—spending approximately $335 billion a year on buying and transporting goods from abroad.

Amid all this gloom, there are glimmers of hope that U.S. industries are considering to bring back manufacturing jobs to the U.S.—led by a $100 million investment by Apple to produce some of its Mac components and a $1 billion investment by GE to build an appliance assembly plant. Apple's iPad and iPhone products, which amount to 70 percent of its sales, continue to be made in China, mostly at Foxconn, the largest factory in the world. Actually a $100 million for Apple is like "a drop in the bucket," but optimists feel it's a start for "reshoring" jobs after decades of shipping them overseas.

Although many reasons are given for "reshoring" jobs, a primary factor is that the unions have lowered their expectations, as have the labor force in the U.S. Salaries and benefits for new factory workers are about half the pre-1990 scale—a major factor for growing inequality within the country. But it can be argued that the damage is already done: So much of the manufacturing and high-tech knowledge has been lost to Asia, not to overlook the millions of jobs at home that have also disappeared. The bottom line is that today many high-paying jobs in the U.S. are created by high-tech, innovative companies, but they are being shipped overseas where STEM workers are paid 25 percent of what their American counterparts earn. Moreover, many of the new, high-profile manufacturing jobs utilize robots and thus displace workers; technology, today, is not limited to only replacing unskilled labor, but now includes replacing skilled workers.

The outsourcing of jobs is bound to worsen if America's immigration policies are not softened. What we need to be doing is increasing foreign student visas and pasting green cards to science and engineering diplomas, so these qualified people become part of our economy, rather than losing them to another country and then having to compete with them. The ripple effect of these investments in terms of future science, research and technological jobs is estimated to create four times the number of initial jobs. In other words, jobs create other jobs, and science and technology jobs have a fourfold impact in a growing economy—and the impact continues to multiply so long as there is a healthy economic growth pattern.

The fact is that nations are no longer able to isolate themselves and pursue policies that are incompatible with an increasing global market. The types of jobs and services that generate economic wealth for nations are more mobile than ever, based more on a broadband and Internet connection than geography, and policies that shackle international business hinder economic growth. With globalization, the average U.S. worker is exposed to much more competition and job insecurity. As the world becomes digitally and globally interconnected, jobs became more mobile. In *The World is Flat*, Thomas Friedman points out that computers, broadband and cellular networks and the Internet have leveled the economic playing field. Global trade indicates continuous growth in investments and jobs in China, India, Brazil and other emerging markets, and the slow transfer of trillions of dollars from the U.S. to the Asian rim over the next ten years. If your job can be digitized, it may be only a short time before it becomes movable to the other side of the world—with people willing to work for two thirds to three quarters less than the American scientist, engineer, accountant, teacher or computer specialist.

Our gross national product, standard of living and jobs are connected to the world community and influenced by global events. Hence, the jobs at home that have become more plentiful are for displaced, less-educated or part-time workers—mostly low-paying jobs such as "hamburger helper" or Walmart hostess (also called a "greeter"), which on the pay scale of one to ten (ten being the best) is a one or two. This is the future for our children and grandchildren unless we do something about it now. The situation is best summed by one sentence in a 2014 *New York Times* editorial piece: "The forces responsible for job growth… are weak, wages… are low and work weeks… are short."

Beyond the *Times* description, factory overtime, once a common theme for the working class, has all but disappeared and wages barely keep up with inflation. More troubling, most college graduates do not make full use of their education; they are either underemployed or temporarily employed—sort of a lost generation who are unable to grow their resume and future job outlook. According to

Barron's, "job gains over the last several years have been illusory. Full-time jobs have [declined], while part-time jobs have grown." Federal debt in 2015 was at an all-time high: 74 percent of gross domestic product, more than twice what it was in 2007. Beyond the present decade, the fiscal outlook is grim: Given an aging population, huge increases in healthcare and increasing government subsidies such as Social Security, health insurance, college tuition, etc. The predictions that the economy is improving, as most economists claim, may be overly optimistic. The defenders of capitalism and free enterprise may be defending the system on pure materialistic grounds, because it makes people (top 1 percent) rich, but on a moral basis the system falls flat. The economic system no longer seems to help the majority of the populace. It now helps the superich to become richer.

The Global Village

According to Michael Mandel in *Rational Exuberance*, globalization and technology are coming together and creating the potential for future work and where we work. Offshoring jobs, for example, means that knowledge/information work can be broken into smaller tasks and redistributed around the world. Someone in Bangalore or San Paulo can do one aspect of the work, and someone in Hong Kong or Helsinki can perform another part of the job. Moreover, the Internet has enhanced all means of communication, creating "virtual worlds" and transforming the place of work and the speed of innovation.

For global corporations, the trend is to avoid multiple bodies and large offices in places like Silicon Valley or Shanghai. The idea is to shrink personnel and office space and get workers to collaborate instantly around the world. The typical hierarchical organization, with layers of management, has shifted to small, multiple sites, with an ever-shifting network of employees who work on a team for a single project and who communicate through email, Skype and videocoms. Such corporations now hire people from around the world and then offer courses online to develop talent. People can obviously be hired in any part of the world to do the same work an American engineer or accountant can do—and for considerably less than the American salary. President Obama put it this way: "A child born in Dallas is now competing with a child born in New Delhi."

The "gathering storm" or economic demise of American innovation and knowledge is gaining momentum. American students are unable to compete on international tests in science and math, U.S. science and engineering enrollments are down, the recruitment of top students from abroad has dramatically declined due to visa restrictions following September 11, and the world playing field has been flattened and made more competitive by the Internet. U.S. knowledge, information and technology jobs, and other knowledge producers whose jobs are digitized, can now be replaced by a Google-ready or Windows-ready worker anywhere. Our children can only thank us for making it easier to communicate to the unemployment agency or find some underemployed or temporary job via the Internet.

Skilled manufacturing jobs, at one time the backbone of the U.S. economy and the reason why workers once rose to the middle class in America, have collapsed. In the last 15 years (2000–2015), we have lost some five to six million manufacturing jobs. Now one of the last two remaining industries in which America is still in a leadership role—that is, knowledge and technology—is on the downward slide. Its decline is highlighted by the fact that American values crumbled in the twenty-first century. Rather than investing in long-term products, services or technology, and related innovations that would benefit the nation and its people, short-term profits and reckless gambling and risk-taking have became the norm.

Instead of venture capital coming after a product goes through research and development, the U.S. financial world threw money at Silicon Valley and the Golden Triangle. The money came first, instead of the product coming first. There was nothing being produced, rather ideas were evolving and fees being charged under the guise of "financial products" which helped create the economic meltdown. The outcome was the loss of some six million jobs, the shredding of pensions and 401Ks, as well as the evaporation of trillions of dollars of U.S. wealth. Today, big corporations like Apple, IBM, GE, Medtronic, Carnival and Ingersoll Rand, instead of producing new goods and services, seem more interested in pursuing quick profits by taking advantage of tax loopholes and shifting corporate holdings to Europe and Asia or buying foreign-based companies, where taxes are lower than in the U.S. The outcome is loss of U.S. government revenue, rising U.S. deficits and fewer U.S. jobs. Although the new companies are based overseas, the real headquarters usually remain in the U.S. Once the companies "invert" or merge, there is a permanent loss to the U.S. tax base, as well as jobs, since we can assume these companies are not returning to the U.S. As of 2014, according to *Forbes* magazine, 60 U.S. companies had "deserted," and many more were lining up.

Prior to the Great Recession, politicians from both parties embraced globalization as positive for the economy, without describing the negatives to the U.S. workforce. Big government and big banks "financed" our economy by making loans and credit easy for customers, and relying on inflated housing values to generate growth and mask the trend that wages did not grow and good-paying jobs were not being produced. In fact, U.S. salaries as a percentage of gross domestic product has steadily declined since 1960, according to Sheila Bair, the former chair of the FDIC. While wages have stagnated, corporate profits have increased approximately 3 percent annually.

In the last 15 years, from 2000 to 2015, *Fortune* magazine reports that corporations have generated increased output per work hour (35 percent), but workers' hourly compensation adjusted for inflation was the lowest since 1947, rising 9.5 percent over 15 years, or less than 1 percent annually. In short, U.S. workers are not adequately rewarded as a proportion of output or for increased performance. Excellence in labor is not recognized by big business, and it never was recognized except during the Cold War period when U.S. industries were booming and had minimal international competition. Although the stock market has nearly tripled since the 2007 recession, those who have benefited are investors who receive capital gains and dividends. Hence, the triumph of capital over labor is a constant, and now more acute with the rise of globalization and technology.

If you believe that the economy is interconnected, and every worker is a consumer, then all major sectors of the economy affect the American standard of living. As the U.S. dream diminishes and the U.S. workforce is squeezed, we have a growing number of unemployed, underemployed and temporary college-educated workers (totaling nearly 50 percent in 2015) competing for fewer good-paying jobs in the U.S. When adjusted for inflation, the real salaries of U.S. workers with at least a bachelor's degree remained relatively flat from 2000 to 2015, an unpleasant dose of reality in a society in which education is supposed to be the key to success. Only those with special talent and/or STEM skills, and a few who possess human interaction skills, are able to compete in this new economic environment.

Tech Society, Tech Expertise

Prior to 2000, expansion in technology and information-related jobs raised the income for those with sufficient skills and education to handle complex jobs. Those with minimal skills and lower levels of education did not benefit or receive income gains related to American productivity; the collapse of manufacturing and the union movement played a role that started during the Reagan presidency. The resulting inequalities between the rich and rest of the nation was slightly masked by an increasing number of people receiving higher education degrees and moving up the wage ladder with good jobs. But the "good times" came to an end. Now that outsourcing of high-tech and middle-class jobs is impacting the U.S. economy, we can expect an assault on the middle class and increasing inequality.

Beyond flattened salaries for people with college degrees and having our knowledge and technological jobs moved overseas, we are beginning to experience large movements of skilled workers crossing national borders in Asia and Europe, providing a hint of an increasing interconnected world and global economy. The question arises: Are we witnessing the beginning of a new world of empowered and mobile workers or a "brave new world" of virtual sweatshops—where multinational corporations are able to depress employee wages? The emerging workplace may not necessarily be a factory or assembly line, but don't expect it to be a place where the salaries of college-educated or middle-class workers will keep up with corporate profits or inflation. The difference between excellent and average work performance may soon become blurred, because demand for several skill sets will diminish and fewer people in the U.S. will be left with high-paying jobs.

Hence, we are beginning to witness a growing number of ambitious and intelligent students purposely dropping out of college (called "hacking" higher education): viewing it not as a failure but as a sensible option. Inspired by an early generation of successful college dropouts like Michel Dell, Bill Gates and Steve Jobs, and now by Kevin Rose of Digg, Evan Williams of Twitter and Mark Zuckerberg of Facebook, the thinking goes "why pay money, or worse go into debt, if I can make money? I can make millions by creating an app or producing a computer game before someone else comes up with the idea."

Popular culture is portraying self-made high-tech millionaires who reject the "safe route" of a college education akin to going out west 150 years ago to strike gold. Given this new view, college dropouts in the tech world are considered "free thinkers," "risk takers" and "innovators." They have not been tainted by groupthink, conforming rules or corporate restraints. This type of thinking is highlighted by the likes of Michael Ellsberg's *The Education of Millionaires: Everything You Don't Learn in College About How to Be Successful*. It's reinforced by other academics who question the value (or cost) of a college degree, compounded by mounting student debt ($1.2 trillion as of 2014), impacting 40 million Americans, as well as by a growing number of middle-class jobs being downsized or outsourced. The problem is, however, without a college education the vast majority of youth would be unable to compete for decent jobs. The "whiz-kid" entrepreneur or innovator who drops out of school and "hits it big," making millions or more, is statistically pretty close to one out of one million. Assuming approximately 25 million students attend college in 2015, the odds are that 25 college dropouts annually can hit the high-tech jackpot without finishing college: not a good bet, if you want to be rewarded for job-related performance.

Up to the 1990s information and technology (IT) replaced many medium-skilled jobs such as bookkeeper, bank teller, receptionist, secretary and back-office worker. A computer could defeat a skilled chess player or whiz-kid winner on *Jeopardy!*, but those with advanced professional and cognitive skills and low-skilled workers with less brainpower and more muscle were not threatened. Workers at the two ends of the continuum were safe. Well, it's a new century. IT and the Internet have changed data collection and analysis, and are taking away jobs at both ends of the job market.

At the top end are doctors, lawyers and professors. They engage in work that requires research and analysis, diagnosing and problem solving, interpretation and evaluation. Computer data have become so powerful and sophisticated that the machine can figure out quicker and more objectively what to do than the professionals. Computers can read and determine for relevance millions of documents and sources of information for purposes of advising and decision-making. All this implies the need for fewer doctors, lawyers and professors. Already robots are conducting surgery, computers are predicting when a lawyer should sue or settle a case, and online courses can increase student–professor ratios of 1,000 to 1.

At the opposite end of the skill level, involving less cognition and more physical work, robots are in increasing use for repetitive tasks. We no longer need humans to do the heavy lifting, counting, packing, inspecting and moving of items. In addition, robots work around the clock, on Saturday and Sunday, and they don't get hurt and sue their employers. They may break down and need a new bolt or chip once in a while, but that sure beats a million-dollar lawsuit for alleged discrimination or exclusion from meaningful opportunity. As the *Economist* declared on a recent cover page about robots, they are the "immigrants from the future." We may not see technological replacement and unemployment at the end of the corner, but it is certainly just around it. Protectionism will not solve the problem. Outsourcing, global low labor costs, and technological displacement are converging at the same time and affecting the nature of work.

To be sure, technology is making some skills and jobs more important than previously thought, but as trends seem to be shaping, there will be fewer winners and more losers than we imagined. In the past, technology created more jobs than it lost or made irrelevant and dated. The future turning point in technology may not be so kind to workers at all skill levels. It may be too soon to say who is safe and who is at risk, but we can assume new job requirements and new forms of talent, skills and performance will be sought. Moreover, it's too soon to predict whether college graduates will be in more or less demand. More specialized training will also be required for many jobs—contributing to an increased number of displaced workers and inability of older workers to find viable employment—giving rise to income inequality. In recent years U.S. women seemed to have weathered the workplace better than men, creating new categories of "haves" and "have nots," not thought possible 10 or 20 years ago. Nevertheless, as job opportunities for certain workers diminish, wages will decline. Overall there will be lack of good jobs that pay enough to make ends meet and offer opportunities for advancement.

In a nutshell, we are at the cusp—a transformative moment in society, especially as it relates to the economy and future jobs. What's happening on a global basis, according to Patrick Soon-Shiong, the billionaire inventor and former surgeon at UCLA, is "mobile technology, supercomputing, machine vision, artificial intelligence, cloud storage, mega-high speed data transmission, [and robots] are emerging from the Dark Ages" and creating a paradigm-shift. We are pushing the frontiers of chip technology as well, by shrinking circuits into tiny nanometers, a few atoms wide, and employing quantum physics, carbon nanotubes and brain-inspired (neuromorphic) chips. As we create new technologies, Silicon Valley should benefit from the talent and expert knowledge of scientists, engineers and computer programmers. Others, who are less mathematical and abstract, will find their gifts or abilities less favored and rewarded with fewer range of opportunities available to them in this new society.

Writing an opinion piece for the *New York Times*, Steven Rattner, investment advisor and Obama advisor, tries to distinguish between technology and globalization. He feels technology does not necessarily hurt employment, rather creates more jobs than it displaces and new opportunities for skilled workers whom multinational companies can hire. Moreover, there are many nonautomated, nontech jobs that can be created in the future, human to human: teaching, nursing, rehabilitating services for the elderly, caring for the young, food workers, etc. The problem is, many of these jobs are not high-end, high-income jobs, and thus may increase inequality of income and wealth.

What it may all boil down to in the future is simply whether you are computer proficient or not. Tyler Cowen, author of *Average is Over*, argues that the key skill in the future is working with computers, even if you don't directly work in IT. In an age of mechanized intelligence, your job and wage will depend on how well you work with computers. "Average" is over. Either you complement the computer in a creative way or you lose your ability to compete. You need to understand the strengths and limitations of your software and have the skill to adjust or overrule the system. It's like with your GPS, when driving in a familiar neighborhood, or like if you're a skilled doctor diagnosing a patient where an MRI or CAT scan reveals nothing, but you reach another conclusion based on observation, experience and intuition.

Computers (and robots) are able to calculate a limitless number of options and act smarter than humans. But it's an absolute myth that you can insert mounds of data into the computer or send an algorithm over raw data and have insights, decisions or useful information pop up on the screen. Social scientists and tech workers spend an inordinate amount of time collecting and analyzing data before decisions or conclusions are derived from digital data. The person who can provide direction and overall guidance, and also filter out irrelevant or meaningless data, will be prized by the organization and command good pay. The rest of the workforce who work with or rely on computers and cannot function at this skill level will be fungible and disposable.

Back to Cowen; he concludes (it's merely an educated guess) that about 15 percent of workers will thrive in this new economy, providing technical services or people-to-people skills in management and high-end professions. The remaining 85 percent will have less marketable skills and most of them will struggle economically. Beyond Cowen, in this new world, it can be assumed that superior performance on professional jobs will be limited to those capable of working with tech information and digital information—especially for those who can understand and utilize big data, with the cloud becoming the center of all information and the ability to access it from various devices.

Machines are getting smarter than humans at analyzing information, but in a world that is rapidly changing and highly volatile, human judgment and understanding the big picture is going to be at a premium—and rewarded accordingly in business and finance. The amount of information in front of us is becoming infinite and those people who possess the ability to make sense of it and use it on the job will be rewarded and those that cannot will be penalized. Ellen Richey of Visa sums it up: Big data promises "new connections between dispersed bits of information… identifying and [creating] the next generation of intelligence."

Since fewer people with "average" skills will be needed, and most people are average or near average statistically (based on the bell-shaped curve), increasingly people will dread being laid off, which in turn may affect performance and productivity. Employees will not trust management, rumors and concerns will surface. Fewer people will be loyal to companies; and, as workers become insecure about their jobs, performance and productivity will most likely suffer. More workers will become temporary workers and independent contractors (with no benefits), not a view people want to hear or read.

The big, big question is these robots! Now the idea of robots brings a particular image to mind, depending on your experience and education. Some of us think of Watson, developed by IBM, which processes information more like a human than a computer but more efficiently than a human. For others, it's the movie *Terminator* which helped launch Arnold Schwarzenegger's career, about a cyborg assassin sent back from the year 2029 to 1984. In 2015, the fifth sequel of *Terminator* was released. For those with capital, it's a different story: Robots are simply an investment, with little consideration for what might happen to labor or the reward system for the ordinary worker.

The brains in Silicon Valley predict all types of robots with the possibility that they will be programed to outperform humans in short time. IBM's Watson has read over 200 million pages of medical content and is currently used by an increasing number of doctors and nurses to make major medical decisions. Medicine is being transformed into information sciences and data analysis of patient characteristics—all of which can be collected and analyzed and yield personalized treatments and cures. The mysteries of the human gene may be computationally, statistically and mathematically analyzed. The time is fast approaching when robots will overtake human intelligence and may even understand and display emotions. Theoretically, computers and robots will be able to read every book and article on the Internet. Ray Kurzweil, director of engineering at Google, claims the company is trying to teach robots the meaning to what these documents say. We are at the point, or very close to the point, where computers and robots can reason, think and predict better than we can.

We are also at a point in time when caring for a growing aging population is becoming a world-wide crisis. Many elder people prefer to live independently in their own homes, and not rely on children or nursing homes. Cofounder and CEO of iRobot, Colin Angle, who came to the U.S. in 1977, believes that robots will soon be available on a mass level for people to train and help with chores and tasks. Robots will be able to communicate to and understand people.

In the meantime, IBM has devoted the largest amounts of research personnel in its history to computing and robotic operations with the Watson group. Michael Rhodin, the head of the group, claims that the Watson system will eventually "see, touch, and feel." There are no limits. Computers and robots will get smarter and be able to reason better than humans. CEO Ginni Rometty says Watson "will rejuvenate careers and reinvent industries. It's the [newest] era of technology."

The point is, humans are limited by slow biological evolution (over centuries) and education (K to college, which takes 18 or more years to witness the benefit). Humans can easily be superseded by the development of artificial intelligence. Computers (and robots) can learn and improve much quicker than we realize, to the point that people can be left behind. According to Moore's law (Gordon Moore is cofounder of Intel), computers (and robots) can double their speed and memory every 18 to 24 months. The potential is that machines become smarter than humans, a vision originally set forth by Stanley Kubrick's *2001: A Space Odyssey*. We can even argue they are already taking over the operations and data flow of large corporations, banks and insurance companies, complex medical decisions and the hiring and trading of athletes for teams around the world.

Those who can adapt and function in this "brave new world," sort of a Darwinist perspective, will likely retain their jobs and prosper, but others will be replaced. Not many of us will have secure knowledge-based jobs, since computers and robots will become more efficient than humans—and potentially throw us out of work. The only people who will not be dispensable will be extremely talented people and the CEOs of tech companies. In a future match-up with automated machines, humans may very well join the buggy whip, portable radio and rotary phone—on the dust heap of innovation that today's iPad generation cannot appreciate. The end is coming in the near future: Machines communicate with each other, rise up and force humans to vacate Earth; in fact, the more human-like robots with emotions and feelings help us humans build the rockets so we can emigrate to Mars.

Obviously, the author is being whimsical with "the rise of the robots." But he is serious about a new form of excellence: challenging expertise of the computer or robot—and being right. This kind of decision-making could only be made by a few expert people in a given field: based either on intuitive insight or a mental leap, an educated guess involving life experiences or deep knowledge in a particular field or careful observation and/or understanding the big picture and knowing how all the smaller pieces fit. Such a person should be rewarded accordingly, because it is likely that this person is either refining or adding new knowledge to the field, which the robot has not processed up to that point in time.

The Role of Innovation

Innovation is not invention, the latter of which suggests an improved, new and more efficient product and a major shift in our thinking and standard of living. Innovation is based on a spark or insight often derived in an office or research lab (or in the case of Steve Jobs in a garage), and represents a significant modification or improvement of an existing service or product which (1) creates value, (2) is brought to the market, and (3) boosts productivity. The overall effect is the creation of new jobs and even new industries. Innovation represents 20 percent of the economic output of the world's industrialized countries, supplying efficient products or services and economic growth. Innovation is part of the "knowledge" society and a nation's human capital; it is bottomless and limitless compared to economic capital, which has a bottom line and limitations.

Keep in mind when the talk is about innovation in the U.S., the initial money for funding usually comes from the federal government, especially the military establishment. Conservatives can talk all they want about the need for small government, but it's the government (and the military in particular) that has played the key role in funding the early stages of jet engines, radio, television, radar, explosives and missiles, semi-conductors, computer chips and even the Internet. The government has often initiated the research funding, and large universities and corporations have run with the idea and improved the product.

To be sure, innovation and entrepreneurship are now mainstream, embraced by all political stripes and popular business heroes like Elon Musk, Richard Branson and Jack Welch. It wasn't always like that. Writers for the last 60 years have described the shift in culture in terms of the "organization man," "future shock," "the greening of America," etc. *The Organization Man*, described in William Whyte's best-selling book of corporate America, was a cousin or off-shoot to David Riesman's book about the rise of an "other directed" society—people sensitive to other people and people "keeping up with the Joneses." Published three years after *The Lonely Crowd*, both books described the "successful" corporate model, of people keeping their nose clean, following orders and conforming to company rules and group norms.

Successful business people were not risk takers, innovators or explorers. Knowledge workers sought a "good" job at IBM, AT&T or GE, and they relied on a combination of hard work, merit and social skills. They dressed the part, with gray or blue suits and matching ties, and followed the expectations and preferences of their bosses; they had no interest in being too smart, "thinking out of the box" or creating a new idea or image. Innovative personnel were considered disruptive and not part of the team. Economists focused on traditional factors related to production—capital, labor and equipment—and supply–demand curves. New ideas and copyrighted materials were not considered part of a company's financial statement or list of assets.

I recall my next-door neighbor who worked at Searle, a chemical company located in the Chicago area. My neighbor accidentally discovered a byproduct from an experiment that spilled over on his flask and had a sweet taste like sugar. The chemical had a potency 100 times the strength of sucrose. He had to beg his supervisor for release time to develop the product, which eventually became known as NutraSweet. The company went on to make hundreds of millions in profit from the discovery. His reward: a $3,000 raise and a new Ford automobile. One must understand it was the 1960s, in an age of corporate conformity and when thinking out of the box was not encouraged nor rewarded.[1]

It took several decades for an informal atmosphere, combined with rewarding the creative talents of workers in Google, Facebook and Wipro, and now Twitter,

Yelp and Triple D, to become an acceptable choice for other companies around the world. The current buzz involving innovation is based on a loose federation or network of corporate labs, government-sponsored labs and universities. Talented STEM workers become the core and implementer of new ideas from outside and inside corporate gates. They rely on the world-wide web for collaboration and communication, and they can integrate others' work around the world.

The spirit of innovation and entrepreneurship, what the economist Joseph Schumpeter once called "creative destruction," has been embraced by U.S. business colleges, corporations and government. Schumpeter was one of the first theorists to recognize that the most important competitive factor was not lower land prices or labor costs but new ideas—what I refer to as human capital in this book and what corporations and business pundits call part of innovation (and entrepreneurship). The story of the U.S. conversion from conformity to creativity in the workplace is evidenced by the number of endowed chairs of entrepreneurship in the U.S. business schools, from 237 in 1999 to approximately 600 in 2015.

Creativity may be considered the key to invention and discovery, but it's not easy to define or quantify. Thomas Edison, Albert Einstein, Andy Warhol and Bob Dylan were extremely creative by all standards but considered problem students by their respective teachers and not always accepted by their colleagues or peers. It might be said, in fact, most teachers discourage creativity in the classroom because the behavior and responses generated by creative students are often novel or unusual—the kind of thinking that slows down the classroom lesson and throws the teacher off stride.

In a ground-breaking, pocket-sized book, *The Process of Education*, Jerome Bruner, the Harvard psychologist, referred to creativity as possessing the ability to make mental leaps and go beyond what is known. Basically what he was referring to was the ability to understand the concepts, principles and theories of a discipline, and then to integrate new information so as to form something new. Bruner published his book during the post-Sputnik era; his emphasis on math and science coincided with our intent to win the space race and defeat the Soviets. Nonetheless, his ideas carried over to other disciplines or fields of inquiry. More recently, Soon-Shiong, the billionaire inventor, has envisioned creativity as arranging and rearranging the pieces. "His ability to envision exceeds sometimes the capacity of language and usual representation to express." He maintains that not everyone can see the big picture, or what he calls "the systems-integrative approach." Almost everybody looks at the world in a linear way, "but actually we live in a quantum world."

An original work, a mental leap forward, an *aha* moment or insight is rarely the result of linear or convergent thinking. The difference between a good idea and a breakthrough idea (or product) is rarely the result of precise calculation, rather based on intuitive thinking and some sort of imagination, messiness or serendipity. It's the kind of thinking that teachers, supervisors and middle managers have little time for, rarely encourage or support and that cannot be easily measured or taught in school or developed at corporate (or university) staff meetings.

In the tech world we have just entered, where innovation and inventions are prized, creative thought is recognized and rewarded—and such people are increasingly being given several chances to fail. When companies invest in new ideas, they should expect a certain amount of failure. Kim Jordan, cofounder and CEO of New Belgium Brewing, puts it this way: "If you expect things to always succeed you're probably not far enough out on the learning [or discovery] edge." The idea, if I may add, is not to encourage mistakes, but to be tolerant of them and to ensure from a company's ethos that workers are not afraid of making mistakes. In an increasingly innovative world, there are few templates. As Yorgen Edholm, CEO of Accellion (a software company) says, "You can't think that with the right time and resources, you'll have a 95 percent chance of success. You can't have people thinking 'If I can't guarantee success, it's going to hurt me.'"

Creativity comes in different forms and different stories. Elon Musk and Steve Jobs, two iconoclast inventors of the twenty-first century, had a number of common traits, according to staff reporter Anne VanderMey of *Fortune* magazine. They understood the big picture, thought in terms of total system design, had extraordinary vision, deep conviction (despite people saying "no") and an amazing appreciation of technological potential and capacity to understand the needs of their future customers. Musk and Jobs were not the first people to have their respective insights. Their genius was to take the core idea, and improve it to its logical end, and integrate it into the broader method of how their products could be manufactured and marketed.

Although creativity and genius—that is, the likes of Musk and Jobs—is highly sought after, you need more than highly creative and super-smart people to run a successful organization. You need to recruit good minds, people with above-average intelligence, and then create an atmosphere that empowers and rewards multiple contributions and multiple forms of excellence. Companies, and society in general, need to push economic and innovative boundaries as well as aesthetic and social boundaries. Even though educators are reluctant to put labels on children, they have devised a sorting-out process that identifies and pushes students to the top while at the same time identifying, and in some cases discriminating against, less able students. The school does a good job of pushing high-ability youngsters, but it tends to downplay the pain it causes below-average children and youth. The companies and institutions of society use the school's screening process as a reliable barometer for sorting out promising employees. The schools, however, often fail to identify unusual talent and students who do not fit well or conform to classroom and school rules. In this respect, it is highly doubtful if the insights, vision and talent of people like Musk and Jobs can be taught in classrooms or schools. Here we are talking about a genetic component, a way of thinking combined with an acquired personality trait.

Justin Leverenz, who manages $42 billion for OppenheimerFunds, claims he is a "misfit" in his field. He encourages "unconventional wisdom." To have that, one must feel comfortable being uncomfortable and work outside the norm. He claims that his team of investors spends 70 percent of their time developing deep knowledge in a particular industry, then expanding into adjacent areas. As much as 30 percent is devoted to "peripheral vision" and "crazy things." It parallels Google thinking: Do things that are unrelated because eventually you see connections you otherwise would have missed.

Brad Smith, the CEO of Intuit (a financial software company), is influenced by Peter Drucker's dictum: "The bottleneck is always at the top of the bottle." Innovation rarely comes from the top, but some leaders instill a climate or ethos that encourages innovation throughout the organization. New ideas and products come by encouraging workers to think different ways and solve important problems. He has created 10 percent unstructured time for his 8,000 employees to work on new ideas so they can be more productive than their competitors.

For traditional knowledge workers, innovation is considered part of the R&D spending and product development. In today's fast-changing society, innovation is considered the early stage of entrepreneurship and what may be called "innovation economics." And, it does not take a rocket scientist to figure out that more people around the globe are engaged in new ventures: from the slums of South Africa and Indonesia to big companies like GE and 3M. Then there is the difference between old tech companies and new companies: the Microsofts, Intels and Ciscos vs. 3D Systems, Cypress Semiconductor Corp and Workday, Inc. Given today's global competitive spirit and quick access to information, many corporations now feel they must innovate faster just to stand still. In fact, every large (and every old) corporation today—the Walmarts, McDonald's and GMs of America—must adopt technological and innovative policies to compete on a national and international level. If they fail to do so, they are forced to downsize or reorganize, or worse, fall to the wayside and eventually disappear.

Regina Dugan, director of Google's Advanced Technology and Projects (ATAP) group, is well versed in identifying and developing innovative projects that involve quantum leaps in science and engineering. Her MO is to assemble a core team of experts at Google who collaborate with a wider net of experts from multiple disciplines, industries and academia. This allows her to contact researchers and experts at various places around the world (so far in 22 countries). "Today things are moving so fast that a diversity of skills and points of view matter." John Sealey, who once headed the Xerox research center at Palo Alto, agrees. "Often you need a multitude of disciplines brought together quickly." Projects are limited to a two-year deadline so they don't become open-ended processes. If tangible results are not achieved quickly, the team makes room for another project. Time is essential. "You do something epic and then you go to the next project," asserts Dugan.

And with all due respect to the likes of Google and other tech giants like Apple and Facebook, and given all their profits and power today, there is always the chance they may not last. Growth in these companies has leveled off to slower rates than their peak period and their financial statements have not always met analysts' expectations. Old tech giants like Compaq Computers, Packard Bell and Wang sank slowly and steadily, unable to keep up with technological change. The same problem recently happened to Dell computers and now Hewlett-Packard is splitting in two. John Sealey of Xerox would have to admit that Xerox is not the same cutting-edge company it was 25 or 30 years ago; it is barely hanging on and is trying to stay relevant.

Even Microsoft and IBM, two tech giants, are struggling today to stay relevant. Google invests heavily in R&D, like Microsoft and IBM, and has seen little return on its investment. No matter what perceived or real strength a company has, change is inevitable and incremental. There are no guarantees. Over time, change has unexpected results; it is not always precise or predictable.

The U.S. still leads the world in innovation, having spent approximately 10 percent of the world's $600 billion R&D in 2012, followed by the European Union which spent about 6 percent. Part of the reason for the U.S. lead has to do with its multiple sources of financial markets and venture-capital companies which raise money, as well as the American spirit of risk-taking, the spirit of freedom and spirit of individual achievement. Creative and innovative people need this open type of environment to stimulate, motivate and sustain their fresh thinking and human endeavor. So far America is ahead of the curve in terms of creating an atmosphere conducive to risk, thinking out of the box and failing more than once. What we have going is a culture that celebrates individual achievement and operates within a political and social atmosphere of freedom. The top 50 U.S. universities are first-rate research institutes and the nation as a whole has a long history of venture spirit, capital and entrepreneurship that goes back to the Manifest Destiny and the "winning of the west."

European universities tend to be suspicious of private industry, relying more on government grants than private sector money. However, European venture-capital companies have adopted the American model and investment in new companies grew 23 percent between 2003 and 2006, and 15 percent between 2007 and 2010, compared to less than 1 percent per year in the U.S.—meaning we have reached a "flat" period of innovation. Countries such as Denmark, Finland, Germany, Sweden and England, often criticized by American capitalists as too socialistic, have had more venture-capital industries in relation to the size of their economies than America. We need to swallow our pride and recognize their new innovative spirit and reward system for talent and vision.

For all its economic problems, however, the U.S. still leads the world in new start-up businesses and entrepreneurship—producing more than one million new small businesses every year—some of them rapidly growing into the world's largest corporations, such as Microsoft, Amazon and Google. As many as 22 percent of the nation's *Fortune* 1,000 or biggest companies were created since 1980, illustrating the nation's continuous gospel of innovation and prowess of human capital. Even more impressive, of the *Fortune* 500 companies, 82 were not even on the list 20 years ago. These facts suggest that American entrepreneurship is still "with it" and "venturesome," but it is beginning to flatten compared with other industrialized nations. The reason is not necessarily that the flow of money or spirit of innovation have declined, rather because U.S. companies are moving offices to other parts of the world and the innovative model has become global.

Innovative businesses are also beginning to tap into emerging markets. China and India, which spent less than 1 percent of the world's R&D in 2006, are now beginning to become innovative out of necessity. Globalization and the spread of the Internet and technology have led to the spread of information and creation of new business models in Asia. Whereas originally noted as "copycats" of Western intellectual property rights (which cost Microsoft alone an estimated $100 to $250 million per year from 2008 to 2012), emerging nations are now moving into the innovative process in (1) drug and pharmaceutical industries, (2) motorcycle and auto industries and (3) electronic and communication industries—forming multinational companies and reaching markets in emerging countries in Latin America, Asia and the Middle East.

In the meantime, some of us in the U.S. are rejecting globalization and turning inward—questioning the idea of free international trade, talking about imposing import tariffs, viewing China's economic growth as a threat to our well-being, building fire walls to protect our banking, utility and military systems from computer hackers, and describing the origins of the 2007 recession in global terms or as a conspiracy between international corporations and international banks. A 2012 *Fortune* magazine article described the process as "globalization going backward."

Although we may not fully understand all the connecting components of globalization, or how to manage the massive amounts of data, globalization is here to stay. Every time you Google, Tweet or text, every time you use Facebook, Amazon or eBay, every time you use your credit card, cell phone, iPad or GPS—what you are doing is connecting and networking on a global system built by U.S. innovation and entrepreneurship. Regardless of our location—some rural town in Louisiana, a mountain village in Montana, or on Fifth Avenue in New York City—it's a system that permits us to connect from anywhere on the map to the rest of the world.

China and India—and the Future

It needs to be pointed out that in both China and India the majority of the populace, especially in the rural hinterland, are trapped by the solitude of poverty and almost complete lack of power; the people focus on survival; they wake up, eat, drink, work and sleep—every day, every year. That said, while most of

China's and India's innovators are not well known in the West, they are beginning to challenge American human capital and its innovative and entrepreneurial prowess. For example, India's Tata Motors is producing a "people's car" for $3,000, partially out of necessity, and China is boasting that it has manufactured 500,000 electric cars—also out of necessity. It is also already producing clean-coal plants to cut down pollution in its cities. In the meantime, the U.S. is still debating whether it should drill for oil off shore or tax carbon emissions. More troubling, there are over 500 new computer-chip companies in China, ready to challenge Motorola, Cisco and AT&T.

A new world order is taking place in China. *Fortune* reports that in 2004 40 percent of the world's biggest corporations were headquarted in North America. By 2015, Asia had become the home to more *Fortune* 500 global companies than North America, with China leading with 95 names on the new list (52 alone in Beijing). In fact, three of the world's largest companies are housed in the People's Republic and only two of the top 10 (Walmart and Exxon) are in the U.S.

Keep in mind China and India are annually growing 5 to 10 percent while we are growing by 1.5 to 3 percent, and are incrementally going to have a more competitive advantage than the U.S. because they stimulate their collective talent towards new ideas, new industries and new markets. Moreover, they have several technical universities that almost rival MIT and Stanford. The next big ideas are bound to come from young talent in Asia, from people with hard-to-pronounce names. As you read these pages, U.S. investors are recruiting Chinese and Indian students and financing their ideas. There is tons of money chasing these start-up ideas, and it's bound to happen that young STEM workers from China and India are going to start big companies like Google, Facebook and LinkedIn. Our best days may not be over. But we have to get used to the notion that many innovative ideas in the twenty-first century will be coming from Asian-rim nations.

If I had to bet on China or India, I would put my money on India. It's mathematically inevitable that India will grow faster than China, because it's easier for a small economy to grow faster than a large economy. China's economy was more than three times as big as India's in 2014, after adjusting for purchasing power, market capital and inflation rate. Comparing China and India, the human capital of India is young compared to China's population, which is aging due to restrictions on family size and children. In 2010, India's 14-year-old or younger population was 31 percent of its total, compared to China's 14-year-old or younger population, which represented 20 percent. This means India's workforce and consumer base will expand for many years, while China's labor force and economy will shrink or slow down. The outcome is that India, with its 1.3 billion people and capitalistic spirit, represents greater competition for America's future human capital and potential for innovation than does China.

The Chinese thought process is rooted in the spirit of Confucius—poor innovators but skilled imitators, hard work and perspiration, and a respect for tradition. Its new economy is based on manufacturing, a twentieth-century model, not scientific or technical knowledge (India's prototype), which is a twenty-first-century model. Moreover, the Chinese manufacturing model is now running into stiff competition from several Southeast Asian countries, namely Bangladesh, Cambodia, Laos, Vietnam, Thailand and Myanmar, where cheaper labor has increased their exports nearly 20 percent annually between 2010 and 2014 while China's exports have dropped from 31 percent to 8 percent during the same period.

These six countries as a group are becoming the new China. Though their collective economies are smaller than China's, they are growing more rapidly than China. The reason is related to labor costs. According to *Barron's*, the typical Chinese factory worker earns $700/month while their counterpart in Myanmar gets $110, in Cambodia $130 and $140 in Laos.

An important comparative difference in labor costs is related to child-labor practices and laws that are not enforced in these countries, including China and India. This makes a difference in labor costs, especially in large populated countries. The brightest 10 to 20 percent may get advanced education while many in the same age cohort go to work as children. This practice dooms the majority populace to human squalor and suffering and great difference in wealth and inequality within the nations' class structure.

India is the largest democracy in the world, with more people than the U.S., the European Union, Russia, Brazil and Japan combined. On the other hand, the Chinese political system is run by an oligarchy, discourages political reform and often causes public discontent and disruptions. The country is plagued by pollution problems, which have an underlying, invisible cost, and income disparity, which can lead to increased civil strife. As an indication of a pending crisis, many middle-class professionals are looking to get their money and/or themselves to the U.S., England, Canada and Singapore.

The Indian education system is rooted in the Anglo-American perspective, which puts a premium on educating gentlemen in literature and the classics, but there is also acceptance and respect for creativity, inquiry and independent thought. The Chinese schools prize memorization and rote learning, an ideal that can be traced to a series of 40 dynasties spanning more than 4,000 years, beginning with the Hsia dynasty in 2200 BC and ending with the Manchus in 1912, in which bright students studied diligently to pass a series of civil service exams in order to become scholar-officials and bureaucrats who governed China for the emperors.

The Chinese heritage has revealed persistent efforts to maintain unbroken traditions and cultural continuity, relying on respect for elders and old customs, and further promoted by the teachings of Mao, up to Tiananmen Square more than 25 years ago, whereby students were required to memorize and parrot the wisdom and thoughts of their leader. This kind of rote learning goes back to Confucianism—and studying and testing for government jobs. This type of thinking still characterizes the Chinese academic model in which conformity is crucial and questions by students are frowned upon in school because of fear of appearing stupid in front of classmates.

The learning–teaching process at present in China is not conducive for scientific, high-tech and innovative culture. The knowledge society we live in does not reward facts or trivia data that can be Googled. What, when and who questions and answers fosters memorization and characterizes Chinese education; it is mistakenly assumed that people who know the answer are intelligent. Why, how and what-if questions and answers lead to abstract thinking and discovery; such questions characterize higher education in tier 1 colleges in the U.S. and other Anglo countries, as well as to some extent in India, whose schooling system is based on the British model. Chinese education authorities, with the approval of the central government, are just beginning to challenge traditional educational methods and study the U.S. and British education models, but they still have a long way to go in order to overcome 4,000 years of isolated history before they can laud the innovative mind.

Now it's important to note there is a flipside or soft belly to India's future growth, and that flies in the face of its prospective superpower image. The country is beset by an entrenched smug elite, tied to a caste system and perpetuated by centuries of racism and injustices. Notwithstanding the enormous economic gains made by India, far beyond even what optimists would have predicted a few decades ago, the country is flawed by the dust heap of custom and tradition. Although India's constitution prohibits discrimination based on caste, the professors, doctors and industrialists tend to be from the Brahmin caste; marriages among the upper class are still prearranged within the caste. Its history (and current policies) is plagued by the brutal methods of the police, unethical practices of business people, payoffs and favors expected by an army of government bureaucrats and regulators, and a slow-moving, class-biased judiciary system—all which currently vie to slow down India's economic miracle. Like China, it lacks transportation links, has a poor infrastructure and is plagued by corruption and overleveraged loans related to business and real estate investment.

Even worse, a rape culture exists in India which "winks" at the resulting hardships and hazards felt by women, compounded by a gender bias which puts women at a disadvantage and limits their opportunities to compete and develop their talents. Certain castes tend to occupy particular professions and unskilled jobs; this historic built-in bias still restricts talented youth from lower castes. In fact, one can raise a similar concern about China. Will the poor and rural child benefit from an expanding economy? Nearly half of the population of China and India are buried in subsistence farming and unskilled jobs, still hoping for a brighter future for their children. Hence, the limitation on human talent detrimentally affects the entire society.

It's a problem that not only India and China must face and deal with, but also more than half the world must confront in order to fully enhance its own economic growth and development. We cannot all reach the top of the pyramid.

The point is whether everyone in society, especially in the underdeveloped and emerging world, gets to perform on the same playing field and gets a fair chance to succeed. There might also be reasonable limits to discourage excessive competition (or protect slow participants), but the limits should not be based on gender, class or caste (ethnicity, race, religion or tribal affiliation).

Finally, wizened old men realize the value for caution. The Western mind doesn't fully understand the Eastern mind, and no matter how naïve or immature we think the Asian perspective or philosophy, they know us better than we know them. Given a rapidly changing society that we live in, the future isn't what it used to be or expected to be. Therefore, everything the author says about the Chinese and Indian mind and the spirit of innovation or discovery is nothing more than speculation that can be proven wrong by the winds of change. Even the corruption and mismanagement that characterize the history of both countries can change with new leadership or by a series of unspoken and unforeseen coalition of events.

The Rise of Asia

Curtis Carlson, the coauthor of *Innovation*, captures the trend and puts it in blunt terms. "India and China are a tsunami about to overwhelm us." Millions of jobs are at stake and many are expected to be eliminated in the U.S. As Asia moves to a global center for innovation and new knowledge, most people in the U.S. are struggling to understand what is happening to the nation's economic luster and their own jobs. Are we going the way of the dinosaur—big, old and clumsy? As a nation are we on the downside of Darwin's theory of adaptability? At the beginning of the twenty-first century, the U.S. comprised 4 percent of the world's population and consumed 25 percent of the world's resources. These days are coming to an end. We need to come to the realization that the emerging nations of the world will increasingly share economic power with the U.S. The handwriting is already on the wall. The ordinary person in America will have to adjust to a lower economic position on the totem pole of mobility, opportunity and status. That may not be good for Americans but it's better for the rest of the world. For the time being, we may still be king of the global hill, but we're going to have to get used to more competition and the fact that the world is "flat" and interconnected.

The "copycat" stereotype of Asia is quickly vanishing. The number of engineers annually being produced by India (350,000) and China (600,000) outnumber the U.S. (70,000) by 5 to 8.5 times. These two countries, along with many other Asian countries, consistently outscore American students on international tests in science and mathematics. In science, for example, 27 nations of 65 scored higher than U.S. 15-year-old students on the Programme for International Student Assessment (PISA) in 2012. In math, the results were more dramatic: 35 nations out of 65 scored higher than U.S. 15-year-olds. The seven highest-ranking nations were all in Asia. This test-score difference is bound to accelerate the rate of innovation (and growth of middle-class jobs) in these two countries, as well as most Southeast Asian countries, and challenge Silicon Valley. Figuring a four- to five-year lag between the birth of an idea—from a computer model or experiment to research and development and then to production—in the next 10 to 20 years the U.S. is going to wake up and find out that the low-paid, low-quality Asian worker has been relegated to the scrapheap of history and replaced by a freewheeling, innovative workforce. The likes of Apple, Amazon, Cisco, Hewlett-Packard, Intel, etc. are going to experience major competition from China and India (and even Taiwan, South Korea, Japan, Singapore, etc.).

Americans will find the new Asian innovative models of growth and productivity possibly more threatening than the current demise of the U.S. manufacturing model—and the shredding of millions more jobs to overseas competitors, with a culture and language we don't understand and never bothered to understand. Just consider these numbers: In 2008, as many as 50,000 Chinese students studying in America returned to their homeland. By 2011, the number had soared to 180,000. To be sure, we need our high-achieving immigrant students. They are our job creators, economic engine and innovative talent. They represent the key to our own future growth and development.

Vivek Wadhwa, author of *The Immigrant Exodus*, warns that new foreign-born scientists and engineers are leaving the U.S. on an alarming scale, largely due to government bureaucracy and diminishing job opportunities, and, if I may add, due also to growing nationalism, economic opportunities and intense recruitment practices among emerging nations. In 2013, some 4.3 million people were waiting for green cards, but the number of visas available for that year totaled 375,000. The end result, a huge exodus to Canada, Australia, China and Singapore which sought to attract these global entrepreneurs and STEM workers. Be prepared for a wave of new ideas and inventions from people and countries we used to think were second rate to and unable to compete with Western science and culture.

The only way to reverse this growing trend is to stop the erosion of U.S. innovation by (1) improving math and science education, (2) offering scholarships or free college education to math and science teachers, engineers and scientists, (3) welcoming more talented immigrants and promoting their citizenship, (4) linking start-up companies with venture capitalists, (5) offering tax incentives to U.S. companies that invest in innovative products and services, and (6) discouraging or preventing the likes of Cisco, Intel and Microsoft from building new research facilities and offices in Asia or Europe, for tax advantages. Dean Kamen, a college dropout, author and inventor who holds some 450 U.S. and foreign patents for innovation devices, puts it this way: "We can print more money, but we cannot print more knowledge." That takes a generation to produce, some 12 to 16 years of schooling. More bailouts might help the economy in the short run, but only more people like Bill Gates (Microsoft), Larry Page (Google) and Jeff Bezos (Amazon) can move us into prosperity over the long run.

In the U.S., the pressing need is to focus on talented students and math and science education and other innovative capacities (recommendations 1 to 6) in order to secure America's future prosperity and security. Here we are not talking about a new paradigm or transformative shift in society. What we need to do is to invest in incremental changes, more efficient technology and new computerized, robotic and biochemical industries—steady progress and development of ideas and human capital. In the final analysis, a nation is only as good as its next innovation. Transformative changes come in cycles and over several generations cannot be easily predicted or counted on, unless you believe in a constant flow of "Sputniks." The last major paradigm shift had something to do with computers and the Internet. Unless someone has a crystal ball or a direct link to the Oracle, no one really has a clear idea when the next major shift or invention will take place.

As for developing countries, the situation for women is dim and there is need to broaden their basic rights, including access to education. However, the list of problems include basic security issues—sex trafficking, child marriage, domestic abuse, gang rape as a military tactic, malnourishment, lack of medical care and maternal mortality. The key to understanding history is to stop ignoring the custom of devaluing women and to promote the education of women. If the third world is to prosper, the status of women must be improved, for they represent 50 percent of a nation's human resources. Education can chip away at cultural practices in many parts of the world, and the outcomes are tied to economic growth in a knowledge-based and digital society. But schools alone cannot do the job. Political leaders in traditional societies must have the will and courage to implement reform. It is not the role of the U.S. or Western world to play "global cop" and transform or impose its norms and values on other nations. Every country needs to work out its own notion of excellence and equality, along with a reward system for achievement and performance.

Growing Inequality in America

In a capitalist society, the laws of economic individualism, competition and achievement overshadow an economy based on safety nets and social programs; the free market trumps protection for workers. Although the natural law of competition is sometimes hard on the individual, the old-fashioned capitalist might say: "If the strongest and swiftest win the race, and the rest falter and barely make ends meet, we may be consoled by recalling the sage advice of Shakespeare: 'The fault, dear Brutus, is not in our stars, But in ourselves, that we are underlings.'"

The justification of U.S. inequality has been delineated since the birth of the nation. Going back to Alexander Hamilton, the first U.S. Treasurer; he felt the masses rise to the level that nature had intended and possess all the turbulent passions of an animal. The manufacturing and banking class were guardians of the public good, elevating society by providing people with opportunities to work in factories. The government had to support these economic elites and protect them from the influence of the labor class and "Jacobins" in the populous American towns.

More than two hundred years later Milton Friedman, another conservative pundit, argued that small government was the best government, since the big government jeopardizes individual liberties, especially property rights. Competition is the engine that drives the economy and inequality is the natural outcome when society allows individuals to compete and find their proper level and learn how to do that for which they are fitted by nature and nurture, as well as choice. The type of capitalism espoused by Hamilton and Friedman, where the sky is the limit, rewards efficiency at the expense of equity, excellence at the expense of equality, and creates a social and economic pyramid whereby capital overshadows and stunts labor. It parallels 2,000 years of history. Now the new warlords wear crimson suspenders and power-colored ties, while the remaining populace is expected to remain subordinated in their second-place status.

As capitalist doctrine has evolved, people are by nature unequal. Those who take risks, prove their ability and take responsibility, compete and excel, overcome obstacles and get ahead, are thus entitled to the rewards that may come from their efforts. Two classes of workers emerge within the capitalist system: Performers and *executives*, who entertain the public and/or *generate profits* or revenues for a business or corporation, and salaried employees such as professionals (teachers, engineers and accountants) and laborers (plumbers, hotel workers and janitors) who are considered a *cost factor* or expense item in determining annual budgets. The goal of an organization is to keep costs down and maximize profits. For those workers who increase costs, the idea is to trim their salaries by considering supply–demand trends and eliminating jobs. Those who can bolster revenues or increase the asset column are paid handsomely for their efforts; they are profit units as opposed to a cost unit.

According to *Forbes*, in 2012 entertainers such as Taylor Swift earned $57 million, Roger Waters of Pink Floyd made $88 million and hip-hop producer Dr. Dre made $110 million. Ball players such as Roger Federer (tennis), Tiger Woods (golf) and LeBron James (basketball) each earned more than $50 million, while Kobe Bryant signed a three-year contract for $83.5 million; endorsements amounted to another $42 million for James and another $34 million for Bryant. Tom Cruise and Sylvester Stallone each earned $15 to $25 million per movie. All of these people are brand names who perform for the public and realize profits for corporations.

In 2012 the average worker, a *cost factor*, earned approximately $44,300, while the average teacher earned $57,000 and the average civil engineer was compensated with $80,500. Now compare these salaries with CEOs from the 200 largest companies who for the same year averaged $11.7 million, and those from the top

50 companies who averaged $20 million. On the top of the list, according to *Forbes*, were Stephen Hemsley (United Health) at $102 million, Ed Mueller (Quest) at $66 million and Robert Iger (Disney) at $53 million. Ironically, the runaway salaries of top executives have little to do with performance, since many of the companies that paid the highest salaries often lost money that year. You also have to ask if someone is worth more than 1,000 times another human being, a worker earning $44,300 vs. a CEO (such as Hemsley, Mueller or Iger) earning more than $44 million.

The problem of the often overpaid, incompetent executive is especially upsetting when the rewards are subsidized by the U.S. taxpayer, including the single mother or typical laborer who works multiple jobs to make ends meet. It doesn't only occur when the feds bail out Wall Street. It occurs every day, every week, every year because capital is favored over labor in the U.S. and around the world; money derived from investments and capital gains is taxed at a lower rate than money derived from wages. In the U.S. the difference is apparently twice the tax for labor than capital. If executives, entertainers and athletes are making millions of dollars, it has to come from someone's pocket; this is reflected in inflated prices for rock concerts and baseball tickets and depressed salaries for the average worker in the organization which pays top executives top salaries. If we start adding up the ramifications of all these overpaid executives, there is more than a whisper of public frustration, not yet a shout, to put a lid on executive compensation and to improve the links between pay and performance.

What these kind of disparities create is a new group of "haves" and "have nots," based on a flawed capitalist model that rewards those who make money for an organization and penalizes those who cost money for an organization. There is little reason to promote or defend this system of rewards other than some illogical reasoning based on greed and "the law of the jungle" or some quaint notion that capitalists (now including brand name performers) are "job creators" and receive their fair proportion from corporate profits while wage earners should be thankful for their job and can enjoy a day at the beach on Sunday for free or a fishing vacation in some remote part of the country.

It's like the Roman Empire—with highly paid gladiators who entertain the audience—coupled with the "robber baron" era, with all sensible restraints vanished. The key question is whether Roger Waters is worth 1,600 times more than what a teacher earns or whether LeBron James is worth 625 times more than what an engineer earns, or whether the average large company CEO is worth 264 to 452 times (based on $11.7 or $20 million average salary) more than the average worker (based on $44,300 average salary). Your answer probably depends on whether you believe in the free market system or some form of government regulation. It also reflects your views on human capital and the value you place on talent vs. labor. It also considers whether you believe in a fair or just society, and whether you believe there should be a floor and ceiling in money earned and wealth accumulated over more than one generation.

Allow me to frame the economic issues in moral tones. Consider that the average salary for the top 25 hedge fund managers was $1 billion in 2009, sometimes only with single-digit returns. The total, $25 billion, was equal to what 500,000 of the nation's 2.8 million teachers earned the same year. Here is a pop quiz! Should 25 people who move money around with a mouse and produce nothing, and at worse played some role in the economic meltdown of 2007 (which caused tens of millions of Americans to lose their jobs and/or homes), earn the same amount as a half million teachers who perform an essential service for the nation? Is one person worth 50,000 times more than another person?

Or, consider the following. In 1939 Judy Garland earned $125 per week for her role in *The Wizard of Oz*. The movie took five months to produce, resulting in total compensation (for 22 weeks) of $2,750. That year the average salary was $1,730 (or $721 for five months). In 1964, Julie Andrews earned $125,000 for her role in *Mary Poppins*. A year later in *The Sound of Music*, she was paid $225,000. The average salary in 1964 was $6,000; in 1965 it was $6,450. By 2013, Sandra Bullock had earned $20 million for her role in *Gravity*, plus 15 percent of the movie's revenue, for a total of $70 million. That year the average salary was $45,000. Note the multiplying effect paid for talent compared to labor. Garland was paid less than twice the average U.S. salary. Julie Andrews was paid 21 times more than a person's salary in 1964 and 35 times more in 1965. By 2013, Sandra Bullock was paid 1,522 times more than the average worker. And that was for only one movie!

Now consider leading actors. Fred MacMurray was the highest-paid actor in 1943, with a salary of $420,000, equivalent to $5.8 million in 2014. By 1998, Tom Hanks was the top-paid actor, earning $40 million, equivalent to $57.8 million in 2014. In 2013, depending on the list you read, Tom Cruise and Robert Downey Jr. were the top-paid actors, each earning $75 million. As entertainers go, Beyoncé made $115 million. Hence, all these trends reveal the multiplying effect and growing demand for talent—at the expense of labor.

Then there is supermodel Gisele Bündchen who earned $47 million, or $128,000 per day, in 2013. Her husband, quarterback star Tom Brady, made a "measly" $33 million or $90,000 a day during the same year. Compare that salary to Otto Graham, often called the greatest quarterback in history. He led the Cleveland Browns to the league championship for 10 straight years (1946–1955). As quarterback for the Browns, the team's win–loss record was 114–20, plus four ties. Graham was the highest-paid football star in the 1950s. He earned $22,000 a year. Brady's $33 million is more than 1,500 times Graham's salary, indicating how the pay for talent has multiplied and how the market for certain kinds of talent is very much in demand and has nothing to do with the needs of society.

Another way to illustrate the rise of this new money class is to compare two household baseball names. In the mid-1950s, Mickey Mantle of the New York Yankees was in his prime, earning $100,000 a year. Compared to the average working man's salary (few women worked) of $3,300, his salary was 30 times greater. By 2013, Alex Rodriguez of the same Yankee organization was earning $32 million, not counting additional monies from endorsements, while the average working person's salary was $45,000—more than 711 times what the average American earned.

For those who are boxing fans you may recall Rocky Marciano, the undefeated heavyweight champ (with 49 wins, 43 KOs and no losses) in the 1950s. He had a lifetime earnings of $30 million, most of it siphoned off by his promoter and trainer. (He netted $5 million.) Although $5 million was considered a hefty amount for that period, Floyd Mayweather, the current lightweight champ, earned $85 million for two fights in 2012. In 2015, Mayweather pocketed over $200 million for two fights.

Take the world's most popular sport, which is soccer. In 1960, the highest-paid player was Pelé, who earned $40, 000. In 1980, it was Michel Platini with $300,000. Twenty years later, David Beckham earned $9 million. By 2014, the top-paid soccer players—(1) Cristiano Ronaldo, (2) Lionel Messi and (3) Radamel Falcao—earned between $32.4 and $52 million. (These figures do not count endorsements, which ranged from $3 to $23 million.) In some 55 years, the highest-paid soccer player jumped from $40,000 to $52 million—a 1,300-fold increase. Compare these figures with the U.S. median family income. In 1960, it was $5, 260 and in 2014 it was $52, 750, not quite a 10-fold increase. Put in different terms, in 1960 Pelé earned 7.1 times the U.S. median household income. By 2014, Ronaldo earned 999 times the U.S. median household income, the jump largely due to globalization and technology. Moreover, in certain fields such as business, entertainment and sports, talent is now paid huge amounts at the expense of labor—adding to the rise of inequality between the bottom 99 percent and the top 1 percent.

For older readers who golf, Ben Hogan's top annual earnings was $90,000 in 1948, compared to Jack Nicklaus's $320,000 in 1972 and Tiger Woods's $122 million in 2007. In 1948 the average working wage was $2,300; in 1972 it was $7,100; and in 2007 it was $40,400. Whereas Hogan earned 39 times more than the average worker, Woods earned 3,020 times more. Hence the price of talent vs. labor has skyrocketed. To be sure, wealth vs. work has become increasingly skewed because of mass media and globalization, as well as a tax structure that has increasingly favored the rich since the Reagan administration.

In short, what all these disparities in income reflect is that income growth in the last several decades has been heavily concentrated at the very top, not only in the U.S., but also in emerging nations like China, India, Brazil, etc. The issue can also be stated in basic terms—that is, the pricing of seats for sporting events. In the past 40–50 years, the average baseball ticket increased 300 to 500 percent during the same period when the average blue-collar wage (after considering inflation) remained flat at $16 per hour. Add in parking, burgers and Cokes, and a family of four at the ball game spends a few hundred dollars to sit in the bleachers. Depending on the stadium, what used to cost $1 to $2 per seat to sit in center field now costs $30 to $35 per seat. And, what used to cost $5 to $7 some 40-50 years ago for a box seat now costs $100 to $250 per seat. What used to cost a day's wage for a mechanic or carpenter to take two children to the baseball game and sit over third base in reserved seats and have lunch at the ball park now costs a week's net salary, that is after taxes are deducted. The main reason for the spike in ticket prices is that there is increased competition for scarce seats that corporate people can write off as a tax deduction. The bidding process by the rich for good seats has not only driven up luxury skyboxes from $500 to $2,500 (in Yankee Stadium) per seat, but also the box seats behind home plate, which are second-choice seats.

The same situation holds true for center-court seats at basketball games and 50-yard-line seats at football games, which during the season cost several hundreds of dollars per ticket, depending on what arena or stadium we are discussing, and during a playoff game will be scalped for several thousand dollars. The endless demand by the rich in the sports market, fueled by entertainment deductions for big business and the wealthy, distorts the market and cheats the public of tax revenue. Of course, in the grand scheme of things this coincides with the American capitalist system. One solution would be to limit the amount of deductions for expensive tickets. Another solution would be to cap salaries of modern-day athletes and actors who make nothing of worth for the common good and merely entertain the masses in the way gladiators did for Rome while it was declining, and medieval court jesters with their ornamental costumes did for European monarchs.

As a point of comparison, up to the 1980s, women had slim pickings for a professional career. The best they could hope for was a career in teaching or nursing. We continue to hear from their respective professional organizations they are underpaid, especially when salaries are adjusted for inflation. A 60-year history of teacher and registered nurse pay vis-à-vis the average price of a home reveals a different story. A house is chosen as a yardstick because it is the most important purchase and number one asset for many Americans.

In 1950, the average salary for a teacher was $2,992; in 1970 $9,729; in 1990 $32,880; and in 2010 $56,069. During this 60-year period, their salaries increased 18.7-fold. For registered nurses, the average salary in 1950 was $2,600; by 2010 it was $65,218, a multiplying factor of 25.1. (In both cases, the high range in salary for both occupations in 2010 was about $125,000, depending on education, years of experience, specialization and geographical region.)

Now compare these averages with rising home prices in the U.S. In 1950 the average cost was $14,500. In 1970 it was $26,600. By 1990 $149,800, and by 2010 the price was $272,900—that is, an 18.8-fold increase. In short, teachers' salaries kept up with the inflationary price of an average home and registered nurses' salaries outperformed the rising price of a home. This is not to say that their pay is competitive with other professional groups. Conventional wisdom, along with the teaching and nursing associations, tells us otherwise. Looking at the average 2010 salaries of CPAs ($52,900), attorneys ($69,139) and computer software personnel ($69,986), surprisingly, it is comparable.[2]

Of course, the real issue is all the professions are underpaid, compared to our modern-day gladiators, court jesters and Wall Street barons. Without these professionals and others such as police, firefighters, physicians, etc., the fabric of society falls apart—and all the overpaid superstars and corporate titans lose their influence and/or earning power. As a group, the professionals represent the sustainable energy of society, the glue that keeps it all together. These so-called ordinary people transmit and perpetuate the culture of society; they teach our children, care for and maintain our health, protect our homes and streets, organize and maintain the flow of data, and interpret and uphold the law. You take away these people, and the super-rich (the so-called job creators, entrepreneurs and entertainers) experience a significant loss of profit-making prowess. It's true that a few smart and ambitious people can change the economy and even the world, but without ordinary people opting to be teachers, nurses, CPAs, engineers, etc. most of the people who can transform society fall to the wayside because the foundation of society is broken. There has to be a functioning society that gives no more than two cheers to the likes of Tiger Woods, LeBron James and Lady Gaga, and three or more cheers to Bill Gates, Larry Page and Elon Musk. Take away the professionals in society, along with its plumbers, carpenters and sanitation workers, and all the grand visions, grand lifestyle and grandiosity of the super-rich are reduced or wither.

We need to wrestle with the issues of "profit" vs. "cost" and the subsequent problem of inequality—and not pooh-pooh them away as part of the capitalist system, or simply as that's how the "cookie crumbles." It is our teachers, nurses, scientists and engineers, and other knowledge and high-tech workers, who will save this country, not the hip-hoppers or rappers, not our athletes or entertainers, not our hedge-fund managers. In a fair or good society, if inequality of income persists, it should be based on how much value a person's work is valued by and for the common good. The question then arises whether a teacher's or engineer's service is more valuable than someone who can sing songs or hit a golf ball 500 feet. How can we motivate an MIT engineer student to pursue a job in engineering, where the starting salary is about $60,000 to $75,000, and not be seduced by Goldman Sachs or another Wall Street firm, where the starting salary is $250,000? Who is more likely to serve the common good: the engineer or the Wall Street trader?

What we need to do is find ways to reduce existing inequality. There is a lot we can do that is easy to implement regarding education, social security and healthcare. Canada, Australia, and many Western European nations spend up to twice as much per person as the U.S. does on social programs and safety nets. Why should entertainers, sports figures or CEOs in the U.S. earn $50 to $100 million? Why should hedge-fund managers earn a billion dollars or more? Why do the American people allow it? To be sure, there comes a point where financial rewards become irrational, based solely on profit or greed as opposed to the value for society and the planet we all share.

Despite the titans of industry, the wizards on Wall Street and the disciples of Ayn Rand who believe that "greed is good," in civilized society the tests of restraint, balance and fairness are needed to protect all the "slow" and "average" runners of society. Here we are talking about welfare recipients, mentally challenged people, sick people, disabled people, unemployed people, retired people, elderly people and the working poor—what was once called the "forgotten Americans," "disposable Americans," "silent majority" and now the "moochers." We are talking about millions of individuals and families in America living on the threshold of lost dreams. Charles Dickens in *Hard Times* used darker tones to describe this low-paid, industrialized workforce. Indeed, today, we have the largest percentage of low-paid workers within the industrialized world, about 25 percent, according to the International Labour Organization. In this connection, the rate of unionization continues to fall, from a high of 35 percent prior to 1980, when President Reagan crippled the air controllers' union, to fewer than 7 percent in 2012, according to Eduardo Porter of the *New York Times*.

Proponents of the system rely on free market and trickle-down theories to defend this dark side of the economic system while rewarding "job creators," "innovators" and "risk-takers," and now "entertainers" and sports figures. Myself and other critics would interpret it as a rigged system extending thousands of years into history—a divide between 1 percent (originally called the monarchy and nobility class, now called the rich and super-rich) and 99 percent (originally called slaves, serfs, peasants and indentured servants, now called migrant farmers, miners, factory workers, service workers)—in a nutshell, who we refer to as working people, ordinary people, common people, etc.

Proponents of the system would also argue that people who are "profit" units are worth what they can earn; the sky is the limit; this is how the free market system is supposed to work. Well, there is nothing wrong with a profit; it is what encourages risk-taking and innovation. But there should be a limit on profit, simply for moral reasons, and it should bear some relationship to the overall common good. Profits without limitations do not grow the economy. If fiscally responsible measures are not taken, excessive profits (1) result in growing inequality, (2) lead to producing stuff that people don't often need, (3) shrink the middle class—and together cause economic stagnation.

Conclusion

Every nation that professes to be democratic, humane and/or just, needs to implement a floor and ceiling regarding income and wealth. Where that floor and ceiling should be is beyond the scope of this author, but it should be worked out by members of society through political compromise. Failure to work out a balanced floor and ceiling can lead to the economic decline of any nation: first by choking and shrinking the working and middle classes—the populace or base that a democracy needs in order to function—second by reducing opportunity for most citizens because the income/wealth gaps are too wide to permit a level playing field, and third by increasing the costs of goods and services, which makes the nation less competitive with other nations.

Given the context of the times, some of us would argue for equal results (not equal opportunity), group rights (not individual rights), and even reparations (not saving or investing). Others, including most of my old friends from the schoolyard, along with their children, would still advocate equality of opportunity, where individual perspiration and performance count and produce differences in outcomes. The commitment to provide a fair chance for everyone to develop their own talents remains central to the national creed for the vast majority of Americans; it has deep political roots, and, according to Isabel Sawhill from the Brookings Institution, is what distinguishes us from the history and philosophy of Europe. Virtually no one favors equal distribution of income, for it would discourage hard work, savings, investment and risk taking. Some form of inequality, based on abilities and talent, is the price we pay for a dynamic economy and the right of each individual to retain the benefits of his or her own labor.

Although not all of us would agree to address the outcomes of inequality, the vast majority of us would agree to remedy the causes of inequality. For those on the Left who believe inequality is tied to lack of opportunity, or an unfair and tilted playfield, there is willingness to address the results of inequality. For those on the Right who believe that the market place and meritocracy drive earnings and wealth, there is little need for social and economic change or tax-related reform. A little tweaking, a nail here, a screw there, is all that is needed to ensure that all of us get up to bat and do our best. For those who live on Main Street and believe there is declining opportunity and mobility, and the growing risk of a government of the rich and for the rich, there is the need for raising the floor and lowering the ceiling—or shrinking the income/wealth gap.

Notes

1   As a side note, between 1977 and 1985, Donald Rumsfeld, who is best known as Secretary of Defense under the Ford and Bush II administrations, became CEO of Searle. The company no longer exists and is now part of Pfizer. In 1984, I moved to Winnetka, IL and lived one block from Rumsfeld. In those 15 years, I never met the man.

2   These three salaries may be off by 1 to 2 percent because they were based on 2014 data, then extrapolated downward by reducing the amounts 2 percent per year.

5

BEYOND EXCELLENCE

The Rich, Super-Rich and the Rest of Us

The issues concerning *excellence* and *equality* go back to Greek civilization, when Plato wrote *The Republic* and *Laws* and tried to define universal concepts such as truth, goodness, justice and the spiritual world of ideas. These twin issues continue to impact on society and involve a delicate and shifting scale with regard to the kinds of performance society chooses to reward, resulting in the conditions of social and economic mobility and the degree of stratification within society.

Most liberal and conservative pundits in the U.S. have their own ideas about excellence and equality of opportunity in education, jobs and society in general. Many of us are unable to agree on what is equitable or fair, and how much we can stretch the embodiment of reform or the fiber of society. When large numbers of people perceive the system as unfair or rigged so that no matter how hard they work few rewards are achieved, the people who feel discriminated against will stop working hard and thus fulfill preconceived expectations about their lazy or inadequate performance. The subordinate group may even adopt the terminology of the dominant group, especially if the latter group controls the institutions of society and the media.

Too much emphasis on egalitarianism can lead to mediocrity, indifference and economic decline. Extreme egalitarianism leads to policies that handicap or penalize bright and talented people, whereby the goal of equal opportunity for individuals is replaced by the goal of equal results among groups. Such a society devalues the use of tests and other forms of objective data. On the other hand, excellence carried too far can create social and economic differences, hostilities among groups, and a stratified society. Even worse, overemphasis on achievement and unbridled individual performance can lead to a discussion of the unequal capacities of individuals and groups, and an excuse for keeping people in a second-class status and for violating basic human rights. Finally, when excellence turns into winning at all costs or making loads of money without restraints, the process often leads to cheating or unethical behavior (sometimes criminal behavior).

Democratic societies tend to ignore differences in intelligence where possible; when it cannot be avoided, the blame is shifted to the institutions or agents of society. No group is supposed to be regarded as better or smarter than another group. Whenever differences in capacity are discussed in a democratic society, the politically correct view is that differences vary among individuals and not groups. In a heterogeneous society like ours, when we focus on differences in achievement or economic outcomes, the result can lead to a host of hotly contested issues. And when we compare group differences or outcomes, the debate can become highly emotional—focusing on differences in ability among different ethnic groups, accusations of racism, or using the race card as a means to stifle public discussion.

Given how American society has evolved, the ideal is to search for the golden mean, which goes back to the ancient Greeks, and to achieve a balancing act that rewards merit and hard work and provides a floor or safety net for low-performing, slow-running and weaker individuals. But despite this ideal standard for society, we are confronted with the harsh truth that this nation remains much more stratified than its principles suggest. Moreover, there is very little movement from one class to another in American society. We would like to believe that through merit and hard work anyone can achieve the American dream. Our Founding Fathers rejected aristocracy and inherited privilege.

Yet we are heading toward the creation of a new aristocracy—much worse than the autocratic world that our Founding Fathers feared and tried to avoid. The new aristocracy is rooted in the rise of a new money class: Wall Street and the banking industry, the entertainment industry (including Hollywood stars, pop singers and professional athletes) and the captains of industry. At the same time, we are witnessing the dismantling of the middle class, which is the backbone of democracy. We are also beginning to question whether college is still the main avenue for achieving middle-class status, given the rising costs of tuition and debt incurred for attending college. For example, college tuition annually increased between 5 to 6 percent between 2000 and 2012, according to the College Board, running about two to three times the inflation rate for the same period.

The Value of a College Education

Since the turn of the twenty-first century, college graduates have seen their wages stagnate, while two thirds of all undergraduates graduate with an average debt of $26,000 and masters' students compiled an average debt of over $50,000. The total student debt in 2014 amounted to more than $1.2 trillion, a sum greater than the combined U.S. credit card debt and all auto loan debt. According to the think tank Demos, college debt is expected to spike to $2 trillion by 2025.

The fact is 25 percent of millennials, young adults ages 18 to 34, carry college debt, and a third of these borrowers are considered delinquent in loan payment.

Moreover, some two million Americans age 60 and older are still in debt due to unpaid student loans. The student debt among older people has increased from $8 billion in 2005 to $43 billion in 2014, indicating the effect of constant compounding debt and a fixed income as an adult. The interest on many loans can cause the debtor to spend more on interest than principal over time.

Students borrow heavily without thinking of the consequences or the financial pressure they might face after graduation. Not only does growing student debt have a detrimental effect on the ability of college graduates to afford a home mortgage, the *Wall Street Journal* also reported that people under 40 with student loans have more other debt—credit cards, auto loans, etc.—and less net worth than their counterparts without student debt. As student debt gets heavier, it is safe to assume that other issues surface such as depression, low work morale, low job-performance levels, less purchasing power and in turn a ceiling on economic growth. The worst scenario is to incur a lot of student debt and not graduate from college—more often the case among poor and working-class students than middle-class students. Even worse are the for-profit colleges that target low-income minorities, single women and veterans; they collect billions in tuition from the federal government while students are misled and go into a lifetime of debt, graduating with a worthless degree.

What all this means is that people do not have an equal chance to succeed. Passing laws to eliminate discrimination is not enough. Policies must be implemented that remedy monetary disadvantages with which many people start. In the U.S., that represents about one half of the student population, who cannot afford college and most go into debt to attend college. Trying to compare colleges on how much debt their students accumulate or how much their students earn after graduating is misleading. The rating system is bound to be oversimplified and the information collected by colleges is varied and fuzzy. The need is to provide adequate opportunity for low-income and working-class students to reach their maximum potential and to fulfill their full range of excellence. It should be noted that college tuition since 2000 has increased much more rapidly than the rate of inflation—thus every new class of graduates is in more debt than the last.

A rich society like ours should be able to ensure that all students who have earned a particular grade point average (say 90 percent or higher), can attend a state college for a nominal fee or free. Otherwise, society winds up squandering a great percentage of human potential and talent. Another option, less controversial, is to link student loan payments to future earnings. If someone goes into the Peace Corps or teaches—that is, works in the human/social service area—part or most of the loan should be shouldered by the federal government. The exact amount could vary by years of service or other factors based on future income. Another method is to require all students at the beginning of their college experience to pay 3 to 5 percent of their future earnings for 20 years into a state or federal fund. This would serve as an insurance program for all college graduates despite their tuition costs.

Increasingly, a number of pundits are questioning the economic value of a college education. Given $50,000 per year for four years (cost for college tuition and room and board for many private colleges), that $200,000 placed in a money market or insurance account at age 18, compounded at 4 percent per year for 50 years (18 + 49 = 67 years, the age when Social Security starts), yields a better lifetime return ($1.4 million) than the difference earned between a college graduate and high school graduate (slightly more than $900,000). At 6 percent the yield is $3.7 million and at 8 percent the yield is a whopping $9.4 million or $8.5 million more than the lifetime income between a college and high school graduate. Properly structured with an insurance company or with a financial advisor, federal tax can be delayed until distributions are made or even eliminated entirely.

Another way for questioning the value of a college education is to compare the cost of state universities with private ones. The average cost in 2015 for an in-state resident attending a four-year state institution—including tuition, room and board and miscellaneous fees—was $18,950. A four-year private college cost, on average, $42,420 per year, according to *Kiplinger*. Consider four major state universities, and their annual tuition cost for in-state students for the year 2013/2014. (No other costs are considered, such as room and board, registration fees, books, health insurance, etc.) University of North Carolina—Chapel Hill, $5,800; University of Wisconsin—Madison, $9,200; Ohio State University, $9,750; and University of Texas—Austin, $9,000–$11,200 depending on your field of study. Now compare these figures with the tuition of Ivy League schools: Harvard, $43,900; Dartmouth, $45,500; Yale, $45,800; Columbia, $46,800. Most state universities have their own website to explain in-state tuition policies. The candidate usually needs to be living in the state for at least a year and is financially independent from their out-of-state parents. Rules can vary for married students, veterans and noncitizens.

When it comes to comparing average starting salaries between graduates from the above four state universities and the four Ivy League schools, the difference is about $10,000 to $12,000. But the educational institution has much less direct effect on salaries once we introduce other factors: supply–demand for the particular job, market pay rates for people doing similar work, regional location of the job, candidate's IQ, personality, and work (or internship) experience, parents' network of friends and colleagues, etc. When these factors or variables are introduced, the direct effect of the college on starting salaries is minuscule— often not worth the differences in total tuition costs. Then there is always the notion of luck or the unaccounted-for variance (see Chapter 2). This factor alone may account for as much as 50 percent of the monetary outcomes; that is, the difference in starting salaries and even lifetime earnings. The long and short of all the factors is simple: Predicting an individual's future capacity to perform on the job remains a hazardous undertaking, and considering only one factor (education) oversimplifies the process. When judging talent and ability, or someone's future performance on the job, we must not limit our thinking to a narrow or singular factor for hiring the best candidate.

So the question arises: Is an Ivy League education worth 4.5 to 8 times the price of tuition of a major state university? Does the price differential mean an Ivy League graduate has 4.5 to 8 times better chance to succeed or achieve excellence in their field? Given the issue of student debt, is the extra expense of about $35,000 per year, or $140,000 total, worth attending an Ivy League school? Is going to college in general worth the cost? Most "experts" say yes, because college graduates have a lower unemployment rate and earn more money than those without a degree. But a growing number of college graduates who must pay the debt are questioning whether a college education justifies the debt burden from private colleges. As the *Wall Street Journal* pointed out, from 2005 to 2012 the average college loan debt increased 35 percent, adjusting for inflation, while the median salary of college graduates dropped 2.2 percent. A *New York Times* survey put the decline in salary at 4.6 percent, or about $2,000 a year, adjusted for inflation.

In short, graduates lucky enough to find good jobs will face reduced salaries while a large number will search to find work or settle for under-employed positions and lower-paid positions that do not necessarily require a college degree. Even when the economy recovers, some graduates will never catch up in the job market, affecting lifetime career opportunities and lifetime earnings. The biggest misconception is that a college degree guarantees a good job. That type of thinking represents the pre-smartphone era and the pre-digital world, prior to the twenty-first century.

An opposing view is set forth by economists Jaison Abel and Richard Deitz, who argue that despite rising tuition fees and fewer job prospects among college graduates in recent years, it still pays to graduate from college. Their study, *Do the Benefits of College Still Outweigh the Costs?*, examined data from 1970 to 2013. They found that college graduates earned on average $64,500 annually while associate degree holders earned $50,000 and high school graduates earned $41,000. But figuring 45 years of work for a college graduate age 22 to 67 and for a high school graduate, 49 years, from 18 to 67, the total difference ($2.9 million vs. 2 million) is only $900,000. If we only consider monetary differences, investing the $200,000 at 4 percent interest when the individual is age 18 is a wiser choice.

There are still others who argue that certain colleges which emphasize engineering, mining or technology enjoy a higher rate of return on investment than other colleges and/or fields of study. According to PayScale, the top median salaries of college graduates in the U.S. in descending order were from Harvey Mudd ($2.1 million), California Institute of Technology, Polytechnic Institute of New York, MIT, SUNY-Maritime College, Colorado School of Mines, Stevens Institute of Technology and Stanford University ($1.4 million). The criticism of the survey is that earnings were self-reported and only considered the return on investment for a bachelor's degree. Hence, the data is still uncertain for determining if it's worthwhile to pay a premium for a particular college or major. In the end, the major seems more important than the college. Teachers or social workers graduating from Harvard will not be high earners. Moreover, consider the college with the highest return of investment, Harvey Mudd ($2.1 million), with a $200,000 investment at age 18 at 6 percent return; the investment yield ($3.7 million) is considerably higher. In short, there may be too much hype and optimism about getting a college education. It might also be added that in a democracy, college is not just about getting good jobs. College is about educating and making good citizens who can think, prosper within the norms of society and work to improve it, and understand and appreciate humankind. Reading Shakespeare or Cervantes helps understand life, listen to people and appreciate the power of language.

Don't ever assume that college is the only answer for achieving economic independence or success. The sorting-out process in the U.S. gives the edge to the business person and techie who may not necessarily have a college degree, as well as the entertainer or sports figure. What a college degree seems to guarantee, if we consider all types of careers, is a lower-middle-class job. The rest of the mix is related to social skills, networking, politics and luck. In short, the identification of talent is not perfect and neither is the sorting-out process.

The result is some confusion and room for disagreement over the value of a college education, and to what extent it is related to future earnings in a white-collar career. For example, the argument can be made that American students are over educated, given the market place. In 2013, 34 percent of Americans ages 25 to 29 had at least a bachelor's degree, compared to 25 percent in 1995 and 11 percent when the author graduated from college in 1962 (when the gross national product was expanding at twice the rate now). Today, for some jobs, there are 50 to 100 college-educated candidates for one opening.

And just to add salt to the discussion, consider the opinion of Laszlo Bock who heads up the hiring at Google. He admits he is willing to hire people without a college degree. He's not concerned about what you know or where you learned it, rather what value you can create with what you know. In fact, several tech companies are turning to the high schools to recruit promising employees, before their freshman year at college. Many serve as interns, but they are expected to do real work. Among the well-known companies that get young workers in the door as early as 16 years are Facebook, LinkedIn, Square, Yahoo, etc. Then there is the recent argument "why pay for a college education when I can make money as an entrepreneur or start my own business?" Steve Jobs dropped out of college. So did Bill Gates, Evan Williams and Jack Dorsey of Twitter, Michael Dell, Mark Zuckerberg and Kevin Rose of Digg. David Karp of Tumblr dropped out of high school. They're all billionaires! A diploma is still required for most professions, but dropouts are now considered "cool," "free-thinkers," and "risk-takers." All you need to do is create a new app; and do not worry that some day you will be downsized or shown the exit door from your white-collar job.

Of course, if we want an informed citizenry or a baseline for cultural literacy, college has value. If you go to college, you need to acquire more than broad knowledge. You need to acquire skills for the workplace and the ability to apply knowledge and work with data in a logical and systematic way. Going to Harvard or Yale does not necessarily guarantee this kind of outcome. One might even argue that people who have these traits and get accepted to Ivy League schools could develop the same analytical thought processes at state colleges such as Chapel Hill or Ohio State.

Barney Harford, the CEO of Orbitz Worldwide, was previously mentioned in Chapter 3. He's not concerned about someone's college education. He's concerned for the trajectory of the candidate's resume. To get to your current position, "was it a steep trajectory?" Did it take you five or ten years to reach this level of achievement, "because that's going to be predictive of what you are going to do within our company… I'm looking for people who've got passion, energy and curiosity, and I really emphasize that over specific experience or education." The right person with the right aptitude and attitude "can within a week [add] immense value to the organization… You want someone who can learn fast and who will be able to adapt as the organization adapts." That can be someone from Hofstra or Harvard, or from a state university or a person who graduated from a community college. In general, the nature of adult learning and learning on the job will often depend on a person's interests, motivation and abilities—and how much overall effort he or she wants to put in to improve on the job. Most of us are suckers for a person from Harvard or Yale—not fully grasping there are all kinds of ways to get into Ivy League colleges, ranging from parental networking, alumni relations, parental donations, as well as grades.

In the meantime, tuition revenues for private colleges are beginning to peak and undergraduate enrollments are sliding downward because of price sensitivity— yielding a smaller pool of traditional students. Over the next several years, according to Michael Townsley, former president of Pennsylvania Institute of Technology, "small colleges with meager enrollments could be in deep trouble" and disappear. Part of the problem is the economy, but students increasingly are heading to state universities and community colleges (where costs are often $5,000 a year or less) to save on tuition.

Hard Work, Competition and Free Markets

In a more egalitarian society, the people who work at unskilled jobs or low-status jobs are paid relatively higher wages than would otherwise be paid in a society that fosters inequality. In such a society, a full range of excellence would be rewarded, and special provisions would be made for those who do not come out on top because of lesser abilities, motivation, drive and/or just bad luck. In this type of society, policies require decent wages and working conditions for those jobs that few people want to perform (i.e., landscaper, hotel chamber maid, sanitation worker, janitor, etc.) but are necessary to society. No matter how excellently they perform in these jobs, their rewards will be limited. For example, how much extra should society pay for an excellent painter or bus driver? Compare that to an airplane pilot, surgeon or CEO of a multi-billion-dollar company.

In an egalitarian society, safety nets and social programs are needed to help the less skilled and less fortunate (who may be skilled but unlucky), including the poor and working people, sickly, handicapped, disabled and aged. Policies also require an education program for all children and youth not only to enhance mobility among the lower and working classes, but also for purpose of the nation's growth and productivity so that nearly all its citizens can improve their standard of living. At the very least, our public school system should provide equal resources and equal revenues for all students; and lessen, if not eliminate, the extremes of wealth and poverty in funding the nation's schools. If all our nation's students represent the future of our society, then there is no reason why one rich school district should spend twice or three times the amount of a poor school district in the same state, as is often the case.

That said, American school districts rely too heavily on local property taxes to fund schools, so that wealthy districts bring in more revenue than those in poor districts. The states make a half-hearted attempt to reduce the monetary gap but fall considerably short in their attempt to assist lower-class districts. We would hope that a policy existed to distribute resources on an equitable basis, not primarily earmarked for wealthy districts, and that all students were treated as equal citizens.

We might also assume that a fair or just society would require some cap or limit on salaries for jobs that are considered highly skilled, high status and high paying. Government policy is appropriate, not only for purposes of protecting the slow and weak runner, but also to curb the potential for meritocracy turning into exploitation or excessive greed and avarice. Here we are going down a "slipping slope," where the "masters of the universe," the titans of industry, and conservative pundits argue that we need to reward high standards of performance to the fullest in order for society to maintain its competitive edge—or achieve greatness. The realities of competition and the "sorting-out process" operate best in a free market, we are told, with no government interference, no regulations, no quotas and no limits on rewards.

In a highly competitive society, where winning counts more than trying your best or doing what's morally right, cheating often prevails and becomes the norm among the "best and brightest." We see it surfacing in all phases of society—with bright students cheating on high-stake tests, with super athletes involved in doping, and with top traders on Wall Street and politicians we elect to Congress relying on inside information for investing or using campaign donations for personal spending. In a highly competitive society, one that fosters social conditions under which the benefits go to a small group of people because of top performance or special talent, class conflict can escalate to the point that the underclass feels left out and threatens the political order. In fact, this is a common occurrence in third world and emerging nations, especially when the common people or masses feel oppressed by a dominant group and/or unable to find viable work with decent pay. Frustration and resentment also exist when one group— racial, ethnic or religious—perceives itself as a minority group with limited rights and power, or as a former colonialized and oppressed group. No matter what the present status, history has a way of shaping and interrupting present events.

When the costs of protecting the more affluent against the masses outweigh the costs of redistribution of resources or wealth, at that point society collapses or is overthrown. Obviously, the U.S. and most other industrialized nations have not reached this point. But we should pause and take heed that hundreds of societies over centuries have reached the point of breakdown or upheaval because of government authoritarianism and corruption, hereditary privilege (membership in a family, class or caste) is viewed as iron clad, and/or the inability of society to constrain human greed and avarice. Recent events in Africa, the Arab world and Latin America reflect this type of flashpoint or revolt. Jealousy of ill-gotten gains among political leaders is acute among the youth and educated cohorts across the globe, especially among the bottom two to three billion people. Today, in the United States, a new day is dawning. The average person (who Alexander Hamilton defined as the "herd") increasingly feels the deck is stacked against him and he has few chances for mobility or success. The public perception is that the big banks and Wall Street will never have to really answer for their part in the "Great Recession." The fines they incurred were small compared to the profits they made—all at the expense of Main Street.

The global financial meltdown of 2007 to 2012 is an example of the near economic collapse of Western society, because the free market was considered the driving engine of the economy, and it was believed by ideologues that the market, if left alone, would correct itself. The idea that competition leads to increased productivity and greed leads to increased efficiency is rooted in the minds of Darwinism and Spencerism, and to a kind of "survival of the fittest" and "law of the jungle." Similarly, the notion that shrewdness and strength will create the rise of obscure and uncultivated men to great wealth is at best a false free-market assumption, based on the philosophy of Ayn Rand, and at worst a class-interest philosophy that ignores the human condition.

In his 19 years as the Chair of the Federal Reserve, Alan Greenspan, a disciple of Rand, was noted for speaking an oblique, oracular and confusing language called "Fed Speak." He did it partially to keep markets and inflation in check. He used his mastery of finance to confuse his critics, protect his cronies on Wall Street and to deflect any form of government regulation of the market. But greed, corruption and the undermining of the law will always prevail when the money class is permitted to act with minimal restraints or regulations. These kinds of values will almost always trump fair play in the pursuit of excellence and equality—sort of a Machiavellian view of the world described in *The Prince* coupled with a Hobbesian view of life described in *Leviathan*.

Fat Cats: Old Money vs. New Money

In his *Life and Letters*, the words of Henry Lee Higginson, the Boston financer, ring loud today as they did some 90 years ago. In his plea to wealthy colleagues to endow Harvard liberally, he bluntly asserted that the wealthy class had firm hold of the world and that superior education was essential "to save ourselves and our families and our money from the mobs." In the twenty-first century, the "masters of the universe" and "financial wizards" of Wall Street and banking continue to prevail, fortified against possible misfortunes through the acquisition of riches and guided by values and interests unconnected with Main Street or the common good. In picturesque words, they have become marred in the crude and conspicuous enjoyment of the feast—evidenced by their king-sized mansions, lavish parties and lifestyle—and displayed and celebrated by the media in popular magazines, cable television and the Internet.

Spokesmen of big business and banking remind the American public, more precisely dupe the people, that the acquisition of wealth has always been the crucial index of civilization and without it no great achievement nor innovation, no long-term productivity nor jobs could be realized. Celebrated in song and story, they squander hundreds of thousands of dollars on private jets and big yachts, on old wine and rare paintings that may be unpalatable and ugly—or worse, counterfeit— and boast on the airwaves and in print how they made their first million or billion dollars and how you and I can still achieve the American dream. Although they provide us with stories about inspiration and perspiration, their view of excellence has little to do with merit or performance. Their achievement is based primarily on political clout and power, the right social clubs and network of friends, or being born in privileged status. It's hard for anyone who believes in the red, white and blue to admit that the American dream is waning—much harder to achieve than when Ike was President and Joe DiMaggio and Marilyn Monroe were in love.

In the most recent bubble, all the profits in the U.S. went to Wall Street and the losses were absorbed by Main Street. It was working people, ordinary Americans, with diminishing retirement pensions and investments for their children's college education, who saw their world shattered. They have paid the bill for the Wall Street and banking bailout—as will their children and grandchildren in terms of government deficits, reduced Medicare and Social Security benefits, and higher taxes and mortgage defaults. As their wages and benefits shrink, they see corporate profits and business executives and bankers doing far better than in prior years. They are aware of government bailouts and special subsidies handed out to big pharma, big oil, big agriculture, big banks and well-connected contractors and special interest groups.

Under the rules of big business and big money, this is how the world operates. The ordinary person who once believed in the system has become pessimistic about his future chances of succeeding. He is working harder and getting nowhere, even worse senses he is going backwards. He is being devoured by the system—at least that is the perception—while the wealthy, with their clout and inside information, game the system. We would like to think we are all in the same boat, one nation indivisible. Then my thoughts drift to the movie *Titanic*—a great metaphor to explain who drowns and who gets to live another day. Because of class differences, Jack was denied space in a lifeboat—and drowned. Most of the first-class passengers were evacuated and given access to boats and lived.

But no one should really be surprised. The fundamental causes of the last financial crisis can be spun many different ways. Timothy Geithner, the former Treasury Secretary and author of *Stress Test: Reflections on the Financial Crisis*, argues the causes are straightforward and fundamental: It goes back to the same old madness of crowd behavior, greed and excessive risk—dating back to the Dutch mania for tulip bulbs. Few people seem to notice what is happening to the financial system until it's too late. It's like being on the *Titanic*: autopilot and moving too fast, while the captain and the rich guys are drinking in first class. No one seems to notice, until it's too late. The drunks in first class have access to the lifeboats; they have inside information, and simply bail out before the others know what is happening. The rest of us go down with the ship and lose our shirts, or worse.

What is just and fair is irrelevant, according to Geithner. What counts is that the financial system must be saved. To try to hold the big bankers accountable is nothing more than moralistic sentiment; it will not change behavior. We will always have financial crises. It's only a matter of time before another ship hits an iceberg. The system will never be truly reformed. Certain people will make vast fortunes from the failure and misery of others. The super-rich will find a lifeboat and survive. The little fish will always be eaten by the big fish.

In the 1950s, Consuelo Vanderbilt, a symbol of American wealth, published the best-selling autobiography *The Glitter of Gold*, which described her miserable marriages, commonly arranged as a "link in the chain" among aristocratic families to cement their wealth. She was indoctrinated by her mother Alva to believe that happiness is reached through "practical arrangements of marriages" rather than romance, what Old Europe would refer to as "the protocol of marriage," in order to build an alliance or enhance wealth between ultrarich families. Fifty years later, in the biography *Consuelo and Alva Vanderbilt* (the daughter of Cornelius Vanderbilt), the mother in a moment of cynicism referred to wives as "paid legitimate prostitutes" who design their lives around finding "suitable" spouses, even if it means traveling across countries or oceans, to hold on to their elite status. The goal is to not dilute their wealth among "lower orders" of society— that is, you and I, or the bottom 99.9 percent. In modern corporate terms, marriage is like a hedge fund. If it works, great. If not, there is always the daughter or son of the Duke of Marlborough or the King of Sardinia. Everyone in a rich man's world is fungible.

The idea of getting ahead through marriage, not to work hard and not to worry about paying your bills, goes back to the Kings and Queens of Europe. Through marriages alliances were formed and wealth preserved. Then, there is Honoré de Balzac's 1835 classic novel *Le Père Goriot*. It describes an everlasting description of getting ahead through marriage rather than hard work in French society, along with the corruption and greed of the nobility. The novel is suffused with sarcasm, and reflective of the author's critical attitude of the corruption and greed of the upper crust of society. The novel takes place during the Bourbon period in Paris. Individuals plot to secure higher social status through marriage or any other dubious way to climb the social ladder. The idea of legitimate work is not considered a viable way to succeed: that is the route for fools and stupid-witted people.

Although some of the titles and symbolic alliances of super-wealthy families have disappeared over the last hundred years, they still retain much of their privileges. Moreover, they continue to manipulate the corporate world and financial markets for their own benefit, as well as domestic and foreign policies of nations through private clubs and social and business relationships. (The U.S. Supreme Court *appointment* of Bush to the presidency in 2000 is an example of this well-concealed web of favors and how "things" work behind the scenes, despite what the people say or how they *vote*.) Although not all of the elite families today are descendants of maligned monopolists or political scoundrels, they manage to live a life of splendor in places like Southampton, NY; Martha's Vineyard, MA; Kennebunkport, NH; Kenilworth, IL, or on some huge Texan ranch, with 500 or more acres, in the style of the old Spanish hacienda from when El Zorro roamed the Mexican countryside and robbed from the rich and gave to the poor.

The ordinary person has no comprehension of the super-rich lifestyle and the only contact they have with these kinds of families is that they serve as their workers or soldiers, as these elites effect business mergers, make trade alliances, determine war and make peace treaties. To be sure, a few thousand families have much more to do than we realize with running the entire industrialized world, and indirectly through world economic organizations, international banks and paramilitary and spy groups, have a lot to say in determining the fate of third-world governments. This is a hard pill to swallow; it shakes the foundation of our faith, especially if we were brought up believing in the spirit of democracy and loyalty to Uncle Sam.

The super-rich even have their own social network and app. Do you know someone who is looking to invest $10 million in a start-up company? How about funding a humanitarian organization to fight hunger? Who do I call to get a one-hour meeting with Bill Gates or the Chinese ambassador to the U.S.? Well, there is network tool called "Relationship Science," or ReiSci for short, that helps the economic "barons" and "dukes" of the world, the world's super-rich and powerful, to communicate with each other. Membership to ReiSci is by invitation only and it promises to provide a database of information concerning the rich and powerful—the global leaders of the world. Annual fees start at $3,000 to find people you might already know or to meet others you want to know. For the super-rich it's about networking and taking advantage of contacts, what LinkedIn might do for you and me but cannot do for the rich and famous.

The White Anglo-Saxon Protestant (WASP), a phrase coined by sociologist Digby Baltzell in his classic book *The Protestant Establishment*, is often the target of criticism: considered as the forerunners of special privilege, unfettered individualism, land and railroad monopolists, and Wall Street speculators. Ironically, the WASP establishment has declined in power, influence and wealth. This is largely due to their exclusion of Jews, Catholics and minorities (reminiscent of the days when signs on hotels and clubs read "no dogs, Jews or Catholics"), and its unwillingness to intermarry and/or allow into top echelons of business or their privileged world talented non-WASPS. A somewhat amusing idiosyncrasy is for the true-blue WASP to avoid any evidence of hard work or striving, as if this might suggest that you are not on top of the pyramid, nor a lord of the estate.

The world being described here has nothing to do with excellence or making money "the old fashioned way"—that is, through hard work and perspiration. Although the players change over time, the cycle is endless. It dates back to the dawn of nation-states, an evolutionary step starting with the early 1 percenters: the warlords and monarchs. It proceeds to the age of feudalism with its gothic arches, great castles and walled cities; to centuries of European dynasties and its nobility class with titles and inheritances; to the Gilded Age in America; and now the rise of Wall Street and big banks and a few other financial centers such as London, Zurich, Hong Kong, Tokyo and now Shanghai. The people involved in this process comprise a highly organized industrial and financial community, a small political elite and a handful of billionaires and chief executives from investment houses and banking who have a lot to say about global markets and corporate capitalism.

This class of people shuttle from multiple homes, travel on private jets and communicate with their Androids and iPhones. They work, but it's not the kind that characterizes how the multitude works, say from 9 to 5. At the top of this pyramid, business is as usual. These people devise self-serving rules, gamble on the market and put at risk the entire world economy, while managing to be sheltered from the dips and stresses of the economy—not because of excellence or genius but because of their political connections, business networks and ability to engineer laws for their own benefit. For example, the person who is supposed to monitor Wall Street as Secretary Treasurer, Chief Economic Advisor to the President or Chair of the New York Federal Reserve is often the former executive of one the banking giants like Citigroup or investment giants like Goldman Sachs.

In a capitalistic society, you have to let business and banking make money or the economy will not work. Similarly, government needs to support and encourage those who own the capital, equipment and/or property to invest otherwise the health and vitality of the system will slow down. Eventually, the question arises: How much regulation is the right amount to protect the people without causing undue business restraint or without hindering the economic system? Milton Friedman, the Nobel Prize economist, and President Reagan, would say "as least as possible."

In pursuing this balancing act between business and government, the relationship is bound to grow in significance. Historically, the answer has always been the same. Politics has marched to the beat of money. Business has always found a way to buy or bribe a critical mass of lawmakers, treating them as pawns who are disposable and interchangeable or viewing them as a racing horse and nothing more than an investment. In the U.S., since the Gilded Age or post-Civil War period, Congress has always been responsive to the policy desires of the rich. (It's been that way except perhaps during the TR and FDR administrations, the latter out of necessity because of the Depression and the need to prop up the working people of America.)

The government has allowed the top 1 percent to make millions over their lifetime because most legislators do not work for the common people. Some may start out with good intentions, but they become dependent for campaign money—or worse, puppets of Wall Street and big business—that is the rich and powerful. Put in different terms, in 2010, some 44 percent of Congress members were millionaires, and they make the laws. By 2014, it was 50 percent. Ten members were each worth more than $100 million and six others had a net worth of $50 to $99 million. To be sure, there are all kinds of bailouts, handouts, tax loopholes and tax cuts for the politically connected and wealthy—and very little for working people and the middle class. And, that has been the way of the world—for the last 5,000 years of recorded history. Hence, it becomes necessary, not precisely to deny the above facts, but to obscure or to interpret them differently. Thus, there are numerous rationalizations and defense mechanisms in place to perpetuate the system.

Citizens United and subsequent court decisions in the U.S. made it legal for individuals and corporations to donate unlimited amounts of money to political groups called PACS, some devoted to one candidate. This means, according to Kenneth Vogel in *Big Money*, the billionaires have hijacked the political system. It's business as usual. The super-rich, the top tenth of the 1 percent, have become the "kingmakers" of government policy based on behind the scene access. The outcome is just about always the same—policies that favor the super-rich. Key political and economic decisions that affect the entire country, if not the world, are made at special conferences at ski resorts or sandy-beach resorts, where admission fees run from $25,000 to $100,000, as well as in luxury hotels and four star (or Michelin rated) restaurants. Like it or not, the world is run by a handful of people—politicians who listen to and are shaped by the preferences of the super-rich, not by or for the people.

There is no moral or ethical dilemma to discuss at this point. The relationship between big government and big business is unavoidable. But steps must be taken in a democratic society to structure rules and policies that protect the middle class. Otherwise, the distribution of monetary rewards becomes overwhelmingly skewed in favor of the money class. What it boils down to is whether government represents the public interest or special interests. When it represents the latter, equality, equal opportunity and socio-economic mobility become meaningless catchwords—coupled with the outcomes of low morale, frustration and resentment throughout the society.

The fact is a small number of families dominate business and political interests in the United States and Europe. They are in the position to provide lucrative favors for each other and amass wealth, more than the old robber barons dreamed of during the Gilded Age. Their key to their fortunes is not based on excellence or individual genius; it has to do with family ties and social and political clout, who they know and who they do business with. It is what one insider, John Perkins, in *Confessions of an Economic Hit Man*, calls "corporatocracy": the bond that ties together families, corporations and government in the United States and other parts of the world.

Nomi Prins, the former managing director of Goldman Sachs, updates the idea of corporatocracy with two recent books: *All the Presidents' Bankers: The Hidden Alliances that Drive American Power* and *Other People's Money: The Corporate Mugging of America*. She points out that wealth is concentrated in the hands of a few families and corporate titans, how this small group of people run the U.S. economy, how money, and greed and influence, shape politics and economics—an eye-popping discussion of genealogy of American power. Since Teddy Roosevelt's relationship with J.P. Morgan and members of the Metropolitan Club (Astor, Gould, Rockefeller, Vanderbilt, etc.), big government has served the interests of big businesses and big banking. It's a well-hidden conspiracy!

The super-rich are not like you and me. They disrespect ordinary people and ordinary workers. The economic system has always been dominated by the wealth class but now, as Berkeley's Robert Reich says, by inherited wealth, in which birth counts more than brains—more than talent, effort or perspiration. The idea of the self-made man, that we once believed and would like to still believe, is almost a relic—earmarked to the dust heap of folklore and myth. It's just too hard to compete against inherited wealth. To be sure, education is no longer the great equalizer, as we once thought. It cannot compete when the game is overwhelmingly skewed one way.

Senator Elizabeth Warren puts the idea of opportunity and fairness in simple terms, as suggested by her new book *A Fighting Chance*. She grapples with the connection between government and banking and income inequality. She concludes the game is deliberately rigged and the middle class is under attack.

Knowing who you are, or what talents and strengths you have, is one thing. Being able to prove your abilities, or show who you are, is another point for discussion. In a society in which there are great differences of wealth, the passage of laws outlawing discrimination is insufficient. A democracy, according to Woodrow Wilson, "releases the energies of every human being." But that is not the case any more, given the influence of inherited wealth and the rise of big government serving the interests of the wealthy. While Reich and Warren are the darlings of the political Left, John Perkins and Nomi Prins are relatively unknown but have the same message and outline their story as insiders of Wall Street and corporate America.

Even in death the playing field is uneven and unequal. In *Who Gets What: Fair Compensation after Tragedy and Financial Upheaval*, Kenneth Feinberg, a lawyer who mediated victim compensation for a host of tragedies (ranging from Agent Orange settlements in 1984 to the Twin Tower fund in 2001 and the BP Gulf Coast oil spill in 2010), argues his strategy is to pay claims promptly and fairly. But what is fair? Should we be guided by moral principles? He concedes that under pressure to pay claims promptly, the fund usually relaxes its criteria and honors claims that would be laughed out of court.

He favors equal payment for every deceased person, under the belief that every life is priceless (sort of a Western philosophy), not to mention it is much easier to dispense the claims. But with September 11, he was forced to honor U.S. tort law—that is, prescribing a dollar value to each life lost. Those who earned more money in life or had greater potential to earn more than someone else were awarded more money in death. If you accept that money is the method for paying claims dealing with death and tragic loss, and those with greater earning potential or talent should be compensated accordingly, then the payment has little concern for equality nor a higher moral standard for society. In the end, few people are happy with how the pie is sliced, despite the sum of money awarded to family members. To be sure, the people at the top are paid more than the people at the bottom of the income scale, even in death.

Wealth vs. Work

When it comes to wealth or assets, a million dollars is not what it used to be—certainly not when I grew up during the Truman and Eisenhower years—when a burger and Coke cost 25 or 30 cents. About 7 percent of U.S. households are millionaires and some may be your nextdoor neighbor, according to Stanley and Danko's recent book, *The Millionaire Next Door*. But you should not assume that it will make you deliriously happy or give you sufficient security to quit your boring job. Ironically, the authors found that thrift, inheritances and social class had stronger correlations with monetary outcomes than did intelligence or education—or for that matter excellence on the job. Most millionaires become wealthy because they are thrifty and frugal. They live in modest homes, avoid buying luxury cars (one third purchase used cars), save and avoid overspending. They accumulate wealth through hard work, prudent behavior and not worrying what their neighbors think of them—characteristics of what Riesman in *The Lonely Crowd* refers to as inner-directed people.

When people of wealth, with at least $500,000 to invest, were surveyed by *Worth* magazine in 2008, as many as 48 percent defined the rich as having a net worth of at least $5 million, 25 percent said $25 million, and 8 percent said those with $100 million were truly wealthy. Now I think it is safe to say that someone is *truly rich* with $25 million in assets and *super-rich* with $100 million—that is, "mega wealthy" or just "plain wealthy" if you like vanilla ice cream. By 2014, according to *Fortune* magazine, admission to the top 1 percent club, when measured by income, varied by the year with the ranges of $350,000 to $400,000 and a net worth of $8.5 million. Only half the 1 percenters (or 1.4 million tax payers) qualified in both categories.

The mega-rich are sometimes called the "super-rich" (as opposed to just being "rich") or the "have mores" (as opposed to the "haves"). Those at the very top of the pyramid, the top tenth of the 1 percent, are pulling away from the mere rich. A new consumer market is being created to service the upper crust in terms of mega yachts (300 feet or longer), private gulf-stream jets and mega houses with 20 to 30 rooms on 5- to 10-acre lots. According to Berkeley professor Emmanuel Saez and London professor Gabriel Zucman, almost all of the increase in American inequality over the last 30 years can be attributed to increased wealth of the top 1 percent and much of that by the tenth of the 1 percent. Those at the tiptop category (one tenth of 1 percent) have seen their fortunes grow twice or three times as fast as the 1 percenters. The mega wealthy are insulated from fluctuations of the economy, and their wealth is becoming more concentrated since they invest and create more wealth, as opposed to working for a living, which has limitations on how much a person (perceived as a cost unit) can be paid.

Now for the time being, forget about the 1 percent in the U.S. In Russia, according to the *Economist*, 110 people (out of 140 million) own 35 percent of the wealth. In this case, we are talking about extreme corruption, absolutely nothing to do with excellence or the concept of opportunity and mobility based on a fair playing ground. Here the decimal is moved to .000001 percent. There is enough U.S. history to conclude that Americans pursue money and admire their wealthy, who gained it through their efforts. Alexis de Tocqueville, the French scholar, chronicled America's love of equality as well as money as far back as in the mid-1830s in his book *Democracy in America*. But it is doubtful today that average Russian citizens admire their super-rich, given the fact that few gained their wealth through sweat and hard work. This group consists of a large number of former government bureaucrats who were in the right place at the right time (when the U.S.S.R. was breaking up). Here luck and larceny play a role in the economic outcomes of life, not achievement or merit. Regrettably, more wealth in the U.S. recently comes from moving money round or being paid unusually large sums of money for special talent. However, when you look beyond the rhetoric about the super-rich, most Americans and Russians, as well as citizens around the world, merely seek more opportunity—a fairer playing field.

The difference between wealth and work is simple. In the U.S., wealth is passed on from generation to generation, and includes assets that are taxed at a lower rate than work. In 2013, capital gains were taxed at 15 percent while earnings of $50,000 or more for a single person were taxed (including federal, state and Social Security) at nearly 50 percent. It is nearly impossible to accumulate wealth by working for a salary; the tax system prevents it. You may be an excellent teacher or an excellent plumber, but you will not become wealthy. You may spend your weekends on the beach, but you will not be cruising down the Mediterranean. You may be able to afford the blue-plate special at IHOP or Denny's for $5.99, but you will not be dining at Le Bernardin (the coveted 3 star Michelin restaurant) and tasting its $200 pre-fix luncheon special of foie gras and wild salmon or a $30 glass of champagne.

The economy is driven and dominated not just by wealth, but also by inherited wealth. According to the French economist Thomas Piketty, in his book *Capital in the Twenty-First Century*, inherited wealth matters more than talent or innovative enterprise. Performance, talent, character, etc. matter less than we would like to think. The economic outcomes of life, because of family and hereditary advantage, are predetermined for the rich and super-rich. Only a tiny fraction of the rest of us, the 99 percenters, have a chance to grab on to the super rich golden ring.

Based on historical trends, especially during the last 30 years, Piketty concludes that the U.S. and other Western societies are heading toward a plutocracy. In a series of volleys and counterclaims, the critics argue his data is flawed and based on selective and arbitrary statistics. No clear-cut trend on inequality is evident. Piketty, a French economist, maintains his data is correct; and any reasonable changes in his methodology would be small and not alter his conclusions. If he is correct, the implications are disheartening. To talk about varied excellences and talent is misleading because most people cannot succeed; in the long run, excellence is subject to and limited by wealth discrimination and privilege. Moreover, Western society is unwilling to face its own practices and continues to underestimate growing gaps in income and wealth.

Paul Krugman concurs. The former Princeton economist points out in a *New York Times* article, "Wealth vs. Work," that six of the ten wealthiest Americans are heirs to great fortunes and not self-made entrepreneurs. They are children of an elite class that starts with major advantages over the rest of us. For Piketty, the risk of an oligarchy running the U.S. and many other industrialized countries is real. Politicians in the U.S. at the state and federal level depend on donations from this elite group and seem committed in supporting the oligarchy's interests through special favors and tax policies that preserve their wealth. Even worse, conservative pundits seem to defend the super-rich by referring to them as "job creators" and "innovators." But investments in education do very little when the government predicts that most new jobs stemming from the job creators and innovators don't require much education.

Given these conditions, it is nearly impossible to narrow the gap between the *truly rich* or *super-rich* and the rest of us. In fact, the wealth gap is just as unequal in the U.S. as it is around the globe. No joke! About 99 percent of the U.S. population depends on work in order to put bread on the table. They have what is called a job. Less than 1 percent, the super-rich do not work at a 9 to 5 job, rather as members of old money they move around money and invest—thus creating more wealth, based primarily on acquiring stocks and bonds or property. They often live on income from capital gains and dividends, which are taxed at 15 and 20 percent respectively, much lower than the tax on labor and wages. In fact, according to Krugman 1 percent of households in the U.S. accounts for 75 percent of capital gains.

The vast majority of the super-rich do not care about the plight or condition of ordinary people and are more concerned that the masses don't "storm the Bastille" or break down their doors. They care more about which patrician spouses they marry, about their summer homes and gardens, and their charming wine cellars or rare paintings. F. Scott Fitzgerald, the early twentieth-century American novelist, put it aptly: "The rich are different from you and I." It's more than money and wealth; it deals with attitude, lifestyle and social and political connections, and the fact they are part of the system or know how to play the system for their own gain. Hence, it is nearly impossible for individual excellence or talent to match the special advantage the wealthy have over wages and work. The rich love to assert their devotion to competition, but they are ready to take defensive measures and pressure their friends in government if the competition becomes a little too stiff.

New money—athletes, actors and singers and entrepreneurs—do not have the same DNA or breeding as *old money*. New money often lacks political clout, as opposed to old money, who are part of the ruling class. It is not easy being born into old money. These people rarely speak publically about their finances, in good times or bad. Their assets most likely dropped during the Great Recession, but it is doubtful if it will cut into their lifestyle. New money is more overt in displaying their big yachts, fast cars, Rolex watches and $500 hair highlights, and they are less mum about their losses. Certainly, there is no need to feel sorry for them if during the Great Recession they had to cut down on their trips to the Riviera or sell a four-carat diamond with the hope no one noticed that it was gone.

The simple truth is, in the last 30 years, the new money class have had the opportunity to make huge sums of money, largely because of mass media, technology and market globalization. Entrepreneurs make products or provide services, but sports figures and entertainers—well, they entertain us. Their names become brands and faces become images that are copyrighted, merchandised and sold, then plastered on television and the Internet.

It's nice to know the rich and super-rich are human and vulnerable during rocky times. In the last financial meltdown, the nation's 400 top-money people lost a total of $300 billion in 2008, according to *Forbes*. This brought down their combined net worth to $1.27 trillion, about 19 percent. Of course, the super-rich are more insulated and knowledgeable than average folks who work for a living. Their percentage loss of assets was about half the percentage lost by America's pension funds and stock portfolios. Moreover, it can hardly hurt or change the lifestyle of Warren Buffett, the "Wizard of Wall Street," who lost approximately $10 billion or 20 percent of his wealth that year. Nor can it change the life of Kirk Kerkorian, the corporate raider who lost $8 billion and had only $3 billion left. Then there is Bill Gates, the number one "geek" and America's richest person for the 16th straight year. He lost $7 billion or about 12 percent of his wealth.

But the surging stock market and property values have lifted the fortunes of the rich. Nearly ten million people around the world became millionaires between 2008 and 2013, raising the number to 13.7 million among 23 industrialized nations, according to the Royal Bank of Canada. Their combined net worth was $53 trillion or $38.7 million per person. The accelerating pace of millionaires correlates with the increasing gap between the rich and the rest of us. In the U.S., it is estimated by Emmanuel Saez, an economist from Berkeley, that the 1 percenters saw their incomes rise 31 percent from 2009 to 2012, after adjusting for inflation, while the bottom 99 percent saw wages rise 0.4 percent.

Inequality of income and wealth is a byproduct of capitalism, pushing the well connected, under the guise of the best and brightest, to the most profitable positions. But the system falls apart when the plutocrats run the world as if it was their playground. They may encourage young college students to work hard and start their path to Wall Street or banking. However, the system is not sustainable if the vast majority of workers are told they must excel on the job for a $1 more per hour (a waitress or landscaper) or $1,000 to $2,000 more a year (a teacher or police officer), while the upper crust gobble up tens of millions in one year. Lloyd Blankfein, CEO of Goldman Sachs, is constantly in position to talk about inequality. He concludes that growing "inequality is destabilizing America" and other parts of the Western world. Similarly in *The Price of Inequality*, Joseph Stiglitz warns the growing financial divide is crippling the U.S. economy and if not checked or reversed it may eventually affect the value of stocks and property owned by the super-rich. For our purpose, the increasing financial gaps of income and wealth kill off the idea of merit and hard work because it is more difficult to succeed when a growing share of the economic pie is siphoned off by the "lucky" few.

Ruling the World

So in a nutshell, who is the ruling class? Who runs the world? Certainly not those families earning $250,000 a year in 2013, a magical number the Obama administration initially wanted to use for increasing taxes (Obama got the message; he wound up with a higher income level for raising taxes). In fact, on the East and West coasts, where living expenses are higher than the rest of the U.S., $250,000 suggests nothing more than the middle class or upper middle class. For some pundits, however, $250,000 suggests the top 2 percent. As for running the world, ordinary Americans (the bottom 99 percent) have no say. According to a *CNNMoney* report, the majority (76 percent of Americans in 2013) live paycheck to paycheck; in fact, most Americans live just above subsistence level but don't realize it—until they lose their job. Only 50 percent of working Americans have sufficient savings to cover three months of expenses in the event they lose their job, and 37 percent have no savings. But, then, that has been the human condition since the crack of civilization. And, we are supposed to be the fortunate ones. As Otto von Bismarck, the Prussian chancellor, once muttered: "God has special providence for fools, drunks, and the United States of America."

The rise of the nation-state, coupled with the global economy, has given rise to what David Rothkopf in *Superclass* calls a "national ruling class" and a "global power elite"—business and financial titans who run large public companies and banks, supra organizations such as the World Bank and International Monetary Fund, and who have huge influence on political leaders around the world.

These super elites have all the characteristics of the old Protestant elite, but with the essential difference that they operate from a global market and they have sway over more money and a larger share of the economic pie. They attend the same elitist universities such as Harvard, Yale and University of Chicago, attend the same forums such as the Council on Foreign Relations and World Economic Forum, travel in private gulf-stream jets, vacation in private ski havens like the Yellowstone Club, where they can mingle discreetly without bodyguards (since the place is protected by the Secret Service), invest in the same hedge funds such as the Carlyle Group and Blackstone Group and often illegally bury money off shore and thus avoid or delay for years the need to pay taxes, and use tax loopholes to gift millions to their descendants without paying estate taxes. They get together at meetings and resorts with former presidents, prime ministers and CEOs; invite or nominate each other to corporate boards and foundations; trade inside information; and make each other richer. You would think that given the rise of a knowledge-based, high-tech society men and women with talent and ability would be in high *demand*. Given a world tilted in favor of the super-rich, the demand may be superficial or overrated. Remember throughout history, people with high IQ and creative skills were ignored or lay untapped in a society stratified by the monarchy and nobility class.

It matters little how smart or talented the superclass are; they belong to the right clubs and vacation spots, attend Ivy League universities, and through blood, intermarriage and mentor or father–son relationships continue to maintain power and influence. It is the same system of inherited privilege and political power that allows for the Bushes, Kennedys, Rockefellers and DuPonts to live in splendor and influence, if not dominate the world stage. It is similar to the power, influence and money the nobility in Europe once had, and what the Old World monarchs passed from one generation to the next—and thus built and maintained a stratified society for thousands of years.

Hard Times for Labor

As a nation, we face a choice. Either we build an economy in which the vast majority of workers can earn enough to adequately support their families or we build a government that is prepared to support or subsidize an increasing population; that is, the American labor force being left behind. Many workers in lower- and middle-skilled sectors can no longer count on full-time employment or employment at a decent pay scale. Moreover, their hours can be cut sharply from week to week based on the weather or business outlook. They have no union affiliation to protect their wages or working conditions. Moreover, the unions in the U.S. are struggling because of automation and global competition. Nearly half the workforce in the U.S. cannot survive on their own. They need various forms of welfare or entitlements to make it on a daily basis, and thus create a new drain on taxpayers. For example, workers in restaurants, large chain-stores and hotels earned $8.69 an hour in 2013, according to the Economic Policy Institute.

Although a number of blue-voting states have recently increased the minimum wage to $9 or $10 an hour, conservative politicians are reluctant to increase the minimum wage because of concerns for increased unemployment among unskilled workers and that extra labor costs will strain small businesses. The American workforce has been hollowed out for the last three decades—losing semi-skilled and skilled manufacturing jobs that can be performed more cheaply by machines or foreign workers. To some extent, it has splintered the working force into less educated workers (hotel, retail, food, etc.) and professional service workers (teachers, nurses, police, etc.) who cannot be easily outsourced or mechanized. The workforce can also be categorized into full-time workers, with some health and pension benefits, and "independent contractors" without benefits who receive a "1099" tax form at the end of the year. These workers are locked into this new category because they cannot find regular jobs. The system has found an easy and cheap way to hire workers with minimal overhead as well as protection against employee rights, litigation, strikes, etc.—and no minimum wage. The system can hire and fire these independent contractors at will, as the economy expands or contracts.

There is no doubt that the American middle class has shrunk; about 55 million households are classified as middle class or about 43 percent of U.S. households, according to the U.S. Census Bureau. Although we can question the definition of middle class, there is no question the middle class in America has changed from their predecessors: from working people to households headed by people 65 years and older who are receiving pensions and Social Security. Also, older Americans (65+ years) are increasingly working to supplement their incomes; approximately

20 percent were in the labor force in 2013, nearly twice the number as in 2000. While the median household income has dropped 9 percent since the turn of the twenty-first century, reflecting the shrinking of the middle class, it has increased 14 percent among households headed by adults over 65. The point is, as a result of the Great Recession, the U.S. lost a large number of middle-class jobs and gained a lot of low-paying jobs. The change in pay partially reflects the decline of industrial jobs and the loss of union influence.

Most Americans who call themselves middle class still believe in the American dream and still think if they work hard, with a little luck thrown in the mix, they can get rich. Statistically, it will not happen; that goal is out of their reach. The fact is, when ordinary people look up they see the rich getting richer. Rewarding excellence is becoming a harder phenomenon because equality of opportunity is not a simple process and it is becoming more difficult to put into practice—given increasing inequality of income and wealth characterizing the new global economy. The point that very few Americans get rich is not a threat to society so long as the basic needs and rights of the people are ensured, and so long as they believe some opportunity still exists.

The U.S. labor force is also characterized by a growing skill gap. A recent study by the Organisation for Economic Co-operation and Development (OECD) assessed 22 advanced, industrialized nations and 160,000 workers. Fewer than 12 percent of Americans passed in two or more of the six levels of literacy. While younger cohorts are generally better skilled and educated than older ones in other industrialized countries, in the U.S. the younger workers are less skilled than the rest. This suggests that the workforce skills in other industrialized nations will continue to overtake the U.S. It also means that "human capital" in the U.S. is waning. While the nation still rewards skilled workers, the supply is not keeping up—suggesting growing inequality of income among U.S. workers; skilled vs. unskilled. Those trends parallel the fact that 22 percent of U.S. high school students drop out of school, which is among the highest amounts compared to other OECD countries.

In another study, *Social Progress Index 2014*, involving more than 100 countries, Michael Porter of the Harvard Business School reported that U.S. citizens rank 39th in basic knowledge, and 70th in health and wellness; moreover, he concludes there is no direct relationship between economic growth and social/medical wellbeing. This is especially true when economic growth is not equal among the nation's population; or, if I may add, when business profits are earmarked to a tiny group or when we believe we live in a meritocracy in which great wealth is earned and deserved by only "job creators" or entrepreneurs who risk capital.

Profits vs. Wages

In the meantime corporate profits have increased dramatically, as evidenced by a robust stock market, even at the expense of workers with education or skills that are supposed to lead to success. One reason is that technology is displacing workers of all kinds, including those doing semi-skilled and high-skilled white-collar jobs. As pointed out by Erik Brynjolfsson, in *Race Against the Machine*, computers and robots are replacing workers, even people with excellent skills. He points out that "there is no economic law that says technological progress has to benefit everybody or even most people. It's possible that productivity can go up and the economic pie gets bigger, but the majority of people don't share in the gain." This includes even people who excel on the job; simply put, labor is not necessarily rewarded, because of supply–demand and the market place. Corporate profits increase but salaries limp along or are frozen. Moreover, corporations tend to use their "monopoly power" and "too big to fail" status to raise prices at the expense of Main Street and without passing the profits on to the majority of employees. The share of profits goes to the top executives, thus increasing inequality.

It would be nice to frame corporate policy to increase profit-sharing with employees. But when earnings are announced quarterly, the values of stock rise or fall upon performance based on pennies. There are repeated instances in which the market value of a corporation has lost billions of dollars because it missed estimates by a penny or two. This suggests a benevolent corporation that gives raises to its rank-and-file workers or contributes to the well-being of the community (or common good) can have its stock sharply decline. Diverting money to labor puts the company at risk; better to give the money to stockholders in the form of dividends. Given the real world of corporate behavior, there is little incentive for big business to raise salaries or living standards of their employees. The idea is to keep wages down. You would like to think that wages are considered in context with ability, character and hard work. But on the whole, this notion of work and wages is rarely borne out in the real world of corporations. Salaries are capped for workers with average and even above-average abilities—and that tends to force people with above ability to explore other options.

We are thrust into a highly competitive economy, where excellence counts less at all skill levels (including those with a college education), because job opportunities are fewer and labor unions are on the defense. According to one recent study, fewer than 7 percent of workers in the private industry are unionized (a far cry from the 1950s and 1960s when one third of the labor force was unionized). The nation has the largest share of low-paid jobs among all the industrialized countries, asserts the International Labour Organization. Even worse, wages have fallen to record lows as a percent of the nation's GDP. For example, according to the Economic Policy Institute, from 1973 to 2011, worker productivity grew 80 percent, but median hourly compensation, after inflation, only grew 10 percent. In the last 16 years, between 1995 and 2011, productivity increased 38 percent but the medium salary of full-time workers with a college education increased 13 percent and workers with a high school education increased 6 percent. All these trends lead to the conclusion, according to Jefferson

Cowie, a professor of labor history at Cornell University, that underpaid workers in the U.S. are trapped in growing inequality and rigid mobility patterns.

That said, it might be concluded that the notion of meritocracy is limited to a fraction of the U.S. population—an unhealthy situation which allows less-wealthy nations (such as China, India, Brazil, Chile, Indonesia, etc.) with high-performing schools and less inequality to catch up or make impressive economic gains relative to U.S. growth. If things remain as they are, nations that lag behind us will one day catch up to us. Because of our nation's past successes and present influence, U.S. citizens cannot envision such an outcome on the distant horizon. But we either learn from our competition, and make policy changes that welcome and reward meritocracy involving labor (not only capital), or fall further behind.

Manufacturing in the 1960s represented 35 percent of the U.S. workforce and now it is less than 10 percent. Politicians have watched labor groups suffer without lifting a finger. The class war has ended. The people lost. Throughout history, they have always lost. Capital has always had more power than labor, and you don't have to be a Marxist to understand that capital has always gobbled the lion's share of a productive economy. The global pie has expanded, as has the nation's productivity, making the rich richer. But for every super-rich person, there are millions who are barely making it day to day, paycheck to paycheck. There were days when a few giant firms like GM, Sears and U.S. Steel dominated the market place in the U.S. and abroad. They made sufficient profits to make peace with the labor unions and pay decent wages to working people thus allowing them to become middle class. That period lasted about 25 to 30 years, from the post-World War II years to the 1970s. Now more than two thirds of their jobs have vanished overseas where labor costs average $2 to $5 day—and U.S. workers are forced to compete.

More threatening, in the battle between profits and wages, white-collar jobs requiring a college education and noted as the cornerstone of our knowledge and high-tech society, have slowly disappeared. Starting in the 1990s, these jobs have been outsourced by American companies to Asia and Eastern Europe. Many people who used to earn $75,000 to $150,000 have now been displaced by their counterparts in China, India, Singapore and the former Soviet bloc in Eastern Europe for one third or one fourth the cost. Middle-class Americans have lost many of those jobs, and have been forced to join the ranks of the unemployed and underemployed. The result is that for every job that pays $50,000 or more, there were 25 to 100 applicants in 2010.

Between 2000 and 2010, much of the growth of U.S. companies came from abroad; the revenues of multinational companies from the rest of the world were up while sales at home were down. In 2005, the *Wall Street Journal* reported that 41 percent of the revenues for the S&P 500 companies came from overseas operations. Five years later, more than half the revenues of American venture-capital firms were raising money to invest hundreds of billions overseas. This trend increased from 25 percent of the total raised in 2001 to more than 50 percent in 2010. This economic pattern translates into a loss of U.S. middle-class jobs, mostly the high-paying, high-tech types. The sad truth is that globalization equates to a massive loss of American jobs, much more than is generated from exports. There are many apt polemics (aphorisms) to describe the employment meltdown. Thomas Friedman, in his recent book *The World is Flat*, warns that U.S. workers must now compete with knowledge-based and tech workers around the world. Because of the differential in pay scale, the middle-class population is unable to compete—despite disbelief and counter claims among conservative pundits of the success of free market capitalism.

We need to recognize that automation, globalization and increased efficiency have increased unemployment and underemployment among middle-class Americans. As James Huntington, author of *Work's New Age*, claims: "We no longer need the share of people working that we have had in the past… It's clear that the [new] job crisis is permanent and will not go away with better economic times."

Added to these ranks of people who once thought they were middle class are divorced women with children (nearly 18.1 million under age 18), college graduates burdened by massive debt (some 40 million), retirees (some 75 million) whose pensions have dwindled (and are now looking for work during their golden years), and people who have experienced huge medical bills. All these people are products of bad judgment or bad luck, wrong decisions and wrong choices, or being in the wrong place at the wrong time. Just a few curves or wrong turns on the so-called road to prosperity, or some burst of bad luck, and the terrain becomes bumpy.

A macro event that is uncontrollable, such as a recessionary economy, a housing bubble, a dip in the stock market or the fact that the world is now "flat" (meaning that people now compete for jobs on a global basis)—and life can shift abruptly for most Americans from prosperity to hard times. Increasingly, more Americans are treading dangerous waters and hardly keeping afloat. You can talk all you want about merit or talent—and how to reward the notion of excellence, but when society undergoes a major social and economic shift only those at the very top or those with inherited advantages will remain in their privileged status. Sorting people into bright, average and slow categories or high-skilled and low-skilled workers makes less and less sense if there is less and less opportunity.

We are living in an "upside-down" economy where new inventions and technology have increased productivity on a national level and lowered the standard of living for most Americans, because the economic gains have been gobbled up by a few who have become part of the wealthy class—the group of taxpayers earning approximately $400,000 or more per year as of 2014. The rich don't care, so long as the rest of us don't bang down their doors or seek to overthrow the system.

The only time the rich and super-rich ever cared about the plight of the common people was during the Great Depression in the 1930s, when unemployment reached 25 percent, millions of men were homeless and soup kitchens were overwhelmed—and it looked that the social/economic structure was about to collapse. Then, for a short period, the economic elite, concerned about their own lifestyle and wealth, relinquished their grip on the people and the seats of power. They reluctantly permitted the Roosevelt administration to implement social and work programs for the victims of the Depression and allowed government meddling—in the formation of the Federal Reserve and the Securities and Exchange Commission (SEC). If you think there is another reason other than fear, why the business and financial sector helped the common man or permitted increased government tinkering of free markets, then you need a reality check.

Amity Shlaes, a conservative stalwart and former writer for the *Wall Street Journal* presents the usual verbage by and for the political Right. In *The Forgotten Man*, she argues it was a "lack of faith…in the market place [and] government regulation…from 1929 to 1940 [that] helped to make the Depression Great." The book's title is an ironic twist. Roosevelt referred to the "forgotten man" as a victim, someone at the bottom of the economic heap. But William Graham Sumner, a Yale sociologist and disciple of laissez faire economics, first used the term in 1884 to describe the average working American who was being cajoled into believing the down-trodden people needed safety nets or relief programs— the very stuff and soul of Roosevelt's New Deal to combat the Depression.

Roosevelt's critics saw him as a traitor to the comfortable world of the patrician class and business class, but the American people knew better and elected him four times as president. When Bush II became president, he not only made great efforts to reshape and move Social Security into the private sector, but also he went to great pains to provide Wall Street a free hand by weakening government regulation and the controls imposed by the Federal Reserve and the SEC. In 2010, the rich, the top 1 percent of the income bracket, held the working class and middle class "hostage" to ensure high-end tax cuts. The word "hostage" referred to the American people, ordinary Americans. By 2013, slight tax increases for the rich were enacted; that is, for those earning more than $400,000 a year. The point is the rich did not fear the collapse of the system nor that all the people living paycheck to paycheck, the majority of Americans, would bring down the system. To be sure, those who earn over $400,000 a year should show their appreciation to the country that provided the infrastructure and permitted their success; they should be glad to pay the extra tax to help out ordinary people who work for them, buy their products or services and/or built or protected the systems that contributed to monetary gains.

As we travel through time, or move from country to country, the notion of excellence and equality may change and different forms of excellence and equality will be redefined, but those who are politically connected and/or privileged at birth will somehow usually succeed. Not everyone will find the proper time period to succeed. Some people will succeed in certain centuries more than other centuries, and some forms of excellence may make more sense in certain periods of history. But a particular society at a given moment must always think of its people—ordinary people since there are so many of them—if it is to claim the characteristics of a democracy. If there is a lack of opportunity for the common people, and if they do not share in the wealth of the society, then that nation-state is not a democracy. The foundation of a democracy is based on the masses first having sufficient food, shelter and security, then believing they have sufficient chances to succeed and sufficient mobility. We must always ask ourselves, if we profess to be a democracy: Have we restrained hereditary stratification and privilege? Does society foster a fair chance, real opportunities for striving and achieving? Does society reward performance in several fields? Does it recognize different forms of excellence—not just in business or financing, but also in the arts and sciences?

Where the U.S. is Heading

Alan Beattie, the conservative editor at the *Financial Times*, contends that every country is in control of its own economic destiny; our own fortunes depend on what political leaders decide to do. Beattie maintains that the choices we make as a nation determine our future economic health. He fails to consider, however, that the ordinary working person has little to say and depends on his political leaders who are often influenced by special interest groups and large donors who are usually in bed with the finance and banking industry and the corporate world. Make no excuses. The big banks and big business are fueled by profit and self-interest. Obsession with money usually overtakes morality and concern for the common good. As the Abba song goes: "Money, money, money … it's a rich man's world."

Given the real world of economics, it's the financial and corporate world, not the government, that determines how the world is shaped and what opportunities people have in life. It matters little how smart you are, what talent you have, if you live in a corrupt society. On a theoretical level, there is always the chance of reforming government, but big money and corporations will always close ranks and serve their own interests. While Beattie and other conservatives talk about personal responsibility, choice and free markets, they also mention how the role of history plays in the economic success or failure of a nation. In *False Economy*, Beattie argues that neither the laws of nature or scripture, nor luck or even abundance of fertile land or natural resources, explain why some countries end up rich and prosperous and others poor and unstable. Economic outcomes of a country largely depend on choices of its political leaders and the innovative spirit and creative passions of its populace. These are all intangible or hard-to-define items, but they often make the difference between how nations manage and build or mismanage and squander their wealth. While a "tyranny of talent" may narrow the chances of high-ability people in specific fields to succeed, talent still needs to be rewarded for society to fully develop its resources. If the aim is to be economically productive and efficient, especially in a high-tech society, nurturing the talents of a Mozart, Miro or Mickey Mantle may not be the best use of time or money. The odds for recognizing excellence and being rewarded in these endeavors are limited. Anyone seeking to play the odds and function effectively in a highly productive and efficient society would be better off focusing on other pursuits and performances related to science, math, engineering or finance.

Obviously, history has been kind to America, not only in terms of geography (the oceans protected us until 9/11), but also in natural resources (abundant in America) and climate (mild weather has allowed for abundant food production) and opportunities for a full range of talents to succeed. But, given the historical context of America, Beattie and others fail to consider how the corruption of the Gilded Age of the late nineteenth and early twentieth centuries served as a model for the Gilded Age II (the last 30 years). He fails to see or admit that the flaws in our government and financial system can break our economy, that the growth of inequality and shrinking of the middle class (for the last 30 years), unless curtailed, can lead to a financial oligarchy and the collapse of American democracy.

The recent Gilded period has shown that people on the top of the pyramid are just as unethical, arrogant and fraudulent as they were when they were called *robber barons* more than 100 years ago or *warlords* more than 1,000 years ago. The difference is that more money is now at stake because the market has expanded on a global basis and there are more ways to fleece the public. Although schools and colleges are supposed to provide able youngsters the opportunity to succeed, the sorting-out process becomes more competitive when the economy begins to shrink or when the resources and wealth of the nation are increasingly concentrated in the hands of a few people or smaller segment of society.

The extremes of wealth in the Western World and the "old boy club" of the rich nations of the world, notably the G8, reached its apex at the turn of the twenty-first century. Gone are the days of Pax Britannica (Roosevelt–Churchill to Reagan–Thatcher era) and Pax Americana (Bush I to Bush II era), when Britain and the United States determined the rules of the world order. Economically, the new world we live in is highlighted by America drained by military overreach and China clutching a fistful of dollars, actually U.S. banknotes, but also the stark reality that the U.S. consumer can no longer prop up the global economy and continue to chalk up increased debt.

Capitalism naturally leads to inequality, where a tiny minority controls the capital, equipment or land—and runs the show. The remaining populace offers their labor and work skills to earn a living. At the apex of the pyramid, the U.S. capitalist system is characterized by a tiny minority making piles of money while millions of Americans are plagued by debt, struggling with unemployment or underemployment, and worried about how much money they have left for retirement and their children's college education. In the meantime, our presidents speak at international meetings and continuously assure the leaders of the world that America is not in decline. For example, we are reminded by President Obama that all this negativism flies in the face of "a vibrancy to our economic model, a durability to our political model, and a set of ideas that has sustained us through difficult years." All well and good, a great piece of rhetoric, and an uplifting group of words with a pinch of sugar and spice.

But go tell that to the average worker in Wisconsin, Ohio, Indiana, or elsewhere in the Midwest and South who is fighting to retain his or her rights to collectively organize. Conservative governors claim the unions are breaking the middle class. But progressives claim unions are the backbone of the middle class. The titans at the top, the rich and super-rich, are pitting ordinary workers against each other, union workers against nonunion workers under the guise of "shared sacrifice" and balancing budgets.

Recent pundits have failed to consider that the U.S. has moved from a manufacturing society, whereby Americans made products for the world, to a financial-based economy, whereby services are provided for a fee which in the long run is unsustainable. The new model is based on quick profits and phony profits. Much of the financial industry hoodwinks and traps consumers and homeowners with the small print that few people, even with a PhD, can understand. It produces windfalls for bankers, mortgage brokers, hedge-fund managers and insurance agents—and resentment for the rest of us. It drives up the cost for everything—from the cost of a hamburger to a house—until the cost becomes unreasonable, which in turn leads to a correction or bubble in the economy. In simple mathematical terms, as many as 25 percent of the *Forbes* 400 richest people owe their fortunes to the financial sector, compared to the 10 percent in 1982 (when the U.S. was still a manufacturing society).

Our economic system is partially based on a culture that thrives on independence and individualism, not on the collective good or about what happens to our neighbor. It is fueled by the spirit of hard work and inner-directed (not group-based) behavior. If I work hard, and with a little luck, I'll get what I need and I don't have to be concerned nor worry about the person who cannot or will not work as hard. A college education is not necessarily needed. Excellence will be rewarded! The Horatio Alger heroes rarely held college degrees, so a person of ability doesn't necessarily need a college education to succeed in America. Witness Alex Rodriguez and Taylor Swift. Then, of course, there are the CEOs and founders of well-known companies: Bill Gates (of Microsoft), Larry Ellison (of Oracle), Michael Dell (of Dell), Sheldon Adelson (of Las Vegas Sands), Carl Icahn (of Icahn Capital), Leonardo Del Vecchio (of LensCrafters and Sunglass Hut), Harold Hamm (of Continental Resources), Mark Zuckerberg (of Facebook) and Evan Williams (of Twitter)—all of whom are worth $20 billion or more and dropped out of college or never even went to college.

Our economy pretty much sums up Western values and the notion of individual freedom, risk taking and spirit of enterprise in the U.S. Not only does this point of view prune away the "weak links" in society, it also corresponds with the notion of Social Darwinism, popularized in the nineteenth century, and the Gordon Gekko model (in the movie *Wall Street*) that greed (sometimes called self-interest) is good. So what is the average person to do?

Deciding to eliminate your daily coffee mocha at Starbucks, or taking your lunch to work, will not help as much as you might think. The fact is the average U.S. household net worth has dipped nearly 40 percent between 2007 and 2010. Education levels, technological change and globalization may explain why uneducated workers and poor people have lost ground, but now college graduates and professional workers are losing ground. But it does not explain the growing inequality between the super-rich and the rest of us—nor why the middle class is drowning and slowly disappearing. You might say that hard work and luck help explain the differences, but that's old hat. Most ordinary people are beginning to think the system is rigged—where the powerful and rich play by one set of rules and the rest of us play by another set of rules, one group is born on third base with a batch of trusts and the majority are merely trying to get up at bat and get a decent education and job. Under these circumstances, opportunity is limited to inherited privilege, and excellence counts very little. When this happens, and it becomes common knowledge, the high-aptitude, high-achievers and highly talented either stay home and count cars, hang out in Starbucks, or just go to the beach to sun and surf.

One group (about 1 percent of the American populace) is front and center with a long-standing mix of huge salaries, bonuses and pensions while ordinary Americans are struggling and angered. They are barely getting by, sinking in debt and worried about their jobs—and whether they will be able to continue to pay their home mortgages and save enough money to pay for their children's college education. A growing number—the poor and near poor, unemployed and underemployed, low skilled and semi skilled, disabled and sickly, etc.—are worried about putting sufficient food on the table. They are living on the edge—paycheck to paycheck. We have slowly descended into a two-tier society, a country run by a financial oligarchy (the political and economic elite), and a social order (in terms of inequality) that mirrors the one that existed before the French and Russian revolutions. The average American still refuses to admit that the deck is stacked, the bubble is about to burst and the so-called dream is slowly becoming more folklore than reality. Be prepared to say: Kiss Horatio Alger goodbye, kiss the notion of succeeding goodbye, at least for many Americans. The increase in global competition adds to our economic downward slide, particularly at the bottom and middle ranges of the American workforce.

The economic system that has evolved rewards people who are in a position to make *profits* for a large corporation or financial institution by moving money around with a flick of a mouse, by fleecing the public and/or by entertaining the masses (as actors, singers, ballplayers, etc.) through the media. It penalizes people who are considered a *cost* factor for an organization or business, and thus wages are capped. We have unwittingly created a distorted system of rewards—a rigged game and an upside-down economy. The system has allowed the financial sector to become so gargantuan that when mistakes are made, they receive government bailouts so they can survive at the expense of the people who are struggling on a daily basis. This is not only stirring up questions of fairness and equity, but also old vestiges of class resentment.

For conservatives to yell foul—and put down or stifle critics of the system by labeling them as unpatriotic, jealous or stirring class warfare—is to mask the hypocrisy of big business and big money, and the negative effects of multimillion-dollar contracts and salaries. Conservatives argue there is danger in taxing the rich, restricting their bonuses or regulating their behavior. The system works. The vast majority of Americans work. Most Americans are middle class. But helping them should not mean making them more dependent on government programs or entitlements, nor should it mean that the rich and super-rich pay for everything. But the top class fails to consider that anger on Main Street is growing toward the money class. When it comes to people who have earned their money in big business or the financial sector, there is an increasing number of people—average working Americans—who feel it is wrong. A class divide is growing. For some of us, there is the feeling that the wings of the investment bankers, hedge-fund managers and Wall Street executives need to be clipped and that windfall profits, bonuses and retirement packages (often called golden parachutes) should be taxed at higher rates. For others, there is a jumble of alarms and outcries; there is something wrong with the system, but it's too confusing and the system is too big or too corrupt to change. For still others, this is the age of instant, mass media; there is no need to feel useless; change is inevitable and it can come from the bottom up, since the people have the voices and votes.

The fact is the wealth of the nation (and other nations as well) has always been in the hands of the wealthy—not the working people, not the so-called middle class. This may seem somewhat surprising to those who did not create the wealth. But long-term, if the wealthy are to survive over generations, they must allow other classes to change their class status, allowing for some opportunity and mobility, so those who increase their efforts or exhibit ability can obtain greater income and then turn their income into investments and wealth. If the wealthy refuse to allow such mobility, they risk revolution from the bottom, class warfare and the overthrow of the system, as in nineteenth-century Europe and twentieth-century Russia and China.

Conclusion

The economic calamity of the Great Recession should have shattered some of the cherished tenets of capitalism. But John Cassidy, a financial journalist, sizes up the problem in *How Markets Fail*. He points out there are no hard-and-fast principles to eliminate or modify. Capitalism means different things to different people;

liberals and conservatives have very different views on how to reform it. It so happens that the free market system has dominated American thinking since the election of President Reagan, whose goal was to downsize government and reduce taxes for the rich. Alan Greenspan, the chairperson of the Federal Reserve from 1987 to 2006, added fuel to the fire. He sold Americans on the ideas that financial markets are rational and self-correcting mechanisms. The outcome was the worst financial crisis since the Great Depression, with no one held accountable or prosecuted for their role in the crisis (except in the case of overt fraud—such as with Madoff).

The conservative movement in the U.S. is for small government and resents government regulation of corporate America. It views government as "Big Brother." So long as the American economy is marked by the closure or bankruptcy of plants making cars, clothes and electronics—where the losers are working people—then there is little concern among conservatives for government regulation. When banks and Wall Street go under and stocks plummet, conservatives rally and come forth with government assistance. The argument is these institutions are "too big to fail" and must be saved in order to ward off financial disaster and save jobs.

Then there is the government–capitalist divide—or myth. More government regulations are considered a violation of individual liberty; they supposedly limit the vitality and innovativeness of society, and hinder workers and work productivity. The conservative pundits rely on a "Trojan horse"—a backdoor attack for limiting the size of government in order to enhance free markets—whereby the winner is the corporate or banking titan (or capitalist) and the loser is the worker. Why ordinary people are seduced by the notion of free markets probably has something to do with partisan politics and cultural issues that divide the nation. Of course, there is always Alexander Hamilton's viewpoint. The masses are stupid; they adopt herd behavior, and they will always be second class to the banking and manufacturing class.

We need to recognize that *extreme* inequality is harmful to society, as opposed to *moderate* inequality, which reflects the (1) result of striving and success of people, (2) in a society that distinguishes between excellence and mediocrity and (3) rewards people according to their performance. Extreme inequality and low economic growth are associated with each other, and the greater the inequality the slower the economic growth for that nation. Inequality impacts on macroeconomics, the large trends that ordinary people cannot control or influence. It also increases financial risk—that is, when there is too much disparity in income—and stifles opportunity among average and even above-average achievers. Not everyone would agree. The conservative argument is that the American dream (and opportunity around the world) is in decline because of (1) government intervention, (2) lack of personal responsibility, hard work and family structure, (3) growing entitlements which curtail productivity, creativity and risk taking and (4) redistributive tax policies.

The other side of the political divide would say that the American dream (and opportunity around the globe) is in decline because (1) real wages for working people (after inflation) have remained flat for the last 30 years despite rising corporate profit, (2) health services and access to education are limited for those who are not well off, (3) tax policies favor the rich (redistribution policies should not be excessive since this will stifle growth) and (4) there are too many tax havens and places to bury illegal money. Then there is a host of "dark" individuals and groups who have no interest in social or moral issues, nor the common good; their only interest is for profits without concern for people. Finally, by its very nature, capitalism leads to inequality—and inequality increases as the economy expands, since the return on *capital* grows much faster than the return on *labor* or the economy in general.

In a democracy, people love the idea of free and fair competition. Everybody should feel they can get a decent job. People should feel a sense of opportunity and that life can get better, especially for their children. The idea of fulfilling human potential of all its citizens should be embedded in the social system, a belief that all individuals have the right for maximum fulfillment and to achieve the best they can. But when a critical mass of people feel they cannot get a decent job, the system is rigged, or they are not treated as part of the larger community— that leads to divisiveness and polarization. Everybody should feel there is a place for them in society, and if you're good enough in school or on the job, you will be recognized and rewarded. Economic growth must help those at the bottom of the pyramid, and not just those at the top. A full range of talents must be nurtured and the discriminatory or authoritarian process of narrowing talent must be curtailed.

The best way to nurture excellence is to build a society that discourages and limits inherited wealth and privilege and fosters a balanced playing field with real opportunities for ordinary people. The need is to recognize and reward different forms of excellence, and to provide special provisions for those who are slow, weak or less than average since more than 50 percent of the population fall into these categories at any given period. Statistically speaking, your time will come, when you need government assistance or entitlements such as Medicare, Social Security or other safety nets. If we only reward the fast, strong and above average, inequality is bound to grow. We need floors and ceilings to reduce inequality, sort of a balancing act, which must be worked out by political compromise.

More equality is possible in a democracy if citizens choose it. What the people need to do is to use their voice and vote for political leaders who will put people before property, legislate a floor and ceiling in income and wealth, and pay people based on how their performance (or job) influences the common good—and not as a profit vs. cost factor. There is some merit in periodically storming the Bastille, eliminating the old guard who have become entrenched (since power corrupts), and hanging a few rotten politicians in the village square—especially those who have betrayed the people and gotten fat and rich off the people's sweat and labor.

In the final analysis, *opportunity* is the key. The U.S. may not be a perfect country, but here someone (from a meager or disadvantaged background) has a chance to advance: to attend college, to get a decent job, to raise a family, to attend any church. Most ordinary people will not get rich, but if they can "deliver" in the way of performance, combined with character and motivation, they can rise and enhance their mobility. In a stratified society, there is little chance to rise in status. There are all kinds of aptitudes, abilities and talents, all kinds of "intelligences." We may not always agree on what capacities count more or should be rewarded more. But so long as society is willing to recognize multiple talents and provide multiple chances, as well as chances for "late bloomers," we cannot ask anything more.

Problems and handicaps related to background are obvious. We don't start at the beginning gate on equal terms. Some of us start as the son or daughter of a sanitation worker or janitor, and others start as the son or daughter of a physician or attorney who attended Harvard University. Still, some of us are born into a one-headed household. Marked inequalities exist. But the great difference of America, compared to the old world, has been the opportunity it provides for the poor and ordinary people—vividly symbolized by the Statue of Liberty which welcomes the "tired," the "poor," the "huddled masses all yearning to breathe free," the "wretched refuse" and the "homeless, tempest-tossed" people from all parts of the world. Thank your lucky stars if you live in America. There is no yoke, no bloodline, no warlord, no whip holding you down—stifling your chances, choking your aspirations, limiting your opportunities. God has blessed this land.

REFERENCES

Albergotti, Reed and Vanessa O'Connell. *Wheelmen: Lance Armstrong, the Tour de France, and the Greatest Sports Conspiracy Ever* (New York: Gotham, 2014).

Apple, Michael. *Teachers and Texts: A Political Economy of Class and Gender Relations in Education* (New York: Routledge & Kegan Paul, 1986).

Averch, Harvey A., et al. *How Effective is Schooling? A Critical Review of Research* (Santa Monica, CA: Rand Corporation, 1972).

Baltzell, E. Digby. *The Protestant Establishment: Aristocracy & Caste in America* (New Haven, CT: Yale University Press, 1987).

Barry, Brian. *Why Social Justice Matters* (Cambridge, UK: Polity, 2005).

Beattie, Alan. *False Economy: A Surprising Economic History of the World* (New York: Riverhead, 2009).

Bell, Daniel. *The Coming of Post-Industrial Society* (New York: Basic Books, 1973).

Blau, Peter M., and Otis Duncan. *The American Occupational Structure* (New York: Wiley, 1967).

Brooks, David. "Karl's New Manifesto," *New York Times*, May 29, 2005.

Bruner, Jerome S. *The Process of Education* (Cambridge, MA: Harvard University Press, 1960).

Brynjolfsson, Erik and Andrew McAfee. *Race Against the Machine* (Lexington, MA: Digital Frontier Press, 2012).

Carlson, Curtis R., and William Wilmot. *Innovation: The Five Disciplines for Creating What Customers Want* (New York: Crown, 2006).

Cassidy, John. *How Markets Fail: The Logic of Economic Calamities* (New York: Farrar, Straus and Giroux, 2009).

Chakrabarti, Vishaan. *A Country of Cities: A Manifesto for an Urban America* (New York: Metropolis Books, 2013).

Chua, Amy and Jed Rubenfeld. *The Triple Package: What Really Determines Success* (New York: Penguin, 2014).

Coleman, James. "The Concept of Equality of Educational Opportunity," *Harvard Educational Review*, Spring 1968.

Coleman, James S. *Equality of Educational Opportunity* (Washington, DC: U.S. Government Printing Office, 1966).

Collier, Paul. *Exodus: How Migration Is Changing Our World* (New York: Oxford University Press, 2014).

Collins, Jim and Morten Hansen. *Great by Choice: Uncertainty, Chaos, and Luck—Why Some Thrive Despite Them All* (New York: Harper Business, 2011).

Conant, James B. *Slums and Suburbs* (New York: Signet Books, 1961).

Conant, James B. *The American High School Today* (New York: McGraw-Hill, 1959).

Cowen, Tyler. *Average is Over: Powering America Beyond the Age of the Great Stagnation* (New York: Dutton, 2013).

Cremin, Lawrence A. (ed.). *The Republic and the School: Horace Mann on the Education of Free Men* (New York: Teachers College Press, 1957).

Cubberley, Ellwood. *Changing Conceptions of Education* (Boston: Houghton Mifflin, 1909).

Deresiewicz, William. *Excellent Sheep: The Miseducation of the American Elite and the Way to a Meaningful Life* (New York: Free Press, 2015).

Dowd, Maureen. "Silicon Valley Sharknado," *New York Times*, July 8, 2014, p. A25.

Ellsberg, Michael. *The Education of Millionaires: Everything You Don't Learn in College About How to Be Successful* (New York: Penguin, 2013).

Eng, Norman. "Demographics and Education in the Twenty-First Century," in A.C. Ornstein (ed.), *Contemporary Issues in Curriculum, 6th edn.* (Upper Saddle River, NJ: Pearson, 2015), pp. 164–180.

Feinberg, Kenneth R. *Who Gets What: Fair Compensation after Tragedy and Financial Upheaval* (New York: PublicAffairs, 2012).

Fishman, Ted C. *China, Inc.: How the Rise of the Next Superpower Challenges America and the World* (New York: Scribner, 2005).

Friedman, Milton. *Why Government Is the Problem* (Stanford, CA: Hoover Institution, 1993).

Friedman, Thomas L. *The World is Flat: A Brief History of the Twenty-first Century* (New York: Farrar, Straus and Giroux, 2005).

Fussell, Paul. *Class: A Guide through the American Status System* (New York: Summit, 1983).

Gardner, Howard. *Frames of Mind: The Theory of Multiple Intelligences* (New York: Basic Books, 1983).

Gardner, John W. *Excellence: Can We Be Equal and Excellent Too?* (New York: Harper & Row, 1961).

Geithner, Timothy F. *Stress Test: Reflections on the Financial Crisis* (New York: Random House, 2014).

Giridharadas, Anand. *The True American: Murder and Mercy in Texas* (New York: Norton, 2014).

Goldstone, Lawrence. *Birdmen: The Wright Brothers, Glenn Curtiss, and the Battle to Control the Skies* (New York: Ballantine Books, 2014).

Grissmer, David. *Improving Student Achievement* (Santa Monica, CA: Rand Corporation, 2000).

Harari, Yuval N. *Sapiens: A Brief History of Humankind* (New York: Harper, 2015).

Heckman, James J. "The Economics of Inequality," *American Educator*, Spring 2011, pp. 31–35, 47.

Herrnstein, Richard. *IQ in the Meritocracy* (Boston: Little, Brown, 1971).

Herrnstein, Richard and Charles Murray. *The Bell Curve: Intelligence and Class Structure in American Life* (New York: Free Press, 1994).

Hoover, John. *How to Work for an Idiot* (Franklin Lakes, NJ: Career, 2004).

Huntington, James B. *Work's New Age: The End of Full Employment and What It Means to You* (Eldred, NY: Royal Flush, 2012).

Hurwitz, Michael. "The Impact of Legacy Status on Undergraduate Admissions at Elite Colleges and Universities," *Economics of Education Review* 30(3), 2011, pp. 480–492.

Isaacson, Walter. *Steve Jobs: The Exclusive Biography* (New York: Simon & Schuster, 2011).

Jencks, Christopher. *Inequality: A Reassessment of the Effect of Family and Schooling in America* (New York: Basic Books, 1972).

Kristof, Nicholas. "An Idiot's Guide to Inequality," *New York Times*, July 23, 2014.

Krugman, Paul R. *End This Depression Now!* (New York: W.W. Norton, 2012).

Lohr, Steve. *Data-ism: The Revolution Transforming Decision Making* (New York: HarperCollins, 2015).

Macur, Juliet. *Cycle of Lies: The Fall of Lance Armstrong* (New York: Harper, 2014).

Mandel, Michael J. *Rational Exuberance: Silencing the Enemies of Growth and Why the Future Is Better than You Think* (New York: HarperBusiness, 2004).

Mayer, Kurt B. *Class and Society* (New York: Random House, 1955).

Mayer, Susan E., and Paul E. Peterson. *Earning and Learning: How Schools Matter* (Washington, DC: Brookings Institution, 1999).

McDougall, Walter A. *Freedom Just Around the Corner* (New York: HarperCollins, 2004).

Merchant, Minhaz. *The New Clash of Civilizations: How the Contest between America, China, India and Islam Will Shape Our Century* (New Delhi: Rainlight, 2014).

Murray, Charles. "Intelligence in the Classroom," *Wall Street Journal*, January 16, 2007.

Murray, Charles. *Human Accomplishment: The Pursuit of Excellence in the Arts and Sciences* (New York: HarperCollins, 2004).

Nisbett, Richard. *The Geography of Thought: How Asians and Westerners Think Differently and Why* (New York: Free Press, 2003).

Noah, Timothy. *The Great Divergence: America's Growing Inequality Crisis and What We Can Do About It* (New York: Bloomsbury, 2012).

Oakes, Jeannie. *Keeping Track: How Schools Structure Inequality* (New Haven, CT: Yale University Press, 1985).

Ornstein, Allan C. *Wealth vs. Work: How 1% Victimize 99%* (AuthorHouse, 2012).

Ornstein, Allan C. *Class Counts: Education, Inequality, and the Shrinking Middle Class* (Lanham, MD: Rowman & Littlefield, 2007).

Ostry, Jonathan and Andrew G. Berg. "How Inequality Damages Economies," *Foreign Affairs*, January 2012.

Perkins, John. *Confessions of an Economic Hit Man* (San Francisco, CA: Berrett-Koehler, 2004).

Pew Research Center. *The Rise of Asian Americans* (Washington, DC: Pew Research Center, 2012).

Piketty, Thomas, and Arthur Goldhammer (trans.). *Capital in the Twenty-First Century* (Cambridge, MN: Harvard University Press, 2014).

Prins, Nomi. *All the Presidents' Bankers: The Hidden Alliances that Drive American Power* (New York: Nation, 2013).

Rattner, Steven. "Fear Not the Coming of the Robots," *New York Times*, June 21, 2014, p. SR 5.

Rawls, John. *A Theory of Justice, 2nd edn.* (Cambridge, MA: Harvard University Press, 1999).

Riesman, David. *The Lonely Crowd: A Study of the Changing American Character* (New York: Bask Books, 1953).

Rosenberg, Jonathan with Alan Eagle. *How Google Works: The Rules for Success in the Internet Century* (New York: Grand Central Publishing, 2014).

Rothkopf, David J. *Superclass* (New York: Farrar, Straus and Giroux, 2008).

Saletan, William. "Taken for a Ride," *New York Times*, April 18, 2014.

Sandel, Michael J. *What Money Can't Buy: The Moral Limits of Markets* (New York: Farrar, Straus and Giroux, 2012).

Sengupta, Somini. "Other Nations Dangle Visas for Foreign Entrepreneurs," *New York Times*, June 6, 2013, pp. Bu 1,7.

Shlaes, Amity. *The Forgotten Man* (New York: HarperCollins, 2007).

Sowell, Thomas. *Conquests and Cultures: An International History* (New York: Basic Books, 1998).

Stanley, Thomas J., and William Danko. *The Millionaire Next Door: The Surprising Secrets of America's Wealthy* (Atlanta, GA: Longstreet, 1996).

Stark, Rodney. *The Victory of Reason* (New York: Random House, 2006).

Stephens-Davidowitz, Seth. "The Geography of Fame," *New York Times*, March 22, 2014.

Stiglitz, Joseph E. *The Price of Inequality* (New York: W.W. Norton, 2013).

Streitfield, David. "Engineers Allege Hiring Collusion in Silicon Valley," *New York Times*, March 1, 2014, pp. A1, A3.

Sutton, Robert and Huggy Rao. *Scaling up Excellence* (New York: Crown, 2014).

Thiel, Peter. *Zero to One* (New York: Penguin–Random House, 2014).

Tucker, Patrick. *The Naked Future: What Happens in a World That Anticipates Your Every Move?* (New York: Current, 2014).

Tyack, David B. *Turning Points in American Educational History* (Waltham, MA: Blaisdell Publishing 1967).

Vogel, Kenneth P. *Big Money* (New York: Public Affairs, 2014).

Wadhwa, Vivek and Alex Salkever. *The Immigrant Exodus* (Philadelphia, PA: Wharton Digital, 2012).

Warren, Elizabeth. *A Fighting Chance* (New York: Metropolitan Books, 2014).

Wells, H.G. *The Future in America: A Search After Realities* (New York and London: Harper and Brothers, 1906).

Whyte, William H. *The Organization Man* (New York: Simon & Schuster, 1956).

Young, Michael. *The Rise of the Meritocracy* (London: Thames and Hudson, 1958).

Zagorsky, Jay. "You Don't Have To Be Smart To Be Rich," *Wall Street Journal*, May 1, 2007.

INDEX